MW01630376

A Trans Feminist's Past

To Saman,

I'm thankful that OSP connected us. I wish that you find a helpful gem between these covers.

Enjoy the Read,

Forest Handford

A Trans Feminist's Past

By
Forest Handford

Published by
TransGender Publishing

An imprint of
Castle Carrington Publishing Group
Victoria, BC CANADA

2021

A Trans Feminist's Past

Cover design: Forest Handford
Photographs from the author's personal collection (unless otherwise indicated)

ISBN: 978-1-990096-29-7 (paperback)
ISBN: 978-1-990096-30-3 (Kindle electronic book)
ISBN: 978-1-990096-31-0 (Smashwords electronic book)

Published in Canada by
TransGender Publishing
www.transgenderpublishing.ca

an imprint of
Castle Carrington Publishing group
Victoria, BC Canada
www.castlecarringtonpublishing.ca\

For more information see
www.EastCoastGAmes.com

Trigger Warning

This is the most graphic book I've written thus far. It includes discussion of the unacceptable violence and murder that still happens to transgender victims. I will discuss my challenges with sexuality and a detailed description of my personal struggles with suicidal ideation. Transphobia, sexism, homophobia, mental illness, Islamophobia, sex work, and racism will all be explored in this book. Please do not read this book if reading these topics will cause you trauma.

Dedication

This book is dedicated to Marilyn Cazares. As of when I began writing, Marilyn was the most recently reported transgender person in the US to be murdered. Marilyn was a few weeks shy of reaching her 23rd birthday. While Marilyn had wished to become a nurse, a drug addiction led to her becoming homeless. While homeless she turned to sex work to pay for her lifestyle. As a transgender Latina, the odds were stacked against her. Marilyn needed love and support.

Contents

Preface

Before getting into the content, I want to discuss how this book was written, what my blind spots are as the author, and some stylistic choices I have made. As much as my life is about me, many of the choices I've made are a product of the people in my life. As much as possible, I've discussed with the people I bring up in the book what I am including in the hopes they won't be blindsided by it or hurt by it. Unfortunately, there are a few people I am unable to contact and thus have changed identifying information about them, including their names. Please do not hold anything in these pages against others. Truth can hurt. But as it's my truth, I'm the only person who should be held accountable for the content of this book. If you want to hurt somebody because of this book, address it with me, please leave the people in my life alone.

While I have some intersectionality as a transgender woman and single mother of two, I also have a *ton* of privilege. I'm white, I am just above the threshold to qualify as upper class, I have work-life balance, I can trace some of my ancestors all the way back to the Mayflower, I grew up in a middle-class home, I'm the product of multi-generational wealth, and, to my knowledge, I'm neurotypical. Please read this with the understanding that I don't know what it's like to live in the US as anything different. While I know what it's like to live with male privilege and, to an extent, without it, I will never be able to fully understand how hard it is to live without all my other privileges. You cannot blindly apply my life to people who have less privilege. For example, you would be making a serious error if you said that if Marilyn Cazares had made choices more like mine that she would still be alive, wouldn't have been homeless, wouldn't have become a drug addict, wouldn't have become a sex worker, and wouldn't have been murdered. Frankly, if I was a Latina who came out as young as she did with so little support, I doubt I'd have made it to 21. American society favors people with privileges like those I have.

Some medical professionals have an expectation of what the trans narrative is. This narrative is used for gatekeeping medical access for "our safety." Many of us twist our true narrative in order for the gatekeepers to approve our care. When I first began my transition, my narrative was very far from what the gatekeepers wanted. As I've spent more time reviewing my life, I've discovered it is closer to the narrative they want to hear than I originally realized. In reality, our narratives are all different. Please do not use my narrative as a way to judge other trans folks. There are many narratives and lots of them are different from mine. This book holds my unique perspective.

I've decided to order my story somewhat chronologically. While my favorite television show, *Doctor Who*, brings characters to different times, I feel like putting them in order makes it more accessible. In fact, while I love the topics Margaret Atwood addresses in her novels, her reliance on flashbacks drives me batty.

Joan of Arc

Joan of Arc has always been a hero for me. In fact, almost all of my heroes during my youth were women. I thought of famous women as being extra special because not only had they done something to become famous, they did it despite being a member of the oppressed sex. My favorite podcast is *History Chicks* where, in each episode, the two women who run the podcast talk about a famous woman from history.

I don't remember when I first learned of Joan of Arc. I remember making her the topic of a school essay for English class, I don't remember the details behind the grade, but I got an A+ and extra credit. I've read multiple biographies of her, the kind of biographies that have tons of footnotes, which for other subjects usually put me to sleep.

I don't condone violence. It wasn't that she was a military leader. I have complicated feelings about her accounts of hearing angels. But she brought her people back from the brink of destruction. She inspired a revolution. All of this she did in a very short time, as a teen, while being a gender that was treated as far more inferior than today.

Like her, I might have a bit of a martyr complex. She fought in clothing meant for men. As I'll discuss later, I often chose clothing that defied gender norms. Perhaps unconsciously, I believed it was okay to dress as a boy while knowing I would rather dress feminine.

Throughout my life, I have occasionally fantasized about reincarnation and past lives. If I could pick what happens after death, I would pick reincarnation. Of course, as someone who is still living, I cannot say what happens when we die. It's my sincere hope that many of my organs will be used to help people and that the rest of me will have a natural (chemical free) burial in which plants can use my remains as nourishment.

During a high school trip to France, I visited the Cathedral of Reims. Joan of Arc's army got the *Dauphin*, heir to the throne, crowned at the Cathedral making him Charles VII, King of France. The crowning at Reims was critical to the legitimacy of his office. My trip there was like a pilgrimage. I bought a statuette of her there, which I keep on my desk and look upon when I find myself struggling. As of this writing, it is currently in my former office at Affectiva. It's been there since the start of COVID-19 and has remained there even after I was laid off. I'm not looking forward to seeing my former colleagues after the pandemic, but I want her back.

As a teen, my friends and I were exploring hypnosis. Past life regression was my favorite thing to do when hypnotising someone. Invariably, all past lives of the people who I hypnotised were the same gender as the person I hypnotised. The one time I had it done to me, I regressed to Joan of Arc.

About a decade later, when learning about the American suffragettes, I noticed that Alice Paul died right around the time I was born. I added to my reincarnation fantasy that I was her in my last life.

Sometimes, long-term female partners and I would fantasize that we had been together in previous lives but with her as the man and me as the woman. In my reincarnation fantasy, I imagined you pick your gender for your next life. I've always wanted to pick female for my next life.

Perhaps, if reincarnation exists, I picked being male at birth as an experiment for this life to see what it's like and because there is accessible technology to switch genders if I hated it. I also could have picked my parents because I knew how supportive they would be if I transitioned.

Mary Dyer

My great, great, great, great, great, great, great, great, great grandmother was Mary Dyer. She's from my father's side of the family. She was born in England in 1611 as Mary Barrett. She married a milliner named William Dyer in 1633. In England, they followed Puritan beliefs with the hope that the Anglican Church would reform. Like many Puritans of the time, they decided it would be better to live in the new world as Puritans rather than be oppressed in England.

I realize the irony in Puritans coming to North America for freedom as it came at the cost of the Native Americans' freedom and, in many cases, their lives. The Puritans, including the famed Mather family, were pro-slavery. In fact, Cotton Mather owned black slaves. There is no record of the Dyers having slaves.

After arriving in Boston, the couple became entangled in the Antinomian Controversy. The Puritans were divided, and Mary backed Anne Hutchinson. Anne's followers believed in free grace, that once a person believes in Jesus that person gains eternal life. Ultimately, the couple was "disarmed" and forced to leave Massachusetts in 1638. They chose to go South to Aquidneck Island, which would later become part of Rhode Island. Anne Hutchinson and several others went with them.

A year before the Dyers were kicked out of Massachusetts, Puritan minister Roger Williams had been forced to leave because of his views against slavery, about treating the natives fairly, and his belief that people should have religious freedom. He took a group to a place he named Providence, which would later become the capital of Rhode Island. The European settlers of Providence paid the Narragansett tribe for the land.

Anne Hutchinson's group had Roger Williams negotiate their purchase of the island from the Narragansett sachem Miantonomi. In 1638, the male settlers, including Anne's husband, William Hutchinson, and Mary's husband, William Dyer, signed the compact of Portsmouth, which established the town that is on the northern section of what is today Newport County. After a year, some of the Aquidneck Island settlers decided to go to the southern section of the island where they founded Newport. Newport quickly grew and flourished. A group of Jews who fled from the Spanish Inquisition settled in Newport in the 1650s. Eventually, Newport would also become a major hub for the slave trade. Long after Newport was founded, the "woods" between

Newport and Portsmouth was incorporated as Middletown. I married my second spouse in our house in Middletown. We lived there for five years.

In Newport, the Dyers owned 87 acres, an area which is now a naval base. Their house was located where the Naval Health Clinic is located today. They had eight children, but only six of the children made it to adulthood. One of their sons would later become a governor of another colony.

The governments of Aquidneck Island and the neighboring Conanicut Island created an overarching government, which William Coddington had hoped to be an independent colony. William Dyer became the Attorney General for this government. The original Rhode Island official records were written by William Dyer: those he wrote that were stored in Newport were mostly lost during a fire set by the English during the revolution. The records that made it to Providence are in the state house vault. Roger Williams was set on having Providence and the islands becoming a single unified colony. Roger Williams and William Dyer sailed to England to bring the dispute to King Charles II. In 1651, just prior to the trip, Mary had left for England on business, in what many assume was a mission to collect an inheritance. The access that the Dyers had to the crown seemed extraordinary, and the trip coincided with Oliver Cromwell's death, causing the Royalists to regain control of England. There is no way to be sure why she traveled alone to England.

During Mary's five-year trip, she met George Fox. The two believed that the Puritans had not gone far enough in reforming the church. Both believed that revelations were available to all Christians. George had established the Quaker religion and based on the commandment of false idols, the religion rejected the symbols and rituals that were still part of the Anglican church. As a new member of the Quakers, Mary returned to Boston.

While Mary had been in England, Massachusetts Governor, John Endecott, had been getting upset by Quakers who had entered his colony prior to Mary's return. Endecott felt that the Quaker practice of listening to the voice of God within them was not only heresy but blasphemous. Quakers disrupted Puritan services to denounce the ministers. The governor banished all Quakers and ordered that their writings be burned.

Mary's ship arrived in Boston without her knowing about the ban on Quakers. She was thrown into jail for being in defiance of the law.

While in jail, two other Quakers were hung on the Boston Common, a place where I've taken my family sledding and ice skating. Mary was going to be hung as well. Word got to her family and her husband. One of her sons pleaded for her life. At the last minute, Mary was released and told to never return. She wrote the following in a letter to the Massachusetts court:

> *My life is not accepted, neither availeth me, in comparison with the lives and liberty of the Truth and Servants of the living God for which in the Bowels of Love and Meekness I sought you; yet nevertheless with wicked Hands have you put two of them to Death, which makes me to feel that the Mercies of the Wicked is cruelty; I rather chuse to Dye than to live, as from you, as Guilty of their Innocent Blood.*

She traveled to Shelter Island to spend time with other Quakers. In her time on Shelter Island, she considered the news that Endicott was sending a letter to Charles II in order to explain his stance on Quakers. The Massachusetts government hoped this would remove any doubts the King might have about hanging Quakers. She decided to return in the hopes that either the governor would be forced to change his mind or make her a martyr. When she returned, they had the following conversation.

Endicott asked, "Are you the same Mary Dyer that was here before?"

Mary replied, "I am the same Mary Dyer that was here [during] the last General Court."

"You will own yourself a Quaker, will you not?"

"I own myself to be reproachfully so called."

Endicott pronounced, "Sentence was passed upon you the last General Court; and now likewise—you must return to the prison, and there remain till tomorrow at nine o'clock; then thence you must go to the gallows and there be hanged till you are dead."

"This is no more than what thou saidst before."

"But now it is to be executed. Therefore, prepare yourself tomorrow at nine o'clock."

Mary explained, "I came in obedience to the will of God [to] the last General Court, desiring you to repeal your unrighteous laws of banishment on pain of death; and that same is my work now, and earnest request, although I told you that if you refused to repeal them, the Lord would send others of his servants to witness against them."[1]

Mary's husband sailed to England hoping to get the king to prevent his wife's execution. Before he returned, she was brought to the Boston Common and forced to climb the ladder and have the noose put around her neck. She was asked one last time if she would renounce her ways and she said, "Nay, I cannot; for in obedience to the will of the Lord God I came and, in his will, I abide faithful to the death."

Captain John Webb recited the charges and said, Mary "was guilty of her own blood."

She replied, "Nay, I came to keep bloodguiltiness from you, desiring you to repeal the unrighteous and unjust law of banishment upon pain of death, made against the innocent servants of the Lord, therefore my blood will be required at your hands who willfully do it; but for those that do is in the simplicity of their hearts, I do desire the Lord to forgive them. I came to do the will of my Father, and in obedience to his will I stand even to the death."

She was the last Quaker executed in Massachusetts. When the king got word that his subjects were being killed, he sent a mandate to the colonies that there should be no further punishment of Quakers by the colonies. He told them that if they cannot handle the Quakers, then they should send them back to England.

A diary of Roger Williams was discovered to discuss his thoughts about the colony. He wrote that he was glad Rhode Island and Providence Plantations was able to provide a safe home for Quakers, but he believed they were all going to hell.

After Endicott was forced to stop killing Quakers, he tried other ways to hurt them. He was eventually stopped. Boston now has a statue of Mary Dyer that says the following:

Mary Dyer
Quaker
WITNESS FOR RELIGIOUS FREEDOM
HANGED ON BOSTON COMMON 1660
My life not availeth me in comparison to the liberty of truth.

---

1 https://famous-trials.com/dyer/2486-mary-dyer-before-the-general-court-may-1660.

Figure 1: Forest with Mary Dyer Monument

I have a picture of me as a child with that Boston statue. I also have a picture of me sitting on Shelter Island's monument of Quaker martyrs. I was sitting on the stone dedicated to her. My father researched his ancestry after his mother died. His father took no interest in the research. It was through this research that he discovered our Pilgrim ancestors, and he found the Dyers. He found Mary Dyer especially compelling. Why was she treated so well? How close were the Dyers to the crown? Would she have stood out more if she were male? These are all questions he ponders.

It's hard for me to ignore my tendencies to state loudly when I believe something unethical is happening to me or my family. I also frequently speak out for those who don't have a voice, as you'll see throughout this book. I don't have any interest in dying for my beliefs, but I do put myself at risk.

Hazel King Dyer

My paternal grandmother was Hazel King Dyer. Her mother was Mary Alice Allen, and we have a picture of her. Mary Alice Allen is buried in New Bedford, Massachusetts. She married Stephen King Dyer in 1902. She raised two daughters from her husband, who she may have divorced. He did little to help with raising them. Her husband was never spoken of and it was very taboo to divorce back then. Stephen was a teacher at a textile school in New Bedford. Family lore says that, "Stephen liked French Women." Mary worked at a Five and Dime in New Bedford.

Hazel was the valedictorian of New Bedford High School's class of 1923. She married my grandfather, John Albert Handford. She was a manager of an insurance office. My father was her only child and had been a late in life "surprise." Hazel was in her early 40s, which back then was not considered a safe age to have kids.

They originally lived on Hillman street in New Bedford. My grandfather later built a home for them on the family farm on Phillips Road. The house of his sister, Gladys, burned down, injuring their mother, Lotta G. Skiff Handford (who lived from 1875-1949). He also built a replacement house next door for Gladys to replace the one that had burned down. After my grandfather died, my father sold this land to developers who created Monica's Way, Stephanie's Place, and all the homes along them.

Women of the time were expected to stay home and raise their kids. But leaving her job to raise my father was not in Hazel's best interests. She struggled with emotional issues that could have been linked to an undiagnosed thyroid problem. She was eventually committed to an insane asylum, which is what mental health facilities were called back then. My grandmother died in 1964 at the age of 58 due to an organ failure. My father was 17 at the time, a student in New Bedford's Vocational High School. While my father cannot remember her cooking, he was told that his mother was a good cook.

My father and I haven't talked much about her death, but it's a large part of why I have concerns with mental health professionals. I know many are well intentioned, but I think they have too much power. When I started seeing a gender therapist in August 2018, I warned my therapist this might be problematic. When I was a teen, the best friend of my partner was studying to be a psychologist. It was hard for me to be comfortable with her. Over the years, I have come to value the lessons from psychological research, especially on topics related to computer science and leadership.

I generally avoided the topic of my grandmother with my dad. I know it was sad for him and didn't want to retraumatize him. My grandfather rarely mentioned her. Her absence in my life was surprisingly impactful despite never having met her. For the longest time, I wondered if I had any ancestors who took on management roles. I could trace other traits of myself to my parents but both of them were individual contributors in their jobs, which is why they were both in unions their entire careers. It was only recently when I gently asked my father about her that I discovered she led a team in a time when women were rarely in white collar jobs. I can't imagine how few women were in leadership positions at that time, and I suspect nobody kept statistics.

Aline Brassard

My maternal grandmother was Aline Brassard. She was born in Newmarket, New Hampshire. Her first language was French. Aline's parents were French Canadian. She went to Catholic schools until high school. Her family eventually moved to Pawtucket, and she graduated from Pawtucket East, which today is called Tolman High.

She worked at the soda fountain in a pharmacy when she was in high school and possibly until my mother was born. It was at the soda fountain that she met James, a young man whose parents were of Canadian origin, a man I would later know as my grandfather, who I called Pépé. He preferred drinking cola from a bottle rather than poured from a fountain. Sometimes, she would see him and open a bottle in anticipation, only to discover he came on a different errand.

After graduating from High School, WWII was ravaging Europe. Pépé enlisted and landed in Normandy four days after D-Day. He spent most of the war in France and Poland. When he returned home, they married. They bought a new house in Pawtucket on Oakland Avenue that would eventually be passed on to me.

Once my mother was born, Aline did childcare work at home, worked a second shift piecework in a Pawtucket Rhode Island costume jewelry factory, was a clerical worker for a manufacturing company, and finally got her favorite job, working as a school crossing guard for the city. That was when crossing guards wore uniforms similar to police uniforms and children went home for lunch. She had to be at the school a half-hour before it started, stay until 15 minutes after the morning session began, return 15 minutes before lunch dismissal, and stay until 15 minutes after the afternoon session began. Back then, lunchtime lasted 90 minutes so children could go home, eat, and return, so that shift was 2 hours. She would be there again 15 minutes before dismissal at the end of the day, staying until all the children had crossed. During the lunch period, she could wait inside her car or the school building if she was on the lookout for any children who were exiting the building late or returning early. At the time, it was a respected job, which was sometimes hazardous due to standing in traffic. For the time, she received good pay and benefits.

Around 1968, Aline found a lump in her breast. My mother was in her third year at Rhode Island College. My grandparents limited what they told my mother so she could focus on her studies. Aline never lost her hair. She seemed to be doing well until my mother was in her first year as an elementary school teacher. Aline had found a lump in her thigh. It was surgically removed, and she was given more cancer treatments but in May of 1971, she died.

Just as I felt uncomfortable asking my father about his mother, I felt uncomfortable asking my mother about hers. She shared more with me than my father shared about his mother. My mother was proud of her mother, especially because of her job. I had a brief phase where I considered being a police officer. For the regional Burning Man event, I volunteer in a leadership capacity for the safety team known as Rangers. I think that because I knew some of her story and she didn't die because of a human system, I feel less loss about her than of my paternal grandmother. I do, however, deeply sympathize with her.

Compton's Cafeteria Riot

In the 1960s, Compton's Cafeteria in San Francisco was a place that transgender folks, mostly women, congregated. It was a very dangerous time to be trans in the US. If you wanted to legally change your gender identity you were required to:

- have gender reassignment surgery, which had its own gatekeeping,
- be sterilized (often gay people were forced to be sterilized too),
- be unmarried: if you were married you needed to have a divorce because same sex marriage was illegal. If you had kids, you were also expected to cut ties with them.

Some of these "requirements" still exist in some US states and in some foreign countries. Then, there are the countries where being trans is illegal, like Egypt.

Gay bars were popular in San Francisco, but due to transphobia, trans folk were often unwelcome. I equate this to the racism of white suffragettes. Some of the suffragists justified their actions by saying it would be too complicated to include black women in the movement. Some were just plain racist, and I cannot excuse them. There were some, however, who were not racist and fought for female inclusion.

Being trans at the time could take a huge toll on anyone. Those who were married were forced from their family. Very few had family that understood and accepted them. There was no employment protection for gender identity and sexual orientation. Unless you "passed," meaning you looked cisgender, and you had legally corrected your gender, it was unlikely you could get white collar work.

Many trans people have no occupational options beyond sex work. There are lots of stigmas against sex work and very few protections. While there is a demand for trans folk in sex work, there are also dangers, the biggest of which is violence. Sometimes, cis folks who hire a trans sex worker don't realize that the person they have hired is trans. If they discover the truth, it sometimes triggers internalized homophobia. I have several friends (cis and trans) who are sex workers.

In 1966, the cafeteria staff started to regularly call the police on their trans customers because they felt the presence of trans folk was causing other customers to avoid the cafeteria. The staff harassed the trans folk and started to charge them a "service" fee. Customers began to picket the cafeteria until police forced them to leave. One night, there was a trans woman who was in the cafeteria and refused to be mistreated. The police officers had a record of being violent to the LGBT community. Cross-dressing was illegal in California, giving the police an excuse to arrest trans folk, drag queens, and drag kings. A police officer began to arrest the woman and she splashed coffee into his face. That was the trigger for the riot.

The newspapers didn't cover the riot or the protests that followed with trans allies. This was a spark that led to San Francisco creating several support networks for trans folk. At a 50th anniversary event, Felicia "Flames" Elizondo said, "Nobody cared whether we lived or died. Our own families abandoned us, and we had nowhere to go." I consider this the first brick in the foundation of the LGBT rights we have today.

Stonewall Riots

While most people have never heard of the Compton Cafeteria Riot, most Americans know about Pride parades and some know that the first pride was a riot—literally. The Stonewall Inn was run by members of the mafia as a bar catering to the LGBT community. They felt it was a community they could make money off of partly because they had few places to go but also partly because they could extort money from the rich and famous who were visiting while closeted.

The police were upset that they weren't getting kickbacks from Stonewall. The Public Morals Squad decided to shut it down in a raid on June 28th, 1969, three years after the Compton Cafeteria Riot. They planned to arrest everyone who was cross-dressing. After checking IDs, they were going to force all those dressed as women to be checked by female officers and all who had male genitalia would be arrested. Some men began to refuse to show their IDs. Some of the lesbians were being patted down, which everyone felt included some sexual assault.

The police were slowed down as they waited for more vehicles to transport patrons to the station and to seize some of the liquor. Those being arrested resisted being taken out of the bar. Slowly, a crowd began to form outside, composed of onlookers and of the "cooperative" people the police decided to release.

The crowd cheered when the employees from the mafia were put into a police van. The crowd decided to chant and sing, "We Shall Overcome." Some of the customers being arrested decided to fight back and, when one of the patrons resisting arrest asked, the crowd rose to the task by creating a riot. Unlike the riot at Compton's Cafeteria, this one made the news.

That first night, and the following night, lines of police officers were met with chorus kicklines to taunt the police. No one had expected LGBT people to fight back, yet for nights they did.

The next year, a commemorative March occurred that, over the years, morphed into pride parades. I think it's important to note that Marsha Johnson, a black drag queen, was one of the three people at Stonewall who initially pushed back against the police. Marsha co-founded the Street Transvestites Action Revolutionaries with Sylvia Rivera. In 1973, the gay and lesbian committee that took charge of the pride parades banned drag queens because the committee felt they gave the community a bad name. While the two continued to form communities for LGBT people who were Black and Latinx, the LGBT community as a whole forgot them, preferring a more white, male-centric leadership.

I'm not really a parade person. It could be that I participated in too many parades from marching band and scouting. But I felt it was important to go to Pride Boston in 2019. We got there in time to have lunch before the parade. We waited in the shade, but also rotated the family through the spots we were holding so we'd have a good view. I was surprised how commercialized and politicized the parade was.

My second most recent Pride parade was in Providence over a decade ago. That parade was a bad experience for me. A queen had thrown something to my son (maybe beads) and got snippy with me because when I helped him with it, she thought I was taking it from him.

Pride 2019, I had fun dancing when there was music, and when there wasn't. My youngest child, Pon, and I got a bunch of swag. A few people, including strangers, said, "Happy Pride" to me, and that felt really good.

I got very emotional when I saw the Stonewall veterans and shouted, "Thank You," to them. I cried when I saw the people honoring the trans victims. I'm not afraid for myself, but I'm afraid of the impact on my kids if something ever happened to me.

After the parade had been going past us for a little over an hour, Pon said they were tired. Pon's not the type of person to complain unless there is a problem. They asked to leave soon. Sometimes, these things sort themselves out. So, after a few minutes, I asked if they still wanted to go. They said, "Yes." I think Pon was getting too much sun and heat. We left the parade, and I got the kids hydrated. My son, Simon, and I had Italian ice. Pon had ice cream and a pretzel. We cooled off in the shade. While they were eating, I went to get some selfies at the parade. My teeth were stained red from the Italian Ice, so I couldn't get a good one. The best I have is of me looking cross-eyed with my lips sealed.

It's a good thing we left when we did. I had Simon drive and noticed he had gotten sunburned on his right hand. When we got home, I discovered I had sunburn on both of my shoulders. Apparently, my dress had been covering my shoulders when I applied sunscreen but shifted during the parade.

We're all glad we went. Simon even asked, "Are we going to do this every year?" I told him I wasn't sure.

For Pride 2020, most events were cancelled due to COVID-19. Lately, Pride parades have been commodified so companies can market themselves by showing straight models in their logo-rich parade floats. In 2020, many companies created rainbow versions of their corporate logos. Many of these companies laid off their most vulnerable workers before and during Pride month.

Birth

In 1977, I was born in Kent County Hospital. The way my body appeared at birth caused the doctor to immediately, and authoritatively, say, "It's a boy." There was no ambiguity or appearance of intersex traits.

While the world around me adopted male pronouns for me, I don't feel like my parents put any pressure on me to be masculine. They named me Forest Jay Handford. Even if the doctor had correctly said, "It's a girl," my first name would still have been Forest. Most people don't realize that Forest isn't a gendered name because they think of Forrest Sawyer, Forrest Whitaker, and the movie that came out when I was in high school, Forrest Gump. I'm in a private Facebook group for people named Forest and we don't allow people to join if they have two "r's." I never seriously considered changing my first name, in part because I'm a fairly public person. I have a patent and four novels with my name on them. Many of my online account usernames, like Twitter, are ForestJay.

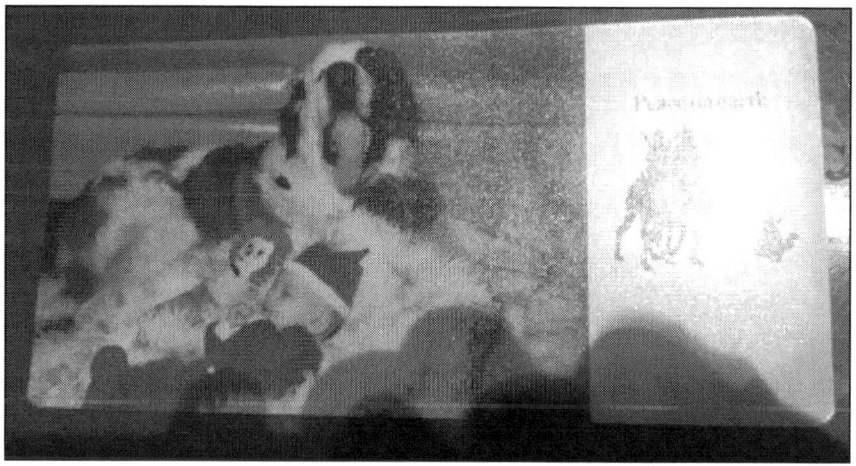

Figure 2: Baby Forest

My parents gave me my middle name in case I disliked my first name. At times, I've enjoyed having people try and guess what my middle initial stands for as it's rare for people to guess "Jay." While Jay has been used in the past for girls, it's popularity rapidly diminished before WWII. Lately, I've taken to omitting my middle name and initial from documents. I've considered changing it to Jaye, but it seems like too much effort.

While I've had my license and passport corrected for gender, I don't currently feel like the paperwork to correct my birth certificate is worth it. If, however, the government maintains its socially conservative course, I might get it changed for safety reasons.

Unfortunately, my childhood is a blur. Even when I was a teen, parts of my childhood were a blur. At times, it makes me wonder if there was some sort of trauma that I tried to suppress from my memory. I'm writing this book partly to uncover more of my past. A question I constantly ask myself is. "Why didn't I consider transition sooner?" It's sadly a question that medical professionals often ask trans people, and their expectation is that in the standard trans narrative, we're expected to have always wanted to be a gender we weren't assigned at birth. At times, I wonder if I've reshaped my narrative in order to have the gatekeepers approve my care.

There are many trans people who regret how long they waited to transition. We see kids who as young as three clearly state to their family that they aren't their assigned gender. I have no idea why I never did that as a kid. I know that I liked gymnastics. I know that I got along better with girls. I know that I hated boy clothing. Maybe I wasn't informed or imaginative enough back then to realize I could transition. Maybe something happened that scared me. Much of this book explores me grappling with why.

My mother preferred that I sit down to pee. My aim was awful for potties because I was too tall and for toilets because I was too short. My father spent time teaching me, but I developed a preference for sitting until my first wife, Elena, teased me enough times that I taught myself. Since then, I usually pee standing up if it's an option.

My favorite toys were robots, Lincoln Logs, Transformers, Legos, and stuffed animals. When I was learning to walk, I had a stuffed bear that could be wound up to play a song. I called it "Blue Bear." I'm sure you can imagine what color Blue Bear was. When I was at the cruising stage of walking, I somehow believed I couldn't walk without Blue Bear. I would take some steps with Blue Bear, and if somebody took Blue Bear, I'd drop to the ground.

As I grew older, I developed a collection of stuffed animals, including two Koosas from the Cabbage Patch Kids collection. My mother bought me a Tesorino, a male doll that you could "feed" and it would eventually "pee." I remember playing with it. She had hoped it would help make me nurturing. At night, I pretended my bed was a spaceship and my stuffed animals were my crew. It made me feel safe from the dark.

I grew up as an only child until I gained older stepsiblings as a teen. Our house was in Western Coventry, Rhode Island, a very rural section of a rural town. Our nearest neighbors were hundreds of feet away. I lived 5 miles from the Connecticut border and only half of my road was paved so that the local farmers could ride, or walk, their horses on a dirt road. I lived directly across from a corn field that made for great games of hide and seek. Unfortunately, it also came with a yearly stench of manure that included dead chickens. Our dogs would often bring some of the chicken carcasses to the house!

My father built me a train set that I loved. He also built me a jungle gym that I liked to play on when it wasn't hot out. We had a pool. For a brief period, we had an old pony that couldn't be ridden. The pony was from a cousin who couldn't care for it. We had a barn and were able to set up an electric fence for the pony. I liked to pretend an old wooden box I had in the barn was a TARDIS from *Doctor Who*, letting me travel through space and time.

We had cats and dogs. When I was old enough, I started getting my own pets. I had a parakeet, but it died young. Next, I had a box turtle, which, to this day, is my favorite type of animal. I didn't know back then how much box turtles hate being far from their birthplace. I had gotten the turtle with the hope it would outlive me. One day, I discovered my turtle had died. I was heart-broken and, to this day, don't want pets.

With nobody my age to play with, I wished for siblings. No amount of imagination or animals made up for the lack of kids to play with. My parents asked me when I was older why I, an only child of only children, have so many kids. I would always reply, that's exactly why! I hated being alone. I'm an extrovert.

Pre-school

I felt, as early as pre-school, that I was stuck in a male body and had better make the most of it. I had no information or role models to show me there were other options. I wished that if there are future lives that my next life would be female. Americans who transitioned as early as 1970 often realized they were trans because of their mental health professionals. Due to my issues with mental health professionals, I didn't seek one out until 2018.

There are three memories I have of pre-school. I remember that, during lunch, I accidentally ate a fly once. I remember the rows of cots for naps. I remember my two closest friends.

When it came to friendships, I always wanted to be "one of the girls." I had much better friendships with girls. Most boys, even prior to puberty, were too aggressive for my taste. While I find some men physically attractive, most men have personalities that put me off. Also, since society was (and is) more accepting of heterosexual couples it was the path of least resistance.

I'm not sure of their names, although I have a guess about one of their first names, my two closest friends were girls. We hung out together a lot. One day, we made a pact that when we became adults, we would have a three-way marriage, not knowing such a thing was illegal in the US at the time.

At some point, I was enrolled in gymnastics. My parents set up a balance beam in our basement that I enjoyed. My (male) instructor got ill and had to stop teaching. The studio was no longer able to hold gymnastics classes, but a female teacher taught dance classes. They wouldn't accept me into the existing classes. The teacher mentioned potentially adding a military tap dance class that I could join, but it never happened.

I didn't take much interest in clothing when I was young. My mother picked out stuff and I just went with it. I do remember having body image issues with swimsuits. I didn't like changing around other kids. I felt uncomfortable swimming without a top. I cut some paid swimming classes at the Seekonk YMCA because of this. Those are the only classes I ever cut.

Sitter

My parents both worked full time. My mother was a teacher in North Kingstown and my father worked as an electrical engineer for New England Telephone. I was sent to Mrs. Trudeau, a babysitter, for care before and after school. Unlike my grandparents, my parents didn't believe in corporal punishment. Usually, when I got in trouble at the sitter's house, I was forced to stand in the corner. There was one time she got so upset with me that she hit me. I think she threatened me not to tell my parents but I'm not sure. I did tell my father, and it never happened again.

Figure 3: Forest and Dad

When I was much younger, I had had a different babysitter. I don't remember much about the first babysitter but at some point, I fell in the bathroom and my chin slammed into the track for the shower's sliding doors. I bled so badly that I needed stitches. To this day, there is some scarring. It's part of why, with a few exceptions, I had a beard from the moment I could grow one until I decided to transition.

I was one of several children who went to Mrs. Trudeau. Her husband did construction work. I was so afraid of Mrs. Trudeau that I would pee my pants rather than ask her for permission to use the bathroom.

One Halloween, she had a pumpkin that she carved. It started to rot and one day it looked like someone kicked it. One of the kids blamed me. There didn't seem to be anything I could do, and I was in trouble no matter what, so I just pretended I had done it and took the punishment for it.

Figure 4: Halloween

Things weren't all bad at Mrs. Trudeau's. I liked some of the other kids, especially playing with the girls. At some point, I bought an Atari 2600. I spent so much time there that I brought it over. After I stopped going there, I was too scared to ever return to reclaim it.

It was at her house that I saw the Challenger explode on television. It was heartbreaking. I thought Christa McAuliffe was so brave. During this period of my life, I wanted to be a scientist. I suddenly had to face the fact that the world wasn't as safe as I thought.

Elementary School

I ran with a rough crowd in my early years of elementary school. Several boys and I were schoolyard bullies. Mostly, we teased other kids. I remember a lot of chasing people. I don't remember having any fights. I do remember peeing outside at times.

I got stuck in a jungle gym once. They called my mother, who drove all the way from North Kingstown. I was wearing a coat and my torso was stuck between the bars. She had me take off the jacket, and then, I was able to slip out.

I was very jealous of the girls' sexual education class. It was fourth grade, and I was stuck with the boys. I remember passing the time by making jokes with the boys like, "GF—we bring good farts to life." It would be at least another year until the boy's Sex Ed class, and I don't remember it at all.

Figure 5: Forest and friend

Near the end of elementary school, our music teacher had us form teams to take part in a lip sync contest. I think my team was me and two boys. We performed a song I picked from The Alan Parsons Project. I don't think we won, but we did so well that some of the other teams said we cheated and used dry ice. There was no dry ice.

My mother and I recently were corresponding because I wanted to show her a sample of my handwriting now that I've transitioned. I loved seeing girls write feminine scripts when I was young and hated having to write the default masculine handwriting. In 6th grade, one of my teachers gave me poor grades because of my handwriting, despite the assignments having nothing to do with handwriting. My mother, who for her entire career was an elementary school teacher, stuck up for me. Here is a quote from her, that she gave me permission to include:

> *I really went after him at our conference, and I'd required the principal to be present. If I hadn't been a teacher myself, I don't know how I'd have handled it, but*

> *I knew what good teachers did and didn't do. Frankly, even then I wondered if he felt somehow threatened by having a gentle "male" in his class. He didn't strike me as someone secure in his own masculinity.*

I don't remember anything about him beyond his moustache and his issues with my handwriting. Maybe I noticed he treated me differently from other male presenting students, and I blocked it from my mind. Another possibility is that because so many adults and peers would take issue with me being more feminine, that his teaching didn't strike me as being unusual. He was also my first male teacher, so I had no other male teacher to compare him to.

Later in life, I created a "secret" handwriting style with my left hand. While I slightly prefer my right hand, I'm almost ambidextrous. I wanted to have two very different styles of handwriting so I could write things that wouldn't match my right-handed handwriting. With my left hand, I developed a font that had every circle and dot look like a heart. Since I've transitioned, I usually write both my old font, which takes less time, and my feminine font with my right hand.

Divorce

One night, I woke up to my parents arguing about whether I could sleep on a couch. They were in the living room, and I was in my bedroom. I started crying. I told them I didn't care if I had to sleep on a couch. I just wanted them to stop fighting.

I was still in elementary school when the divorce happened. It felt like my world was turned upside down. My classmates were all starting to think about dating and junior high, while I was trying to understand what family meant after divorce.

At some point, I was asked if I had a preference for who to live with. At the time, I preferred living with my mother. It's a really awkward position to put a child in. I felt my mother had more stability and structure, which is what I wanted at that age. When I was older, I wanted more freedom and felt it would be better to live with my father.

Ironically, their divorce made me swear to myself I would never divorce. I'm in my early forties and have already had twice the number of divorces as they had. Both of my divorces have been because my partner asked to divorce. I don't know what it says about me, but divorce rates have been declining since the 1980s. While I like the social liberties we have in the US, I often feel like countries with more conservative beliefs about marriage force couples to work out their issues. As utopian as I may see those marriages, I realize many countries have higher rates of domestic abuse. Despite my fear of therapy, I asked both of my marriage partners if they would try therapy before divorce and both declined. It felt like both of them didn't think I was even worth trying to salvage the relationship. I didn't consciously know this at the time, but my mother also had asked my father to try a marriage counselor and he declined.

My parents each had a lawyer, but this was a long time ago and it was long before mediation was a choice for divorce. In my first divorce, we didn't use lawyers or a mediator. I did all the paperwork and reviewed it with my partner before we filed. I tried a similar approach in my second divorce, but my partner was nervous that I might have missed some important details and after we visited the courthouse, she asked for us to see a mediator.

My mother was urged by her lawyer to stay in our home until I graduated. The lawyer felt it increased her chances of getting custody for weekdays during the school year. I spent three out of four weekends with my father, and two weeks in the summer, which we usually used to camp in the Sandwich Notch of New Hampshire.

Around the time of the divorce, my mother had been considering becoming vegetarian. She worried being vegetarian would have a negative impact on her for the divorce, so she decided against it. During my second divorce, I became a flexitarian, only eating meat when cooking meat for my kids.

Figure 6: Forest, Dad and Grandpa 1988

As a parent, I know that I don't want my kids to worry about me. They do though. When I recently had a bilateral orchiectomy, one of my kids said that they were glad I have no short-term plans for vaginoplasty because they feel it is a really dangerous surgery. From time to time, I worry about my mother. I have felt at times that she closed off her heart to new romantic relationships in order to protect herself from being hurt again.

Junior High

Junior high is when I feel like I began to shape my world views. Unlike all my years before junior high, this is also the point when I really started remembering things.

When I first entered junior high, there was a small group of boys from another school system that targeted me to bully. One of them sat behind me once and hit my ear. When one of the smaller ones tried to get in on the action, I challenged him to a fight in the locker room. It was like a scene in a movie with a circle of boys hoping to see a fight. We pushed each other a few times. My opponent quickly realized I was faster and more athletic than he was, and he backed down. I let him go, and nobody bothered me again until high school.

I had a huge crush on Carolyn, a very intelligent girl who was one year ahead of me. Occasionally, we ended up at the library together. I could barely get a sentence out speaking to her. Her younger sister, Jennifer, and I later became friends, which is how I was able to reconnect in the age of social media. I now have platonic friendships with them. Carolyn was the salutatorian of her class at Coventry High School (CHS).

Around the time I found my middle school yearbook in a recent move, I saw a post by Carolyn about the penalty women pay in their careers if they have families. This got me thinking about her class at CHS. Laurie was valedictorian. I remember finding Laurie and Carolyn to both be brilliant and imagined they would go on to win Nobel prizes, be doctors, or high ranked politicians. Jennifer is an air force officer, which is pretty impressive (even to me as a pacifist). Obviously, we haven't reached our peak yet, but how far can somebody from Coventry go? Peter Farelly is from Rhode Island and he's made some pretty famous movies.

I don't remember going to dances in elementary school. I went to multiple dances in junior high. I had a friend who would stand facing the wall near a vending machine while he rubbed his hands up and down the opposite side of his back to make it look like he was making out with someone. The dances generally started with girls on one side and boys on the other, and nobody dancing. It's similar to how adults are terrified of getting on the dance floor until there is a critical mass. In my 20s, I considered the early hours in the night clubs I frequented (like Club Hell) as opportunities to use all of the dance floor.

I joined lots of clubs. I was already very active in scouting. As a cub scout, I earned the Arrow of Light. In Boy Scouts I was quickly working my way towards Eagle.

Figure 7: Eagle Scout

In junior high, my favorite club was the Audio Video club. I know, classic nerd. We were responsible for all of the video recording done for the school. We had high end cameras, a mixing board, and editing equipment. This was when video used analog cassette tapes. The school put on an annual pseudo-talent show. We were responsible for lighting it, handling the sound system, and recording it. After the show, we would take the best video and edit it into a VHS, which we sold. One of my responsibilities from 1990 to 1992 was to log into the internet each morning to print out certain usenet subscriptions that interested the teachers.

I was a part of the school's newspaper when the Gulf War began. During Vietnam, my father had joined the Navy as a 1A and would have been drafted into the army or marines if he hadn't enlisted. He wanted to join the SeaBees, but they were full. He served on the *USS Princeton* as an electrician when they helped recover Apollo 10 and also a mission to "nuke" an Alaskan island. He also served on the *USS Washoe County* and *USS Coral Sea.* When he left the Navy, my father had the rank of petty officer 2nd class in the role of an Interior Communications Electrician. The Navy offered to make him an officer, but he declined in favor of college via the GI Bill and a job with New England Telephone.

Both of my parents had strong views against war. I don't remember what articles I wrote prior to the war but, as soon as it broke out, I demanded to cover it. While I had my own anti-war stance, I worked to show an unbiased view of how the war impacted everybody involved. I never imagined I'd end up working for a CEO who had lived in Kuwait when the war began.

I went with my mother to an anti-war, Quaker vigil. The first protest I ever went to was in Providence where many of us had signs that said things like "War is a Dead End," "Try Peace," and "Bring the War Home." I started wearing a pin that said, "No Blood For Oil."

A more popular reaction to the war was the yellow ribbon campaign to support our troops. As George H.W. Bush was the one that sent our troops to Kuwait, I saw no disconnect between supporting the troops who were doing their job and being against the war. I began wearing a yellow ribbon that had a US flag. I went with my scout troop to a yellow ribbon rally in Providence. There were several speeches given, including one where somebody said the protesters were unpatriotic. This is when I realized most people see politics as black and white. You are either for the troops and the war or you are against them. After the last scheduled speaker, they invited people from the audience to come up and talk. I was very tempted to go up and tell the crowd that I supported the troops but was against the war. I don't remember if I stopped wearing my yellow ribbon, but I didn't go to another yellow ribbon event.

I think the first feminine attire I ever remember wearing was a pair of nylons. One afternoon, probably after taking part in a club, I snuck into the girls' locker room at my middle school. I don't remember why I did this. It may have just been curiosity. I discovered a lost and found box with a clean pair of nylons. I stole them and hid them in my room for years. I remember being afraid of being caught, but I found it a little thrilling. That was the only time I ever went into a female locker room until I started transitioning.

I wore the nylons a few times in private. I felt like it was a fetish, so I wrote it off as a sex thing and, only later, realized that while it had a sexual element, it was also a part of my gender identity. I actually might still have those nylons. A common theme in the stories I've heard from other trans women is that they would start getting women's clothes and then something would scare them, and they would toss them all away. For example, they would start a relationship and not want to explain why they had those clothes. I've never thrown away clothing out of embarrassment.

I caught my love of acting while playing Peter in *The Diary of Anne Frank*. After the performance, we met Judith Sternburg Newman, a survivor of the Auschwitz concentration camp and author of *In the Hell of Auschwitz*. My copy is signed, although the dedication is to my mother. I read it almost immediately. When I visited Auschwitz in November 2018, as part of my last international work trip before I transitioned, I spent a lot of time thinking about her book.

Puberty

I remember clearly when I began identifying as bisexual: it was right after puberty. Until recently, I only ever revealed this information to partners and friends within the LGBT community. Generally, I feel who I choose to have sex with is nobody's business, except for current and future partners. I think part of the reason I was able to accept being bisexual was because it had nothing to do with birth and was fairly common. I had met bisexual people and knew I was one of them.

I wouldn't learn the term pansexual, which I believe is a better description of my sexuality, until I was much older. When people transition, it's common for us to be asked things like, "So, are you still going to have sex with women?" While I think these questions are entirely inappropriate, I knew they would come up repeatedly and I decided to just come out as pan at the same time I came out as trans. I now have a jacket that I've painted the back with the pan flag inside of the trans symbol, which was partly inspired by a family member who painted their nails the bi-color flag and partly from the jacket Jules wore in *Euphoria* that had a trans symbol painted on it.

It was unclear to me, due to having boy parts, when I reached puberty. My mother kept saying things like, "once you've reached puberty," and "during puberty." As much as I disliked talking to my parents about sex, this confusion led me to ask her, "How do I know if I've hit puberty?" She told me if I started having wet dreams then I'd hit puberty. I don't remember having any "wet dreams" as a teen and even as an adult they were very rare. By the time I had asked this question though, I had ejaculated enough times to know I'd "reached puberty."

A lot of trans people experience dysphoria as part of puberty. While I certainly experienced confusion, I never experienced dysphoria due to primary sex characteristics. I did, however, experience an overwhelming libido that would haunt me until I began medically transitioning.

My friends and I used games like "Truth or Dare" to begin sexually experimenting. I went to an overnight Halloween party at the YMCA one year and met two girls my age. I think this was the year I was a California Raisin. I think they had already known each other. We made a fort out of the bedding we had. We played some version of Truth or

Dare that resulted in kissing and groping. We eventually all fell asleep cuddled together.

There was a girl, a little younger than me, who I had been friends with for years. One day, we were daring each other, and it eventually led to oral sex.

There was a guy who was slightly older than me. At first things started with Truth or Dare. We eventually gave up the pretext and became what today would be called "friends with benefits."

It wouldn't be until later that I'd try having romantic relationships. Slurs like "faggot" and statements like "that is pretty gay" were common at the time. This caused me to be reluctant about relationships with men. Eventually, I would come to believe that since I could be with anyone, they'd have to be really special for me to take all the social risks that comes with a same-sex relationship. This was in the era before Clinton signed the Defense of Marriage Act.

Eagle Scout

I doubt there is a list of all the transgender Eagle Scouts, but I'm not the only one. A couple of years ago, they began admitting girls to the program: so, hopefully, around the time this is published some young women will have earned Eagle Scout as women.

I reached Eagle Scout at 14. I ran a bake sale and food drive for my Eagle Scout Project that benefited the Coventry Food Bank. Due to Scouting for Food, usually food drives were not approved as projects. But because I also raised money for the food bank, the district allowed it.

Around the time the approval came through for my advancement to Eagle Scout, I had attended a scout trip that went awry due to poor leadership. After earning the rank of Eagle Scout, I had to make a speech as part of my Court of Honor. My original speech was very inflammatory, but fortunately, somebody talked me down. I rewrote it to be a parable that had similar circumstances but was set in prehistoric times. With it, I urged people to help future scouts.

Somebody recently asked me if I was uncomfortable in the Boy Scouts. I enjoyed scouts at the time. I did wish that I was around other girls more often, but I got that exposure elsewhere. As much as I appreciate the Girl Scout program, I'm not sure I would have gotten as much from it.

It was after I became an adult that I started rethinking my involvement with the scouts. I had become agnostic shortly after I earned Eagle. My religious views and LGBT status were why I never wanted to be involved as an adult. I felt unwelcome. My son, Simon, never showed interest in scouts and when my stepsons got into scouts, I avoided having a role in their pack. I do like that they allow girls now, but I'm not sure if that is succeeding. When Pon showed some interest, back before they came out as non-binary, I was willing to volunteer to help make sure the pack would succeed with girls. We visited the local pack and, for the first time ever, I used my Eagle rank as social leverage. Pon had a close friend they hoped would join. Pon lost

Figure 8: Forest

interest before they finally admitted girls, in part because their friend decided not to join.

I had worked both at Champlin Cub Scout day camp and Yawgoog Boy Scout camp. I don't remember why or how I agreed to wear a dress in the boy scout skit at Yawgoog. I didn't find it embarrassing, except when someone pointed out I had it on backwards. I don't remember any positive feelings about it but also don't remember any negative feelings. I didn't get the fetishistic feeling from it that I got from the nylons. I don't remember connecting this to my gender.

Many people are worried about having co-ed camping. The concern is that due to gender roles, there will be girls who are violated. It's certainly something that can happen as we can see by all the reports of sexual violence on campuses. I think that the Boy Scouts can develop procedures that will limit sexual violence to female campers. Girls aren't the only ones at risk in a Boy Scout camp. There were some adult gay men who were child predators when I worked at Yawgoog. Fortunately, they got fired soon after I left.

Sex is going to happen. I personally had safe consensual sex with a boy at that camp who was a little older than me.

With gendered camping where do non-binary and intersex campers go? Because of the patriarchal state of our country, girls need the option of a safe space. Pon went to girl scout camp before they came out as non-binary. They made a really good friend there. I think that the Boy Scouts opening to girls is overall a positive step. But it will not be smooth.

The Boy Scouts have a camping honor society called the "Order of the Arrow (OA)." As scouts were voted by their troop to join, they often joined years after entering the Boy Scouts and thus "youth" went to 21 instead of 18. I think some of my interest and devotion to OA was because it drew scouts from throughout the district. I think I also enjoyed that we were a service organization. I regularly volunteered in the ceremonial team, which allowed me to make use of my acting skills.

At one event, I drove members of the ceremonial team from where we camped to where the ceremonies took place. As I started driving my VW Rabbit, which was about my age, someone said, "Oh no, it's going to be a hell ride."

In general, I was a very safe driver. But that comment annoyed me, and I decided to show them what a hell ride was really like. The camp roads were all dirt and if there was a posted speed limit, it was probably in the range of 15-25 mph. While I had experience on ice, I had no experience at high speeds on dirt roads. I didn't realize dirt roads reduce the friction needed to stop at higher speeds. I got to at least 30 mph when I noticed a woman crossing the road with her dog. I tried to brake but, due to the sand, I kept going, so I swerved, and we ended up off the road. My oil pan hit a rock and was forever dented and leaky.

I felt awful. I was embarrassed. I was frightened. I felt like I had almost killed my friends, at the time I thought oil was explosive—which it's not. I felt bad for the woman and the dog. The camp rangers had to tow my car back onto the road and they obviously did not let me drive for the rest of the weekend. I apologized to everyone. From that point forward, I was much more careful on dirt roads and it wouldn't be until my early thirties that I would get my first speeding ticket.

I stayed involved with the OA longer than Boy Scouts. I was eventually nominated for the Vigil Honor.

High School

Of all my school experiences, high school was my favorite. What I loved about high school could be summarized as social activities. I had started playing trombone in elementary school. Over the years, I became the first trombone. As an adult, I realize that the rank system for instrumentalists is probably meant to have mentoring. While I worked with the other trombone players, none of us knew at the time how to mentor and never attempted to be mentors.

Composer Richard Wagner once said, "Never look at the Trombones, it only encourages them." That's a fairly accurate statement based on what I know of myself and other trombonists. For whatever reason, those of us who take up the trombone rarely need encouragement. We're often characterized as the hippies of the band.

Band was never more important to me than when I was in high school. Most of my closest friends played at least one instrument. Several of us enjoyed each other's company so much that before school, we hung out in the hall between the music room and the theater. We relished in our status as "band geeks." I also took chorus at some point. It was fun, but not really the same. We were expected to perform in concerts, parades, and at football games. This is where I learned that I have no interest in football.

In elementary school, I had enjoyed soccer until I got paranoid about getting a ball to the face. In general, I enjoy playing sports but with the exception of the Winter Olympics, I hate watching sports. I also have come to detest how few co-ed sports we have and how women's sports are ignored, underpaid, and often ridiculed. The US Women's Soccer Team is awesome.

In high school, I started running Cross Country because I enjoyed running. I enjoyed being part of a team. I even enjoyed that there was some strategy to what otherwise seems like an individual sport. Bishop Hendriken forced all students to take up a sport and many of them opted for Cross Country. As there were no limits to how many could run, this meant they could overwhelm a race. They had sprinters from their track team that acted like rabbits, running really fast at the start trying to get runners from schools like mine to wear out early. We had to learn to ignore these runners and set reasonable paces. I can't say I was ever good at Cross Country. There were a couple of races I finished close to last. There was one race I got stung by a wasp and came in second to last, I probably should have given up that race.

Senior year, it was clear that our coach wanted to make me the captain. Since I was the worst runner in my year, I thought this was an awful idea. I also wanted to take more of a leadership role in the Student Council. For these reasons, I quit Cross Country.

I can't remember if I had joined the Student Council as a freshman or sophomore. At the time, I had this vision of myself being like Ronald Reagan, an actor who became President. While I hated his politics, his way of getting into the White House seemed approachable to me. I felt like, through politics, I could stop the country from entering wars. I had a vision for the country that was very different from what we'd had before. My views were fairly Libertarian at the time. At the end of my junior year, I ran for Student Council president. I lost and decided that despite losing I should put in extra time that year to support the winner. I think that's when I lost interest in politics.

I took all the drama courses available in high school. I was in a couple of plays. Early in my high school career, I had a bit part in *The Twelve Dancing Princesses*, but I went to every rehearsal because I wanted to learn. Even the other theater kids teased me about that. I had makeup to make it look like I had stubble for my character. On one of the performance nights, I accidentally walked into the girls changing room, the embarrassment was amplified by an actress I respected saying, "Eww, get out."

I had a better experience playing the character of Buddy in *The Diviners*. Some of the adults who saw it compared my performance to that of Leonardo DeCaprio's role in *What's Eating Gilbert Grape*.

I felt there weren't enough opportunities in our town for people who aspired to act, so, in my junior year, I co-founded a non-profit called *The Revived Theatre: Those People Who Put on Plays*. There had been a similar company that had folded years before. I tried to recruit from the defunct group but none of them were interested when they discovered most of us were in high school. We successfully put on two plays before I moved on to college. I learned a lot about theater management and production. The company continued after I left, of which I was very proud.

Student council had an intergenerational committee that I joined. We spent time at the seniors' center getting to know the elderly of the town. I found it really rewarding. It was interesting to see how senior citizens are often overlooked. Ageism was a problem they felt because of mistreatment due to their advanced age. I felt people my age were also discriminated against by the lack of self-determinism and representation we had. To this day, I support lowering the voting age to 16.

My best friend for most of high school was a classmate named Lucy. I think that we met in class together. We hung out a lot. One day, years after our friendship started, she took me aside and told me that I followed her around like a puppy dog. At the time, I was upset and avoided her for the rest of high school. We reconnected later in life via social media. For my part, the relationship was always platonic. Thinking back to it now, I wonder if she felt I was interfering with her dating. Perhaps one of her boyfriends felt threatened by me spending so much time with her.

In my senior year, I was the top of my geometry class. With the exception of French III Honors, I had never taken an honors course. I asked the mathematics department head if I could switch to the geometry honors class. He asked me what I planned to do after high school. I said I wanted to act. He said that since it wasn't a math related field, I should stick with the regular geometry class, little did we know I'd have a career in computer science.

Early in life, I had pledged to myself never to do drugs or drink alcohol. I had even been part of a Just Say No club in middle school. There were a few reasons for this. First, there was a friend of the family who had an alcohol problem. Second, I didn't like the thought of losing control. Third, I felt like I had a bit of an addictive personality.

Figure 9: Graduation

I went on our high school trip to France. I also had signed a document saying I wouldn't drink alcohol on the trip, even though it was legal in France. One night, I bit into a chocolate I had bought and realized it had alcohol in it. I ran to the bathroom and spit it out into the toilet. Our first hotel had an elevator that I broke by pressing the door open button between floors. For the rest of our stay that elevator would stop a foot shy of the floor, forcing people to step up and out or down and in. It made me realize how poorly elevators, especially in France, are designed and that their safety is suspect. From that point forward, I take stairs when possible. I found it enlightening that French soap operas and shampoo commercials included nudity on public television. France's acceptance of nudity helped me realize how our Puritan roots have caused us to be afraid of our bodies.

In high school, none of us were out. There was one person who was slightly known by close friends as being gay, but it wasn't until a few years ago that I discovered on social media that there were multiple classmates who were LGBTIA+.

I've realized retrospectively that I grew up in a very white town. The only non-white person I remember interacting with was an adopted Latino boy. I was never close with him, which I also retrospectively regret, as I learned he had issues with depression and had at least one suicide attempt.

Later in high school, a distant friend I knew from a club was in hospital because he had attempted suicide. Another friend alerted me and several of us went to visit him. I think that having us there was helpful, even if I wasn't a super close friend. From this point forward, I have worked to be there for friends struggling with depression. I've also worked to normalize it by talking about my own issues.

Cindy

After my parents divorced, my father began dating. When my father started dating Cindy, I had a hard time accepting her. I had trouble letting go of the marriage my parents had. It felt like my father was replacing my mother. Cindy never resented the emotional wall I built against her.

At times, I was able to let down my defenses and be close with her. She was with us the first time I ever went to a drive-in. It was my birthday present, something I had wanted to experience for years. I still take my kids regularly to the drive-in.

When I was younger, I would wake her up to watch cartoons. This was back when cartoons were only on at certain times chosen by the stations that sent them through an analogue signal in the air waves.

I recently saw a picture of their wedding. I was my father's "Best Man." I looked uncomfortable in the photo, which may have been because I was in the sun.

Cindy was one of those people who silently volunteered in the background. She volunteered both in the Boy Scouts and Order of the Arrow. She was unanimously voted by the boys to receive the Vigil Honor. She was a volunteer forest ranger for multiple summers in Sandwich Notch, New Hampshire. When my stepsister had a son that she, and the father, couldn't care for, Cindy took the boy in. When my grandfather needed it, she provided elder care. She helped her local church run their white elephant sale and served as a deacon. When Sandwich, New Hampshire had its annual fair, she baked food and sent it to the volunteers.

As was true of my biological parents, when she learned I was trans she immediately accepted it. It was around this time that I realized how much I had taken her for granted. Soon after I came out to everyone, I called her and apologized for being so distant throughout my life. I knew she didn't need to hear it, but I felt I needed to say it.

She struggled throughout her life with medical issues due to a genetic blood disorder. She seemed to be in the hospital regularly, often astonishing the doctors with symptoms they couldn't attach to a diagnosis. I believe sexism played a part in how doctors were often dismissive of her.

On her last birthday, I called her in the hospital. The doctors had finally made a diagnosis, Stage 4 lung cancer. As depressing a birthday present as that sounded, she said she was relieved to finally know. She was back at her home a few days later and I visited her. She was in more pain than I had ever seen her. We cried together. She had a pain med that she wanted to take, but she feared it would make her fall asleep. It felt like she chose to bear the pain so she could spend a little more time with me.

Two weeks after my visit, the country went into lock down due to COVID-19. It seemed unsafe to visit her and risk getting her infected with COVID-19. I didn't think I'd be able to see her alive again.

I got a call from my father in May while I was visiting my co-parent. It was rare for my father to call: usually, I call him. We knew it was probably bad news. He told me Cindy was in the hospital and she was expected to pass in the next 24 hours.

It was already late on a Friday night, but we told him we would visit. I drove my co-parent, Nicole, and one of my (former) stepsons. At the entrance, they said they would only allow one person in at a time and that they wouldn't let underage people in. My stepson would have to stay outside. I had Nicole go first. While she was there, I had my stepson write a message that I would read. I spent some time with Cindy helping her with her juice.

The nurses said she was doing better than they had originally thought. She was holding on for a little longer. I returned on Mother's Day. I helped feed her yogurt, lobster, and a popsicle. While I was there, the staff needed to change the sheets. It caused her a lot of pain, which was very upsetting to witness. Her stepsister and minister visited. I was misgendered a few times, but I didn't care. I wasn't there for me. I was there for her. As the day turned to night, I worried that my kids were probably driving each other crazy. When I left, I called my son and told him how to heat up the fries and chicken nuggets that were in the freezer. Cindy died a few days later.

My son and I visited a weekend or two later. I wanted to spend some time with my father. He had some clothing and jewelry of Cindy's that he wanted me to go through. I was surprised at how many of her shirts I liked, multiple purple shirts (the best color) and some scrubs with hearts on them. Scrubs are great because of their pockets. I am wearing one of these shirts while writing this chapter. I have some mixed feelings about wearing her clothes. I'm glad I have them. I really like them, but I'm sad that she's gone.

Due to COVID-19, it wasn't until the start of August that we could have a service. It was only a couple of weeks after my surgery, so I camped outside my father's house as I felt I was at higher risk. Other members of the family stayed in the house.

The service had four ministers, three more than I'd ever seen at a service. She had been very involved in church throughout her life. Listening to them, I realized she had made a much larger impact than I had realized. It was very clear from everyone that she had lived a life of service to her communities.

They gave everyone an opportunity to speak. When her grandson, who she and my father had helped raise, talked about how much she had done for him, I started crying. My father got up and hugged him, which was one of the most beautiful gestures between men I've ever witnessed.

Later, we spread her ashes. My stepbrother and I spread them together. I felt like an imposter. I had taken her for granted for so long, and he had been part of her life for over a decade longer.

On my ride home from Cindy's memorial, "Everything" by Alanis Morissette played. I bought it over a decade ago but hadn't listened to it for years. It struck me as it describes the people I want in my life. People who I, at times, take for granted—like my parents, including Cindy.

Update Enterprises

The first computer I ever used was an Apple IIc that my father had purchased. At Fitchburg State University, my son's computer club recently discovered an Apple IIe. He said it didn't work, it just loaded a useless prompt. I asked him if he had tried running software from a disk or reading the manual. He and his friends hadn't known that back then the operating system interacted via a command line and that all the instructions were in a manual. I did a Duck Duck Go search for the manual and gave him a link.

I think I mostly used the Apple IIc to play *Space Eggs*, which was really fun. My mother later bought me a Macintosh 512k Enhanced. I played a lot of text-based games like *Wishbringer* on that system. I also had *Golden Oldies*, which was a compilation with *Eliza*, *Pong*, *Life*, and *Adventure*. *Dark Castle* was my favorite game for the Macintosh 512ke. I also wrote my first novella on it, which was filed for copyright but never published. One day, I made a drawing of the TARDIS from *Doctor Who* that used up all the ink.

Around high school, my mother bought an IBM 486DX with a whopping 50MB HDD. I think it had 4 MB of RAM, which I upgraded to 16 MB. I also installed a SoundBlaster 64-bit sound card and speakers. She used the computer for a while, but then, she gave up on it and switched to a word processor, which was basically a fancy typewriter. I used BAT files to create a menu system for MS-DOS. From the menu system, I launched my favorite DOS games *Warcraft II* and *Doom*. The menu system also allowed me to launch Windows 3.11. The first software I wrote was an edutainment game that gave math quizzes using random numbers and random operators. I wrote it in QBasic using a manual my father had.

My "computer" friends, who were all male, were using PASCAL for various projects, including a voting tabulation software that would eventually be used to say I lost the election for student council president. I can't remember how I learned PASCAL, but I used it to write a security program that prevented access to my 486 without the password.

This is when I first got an internet connection. I think I briefly used AOL. I certainly used a lot of their free floppy disks. I then switched to a local dialup company. I used the internet to play *Multi User Dungeons* (MUDs), do research (though internet resources were limited), interact on message boards, play *Warcraft*, post *Warcraft* maps, and view porn (which was all pictures or text on Usenet groups). Some of my maps were bundled in a CD with an edition of *PC Gamer*.

For MUDs, I played a mix of male and female characters. Usually for MUDs, my real-life friends were on, I played as a male character named Raoul. Other MUDs I played as Joan, including a MUD to which I contributed some of the DikuMUD programming.

My friends and I had various ideas for startups. Three of us got together and founded Update Enterprises Inc. Our original idea was to create a cyber cafe. We created a business plan and since I had the business experience from The Revived Theatre, I did all of the paperwork. Unfortunately, nobody was willing to invest in two high school seniors and one high school junior.

Our next idea was a patent for a smart remote that would control all the devices in your home. We designed it so manufacturers could ship a card with their appliance that would be installed in a central station. This also faced cost issues.

At the time, CDs had to be mass printed in order for them to be worth a manufacturer's time. Hardware manufacturers had started selling CD writers. We split the cost (about $3,000) and bought one at CompUSA. I had a friend in a band that couldn't afford to mass produce CDs. He was going to be our first customer. Unfortunately, there was a compatibility issue that basically made the CD writer unusable.

Our final attempt at making a business was by selling web development services. One of our members had done HTML work for his father's company. We began cold-calling businesses but, as the internet was still so new, we never made enough for the effort to be worth it.

Elena

Elena lived near my father's apartment when I was in high school. She was a few years older than me and already done with school when we met. For me, it was love at first sight. I hadn't dated before I met her and had no idea what to do. We started as friends. During my summer vacation, my family and I invited her to camp with us for two weeks in the Sandwich Notch at Kiah Pond.

Kiah Pond is where Cindy and her kids would camp for the summer as Cindy did her volunteer ranger duties. Elena and I went canoeing one day. I hadn't done a great job explaining how important it was to stay balanced while in a canoe. Kiah is a beaver pond. I was navigating us past the beaver lodge and, as I pushed my oar into the water on the right side, something caught her attention on the same side, and she peered over, which caused us to flip. We were both good swimmers, but the canoe needed to be flipped and we were fully clothed, good thing cellphones hadn't been invented yet. My stepbrother heard the commotion and walked along the shore to get close to us. He said he was going to jump in to help.

I shouted to him, "Take your pants off."

He said he wasn't going to.

I said, "Take your pants off so it's easier to swim."

He said no and jumped in. I asked him recently why he said no. He responded that he didn't want leeches on his legs. There were a lot of leeches in the pond that year.

After we got back to shore, I felt a little annoyed at Elena. It was ridiculous though because I hadn't warned her.

She and I went on a walk together and I finally asked her out. She thought it was a bad idea because I was still in high school. I said I was mature for my age. I probably enumerated all of my accomplishments.

I tried to let her think about it on her own, but I couldn't help myself from asking regularly. One night, we were playing a game called "Pass the Pigs." It was a game with two plastic pigs that you rolled like dice. Your score was based on how they landed. At one point, I gestured to the pigs and asked, "Is this kinky?"

She shook her head.

I asked, "Want to try something that is?"

She politely declined. As the vacation progressed, I started writing poetry to her. I was in the middle of reading Stephen King's *Dark Tower* series. My poems were full of rose metaphors inspired by the series. Eventually, she agreed to date me.

We were secretive about our relationship for a while. I remember sneaking out of my father's apartment late at night to visit her. As the weeks became months, we realized we could have a future and started telling people. I don't remember getting any flak about our relationship, perhaps because we were known for being stubborn and it was hard to change our minds.

Elena wanted to do visual arts for a career but was working in retail when we met. One of my favorite pieces by her was of a green plant that contrasted sharply with the white paper it was drawn on. I bet my youngest, who is a digital artist, and Elena would have been good friends if they had met at a different time. While many decades apart, their birthdays are within a day of each other.

I had adopted long hair in high school. My father had a ponytail, so I felt like even stuck as a boy, I could have long hair. It was also around the time *Interview with a Vampire* was released with a long-haired Brad Pitt.

Elena and I were at a restaurant one night when a waitress approached us from behind and said, "Ladies, what can I get you?" While I hid that I felt it was a compliment, I realized that facial hair would probably reduce confusion.

When Elena was in elementary school, she had been best friends with a girl. When they got into middle school, the girl tried to gain popularity by saying Elena had tried to kiss her and was a lesbian. This was a hugely traumatic experience for Elena. There was no acceptance for LGBT people in her hometown.

My first wife and I have almost the same shoe size. There was a pair of high heels she had but didn't like. I wore them, with her, in private. I specifically made a point of saying they were a fetish because of that incident that happened to her in school. I was afraid to discuss gender with her and don't ever remember discussing it with her.

She used to tease me because I would sit to pee. I got out of the habit so she wouldn't keep teasing me.

I think I proposed to Elena during my senior year of high school. We got married in Colt State Park the summer I graduated. We both loved the renaissance and had a themed wedding. The whole event was about $800, which was perfect for our budget.

The night before our wedding, Elena and I got into an argument. I don't remember what it was about, but I was upset and wanted her to stop talking. She didn't stop and I got so angry that I shoved her. It's the only time I have ever purposely hurt a partner of mine. I felt so ashamed and guilty. She forgave me that night, but I doubt I'll ever forgive myself.

When I moved to Fitchburg, I found some wedding photos from my first wedding, as in, during the dark ages when we used film and printed pictures. My head hair and my facial features looked far more feminine than now. If I had transitioned then…

Elena and I joined the Society for Creative Anachronism (SCA) as something we would both enjoy. I got involved with their heavy list fighting where I literally got to beat people with sticks! Unlike re-enactment groups, fighting in the SCA is a martial art. In fact, it is deemed the hardest hitting martial art in the world. Like medieval fighters trained, the SCA uses weapons made out of rattan. The armor people wore had to be thick leather, steel, or strong plastic. Our helmets were made with 10-gauge steel.

During my time in the SCA, there was a well-ranked man who was a local leader for my area. One day, he was regaling us with one of his many stories. He mentioned how he was working and bumped into somebody who used to be a fighter and had transitioned to female. He dead named her to try to get her to admit to her past. "Ha, ha, ha, what a freak," the group agreed. It made me realize that I needed to be on guard with them. If only he had been more enlightened and it had been a positive reunion, so I could have asked who she was and not had to wait 15 years to meet another trans woman.

The first time I wore a kilt was around 1997. It was a great kilt that I made with a sewing machine for my character in the SCA, Roderick Loch. While I know of no Scottish lineage in my family, I've always had a fondness for the Scottish people.

We ultimately left the SCA because, ironically, Elena had a falling out with the wife of that storytelling fighter. The falling out made it uncomfortable for her to be involved locally and, thus, the SCA was no longer a thing we could both enjoy.

I didn't start wearing a kilt regularly again until I started to get re-exposed to them at burner events, sci-fi conventions, and nightclubs. My favorite kilt was my Utilikilt. It's a well-made, durable garment that fits comfortably, and that I felt looks good on me. That kilt cost about $125

It's one of the cheapest kilts the Utilikilt company made. Utilikilts are also popular in parts of California, which is where the company is based. California is also the state with the highest number of Burning Man participants. Obviously, kilts are popular in Scotland, although the kilts that are popular there are, to me, a dull descendant of the great kilt. Kilts are not weird, or even counterculture, for some of my preferred communities. Many people I know wear kilts regularly, in normal activities, including work. I wore my kilt because it's comfortable, I like how it looks, I like how it feels, and I love how it moves. The kilt complimented some of the dancing I did.

When Elena and I had first met, I was slightly interested in shopping at Eddie Bauer. There had basically been two styles in my high school: preppy and grunge. There were a few who broke the mold: for example, there were some who went for a Goth look. I was firmly in the preppy camp, although I did have a baggy pants phase in middle school. My favorite shirt was a purple turtleneck, which I still miss. As I got older, I got less and less interested in buying clothes. My only options—male clothing—seemed dull. I very actively avoided shopping, especially for clothes. I'd repair clothes before I ever considered replacing them. Elena got so frustrated with how ratty my clothes would get that sometimes she would replace them. One day, she gave me a pair of shoes that were a size too big. She said her best friend's husband had bought them, but he didn't like them. It took me a long time to realize this was an elaborate lie to replace my old shoes.

Rhode Island College

Around the time I went to college, I saw some problematic movies. The word transgender is fairly new, so I was only able to identify as trans after it was invented, and I read its definition. Prior to that, the word transexual was used. I didn't ever look up that word because I had seen media portrayals that made me think I wasn't one. Those included *Silence of the Lambs* where the transexual character was a psychopath—clearly not me—and *Rocky Horror Picture Show*, where the characters from Transexual Transylvania were transvestites. I'm not a transvestite. I never watched the *Crying Game* because it sounded horrifically depressing. Years later, I watched *Boys Don't Cry*, and seeing Brandon die, I did not want that to happen to me.

In my first semester, I was a drama major. Originally, I had hoped to go to the University of the Arts (UArts) in Philadelphia. I had tried out to join the acting program, but they declined and instead offered me an opening in theatre management because of my experience with The Revived Theatre. I had co-created The Revived Theatre so I could do more acting (although I mostly did producing), so I declined. I think it was the right choice and can't imagine what my life would be like if I had accepted.

Rhode Island College (RIC) was my mother's *alma mater*. It may not have been as elite as UArts, but it had a solid program for a price my mother could afford. At this point, Elena was working fulltime as a sales representative for a business-to-business company. To help with money, I got a part time job with RIC's IT help desk. At first, this was about helping students with print jobs, helping the President with random Microsoft Excel questions (which is how I learned to use spreadsheet software), and updating computers with A/V software.

We also played *WarCraft II* and later *StarCraft* on the college network. In our group, I won most of the *WarCraft* games, which may have been why they were relieved when we moved on to *StarCraft*. With *StarCraft*, we were all pretty well matched. Some of the players were on the web team and asked me to join.

On the web team, we developed the first version of RIC.edu. That same President who I helped with Excel was required to sign-off on the site before it went live. He delayed because he said the web was just a fad. A quarter century later and that fad seems to be doing pretty well.

Between work and classes, I didn't have much time for clubs, but I did join the radio station (90.7 WXIN). We had a radio station at Coventry High School (91.5 WCVY), but I never passed the auditions, though I had tried multiple times. The differences between the two stations were unusual. WCVY could be heard throughout the town and in a few neighboring towns. I even got it in some parts of Massachusetts. WXIN couldn't be heard if you went a few blocks beyond campus. WCVY had to pay for their music, WXIN got donations from promoters. WCVY never had giveaways, WXIN often had concert tickets. At WXIN, we had trouble giving away prizes because nobody was listening. We used tricks like saying we would take the 5th caller: we usually got no callers. We also would say that we had multiples of a prize, so when nobody called, we could try again later.

I usually DJ'd an alternative program, but sometimes I DJ'd a current hits radio program and ran a talk show. On my talk show, I often had debates with ministers of local churches of various denominations. Because so few people listened to WXIN, we had a lot of freedom.

In my first semester, one of my theatre teachers caused me to have a revelation, which is that there is a huge gap between non-profit theatre and for-profit theatre. For-profit theatre included ridiculous union and guild rules that I wanted no part of. At the end of my first semester, I switched to computer science. Since I already knew the faculty and had proven I could program, they let me skip the introductory classes. I specifically wanted to become a games programmer, which, at the time, was a fairly new field. There were only two colleges at the time that had game development majors and I couldn't afford either. At the time, C, C++, and assembly were the most important languages for a game programmer to know. Any class that required, or taught, a different language, I declined. They wanted me to learn Fortran. I have no idea why, and I said no. They wanted me to learn COBOL because of all the code that had the Y2K bug. I was set to graduate in the spring of 2000, so COBOL seemed like a dead end to me. Therefore, I said no. COBOL and BASIC had both been languages my father had learned when he went to Bryant College.

By the end of my second year, I was in classes with students who were about to graduate. I had completed all of the required 400 classes. I didn't want to stick around for the required math, English, and philosophy classes. Modern dance had been fun, I probably could have gotten a minor in it. All my CS friends were going to graduate and get jobs while I was going to be stuck for two more years

.

MEDITECH

I met Andrea Sinapoli at a RIC job fair. She took my poorly formatted resume and got me an interview. At one point, I was interviewed by a director in the company who asked me how long I thought I would work at MEDITECH if I was hired. This is the one time I ever remember lying in an interview. At the time, I had hoped to spend two years working in the industry prior to moving to a game development company. I had reviewed the MEDITECH benefits, and it was clear they were meant to get people to stay at least five years, so I said five years. I got hired in 1998 with a salary of $26,000 a year. I stayed for sixteen years. First, I worked as a Payroll programmer in the General Financial Implementation group. I transferred to the NMI (Non-MEDITECH Integration or Interface) Implementation group a year later.

The timing was excellent because just as I got the job offer, Elena got laid off. We went from her being the primary income earner to me being the primary income earner, which would remain true for the rest of our marriage.

We had been living in a rundown apartment in East Providence. While the smell of pot is fairly common these days, back then it was really astonishing to regularly smell it from our building. We were both horrified to discover that the neighbor across the hall had Johns she regularly brought to her apartment that would be so drunk they would knock on our door looking for her. With my new income, we made a huge financial step and bought a condo in Milford.

I took part in MEDITECH's 1999 talent show. We had them irregularly and several years later I co-organized a show.

For Y2K, we had a giant party. We had made a lot of changes to make sure our code would work. While the party was partly for support purposes, it had activities to keep us busy when and if nothing happened. I remember watching some movies and playing arcade games.

I transferred into MEDITECH's development division group a few months after it was created. I worked on various things there, including writing Medical Archive Management, some work for the MEDITECH Internet Gateway, some work for Non-Procedural Representation, and eventually working with the scanning application Medical Records Management and the Scanning and Archiving suite.

Simon

When Elena and I had started dating we both were in agreement: no kids! I can't remember why she didn't want kids. I felt like kids were going to hold me back in my career. I wanted to be successful, and I didn't want the responsibility of parenting to slow me down.

Everything changed when I met Elena's niece Maya. Elena's sister and brother-in-law had been living in California: but then, they moved to New England, which gave us opportunities to see them. I spent an afternoon playing with Maya. I think her parents were glad for the break. Maya was excited because I didn't object to playing dolls with her.

After more time with Maya, and lots of introspection, I realized I was wrong. I wanted kids, especially a girl but a boy would be terrific too. What would this mean for Elena? She didn't want to have kids. Suddenly, I realized that perhaps my vow against divorce wasn't such a good idea. If she didn't want to have kids, I'd have to choose between Elena and starting over. I didn't want to lose her. I didn't know if I could ever find another partner, but even if I couldn't, there was always the possibility of fostering or adoption. The world was already overpopulated and there are many kids, especially older kids, who need homes. I've always loved the musical *Annie* and one of the characters in my first novel was an orphan.

I broke the news to Elena. I tried not to make it sound like an ultimatum, but I knew it was one. I told her that I loved her, but she would probably be happier with someone who didn't want children. She was upset, but she decided she'd rather not lose me.

We started trying right away. I can't feel guilty for how soon she was pregnant because now I have my son. I do, however, realize that she needed more time to decide on such a life altering decision.

When my first wife, and later my second wife, were pregnant, I told them I wished I was the one who gave birth. They didn't believe me. I didn't push the issue for various reasons, but mostly because I didn't want them to think I undervalued what they did (i.e., give me a beautiful child). I think, however, they did believe me when I said I would love for them to be the breadwinners and for me to stay home with the kids. Unfortunately, my field has a higher income potential than the fields they were in.

Elena felt she was going to have a girl. She had an ultrasound scheduled when I needed to be at work. I think it was less common for women to have partners at their ultrasound back then. She developed a code to inform me of the baby's gender. If I arrived home to blue clothes, it was a boy: pink clothes would mean a girl.

I had completely forgotten about the code when I came home and found her devastated. There was a set of blue clothes laid out. She didn't want to talk about it at first. Eventually, Elena told me what happened and pointed out that I had missed the blue clothes she had laid out. I was surprised how important it had been to her.

The birth didn't go easily. This was in a time when I was more trusting of hospitals and medical professionals. We picked Women and Infants Hospital of Rhode Island. They had a good reputation. Elena had issues with high blood pressure. When we got close to the due date, we were advised to try induction. They began giving her Pitocin. Her blood pressure climbed to a point where they literally strapped her down to avoid a seizure. I can't imagine how afraid she must have been. I was afraid, but I did my best not to show it. The doctor said they needed to perform a cesarean section. I remember watching as they opened her up. Usually, I get faint at the sight of blood. I probably avoided looking as much as possible, but there are a few glimpses that I still have in my memory.

Our son was born in the summer of 2000, which makes it really easy to remember his age. I was twenty-two at the time. I was the first to feed Simon. My wife was hemorrhaging in the ICU and I was so afraid we would lose her. It was one of the worst moments of my life. At the same time, being the first to feed him was one of the best moments of my life.

Hours later, the doctors told me she was all right. I was circumcised at birth and for hygiene reasons we had planned to have Simon circumcised. While we had told the hospital our plan, I don't think we ever signed a consent form. We were never told when it would happen. They showed up in Elena's room with Simon crying. They explained they had just performed it and how to help it heal over the next couple of weeks. We were absolutely horrified. If I had known how painful it would be for him over those next couple of weeks, I would have said no.

Elena had trouble breastfeeding, so we turned to formula. Unfortunately, Simon had gastric reflux. We felt like he was never keeping food down. We tried a bunch of things and finally succeeded with alimentum. A liter of it cost over $10. It was costing us a fortune but, fortunately, our health insurance helped cover the cost. We got him on solid food as quickly as possible, and once we did, he was fine.

Mostly due to my being a light sleeper, when Simon, then later my stepson, and then finally Pon, woke up at night, I was usually the one to get up, feed them, and rock them to sleep. I used to watch MTV while I was trying to get Simon back to bed.

When I would get home from work during my first marriage, I would be the one to take care of Simon (feed him, change his diaper, and play with him) until I went off to work the next morning. It wasn't as easy to play with Simon as it had been with my niece, but we found things that worked for us. We bonded over walks, parks, and video games.

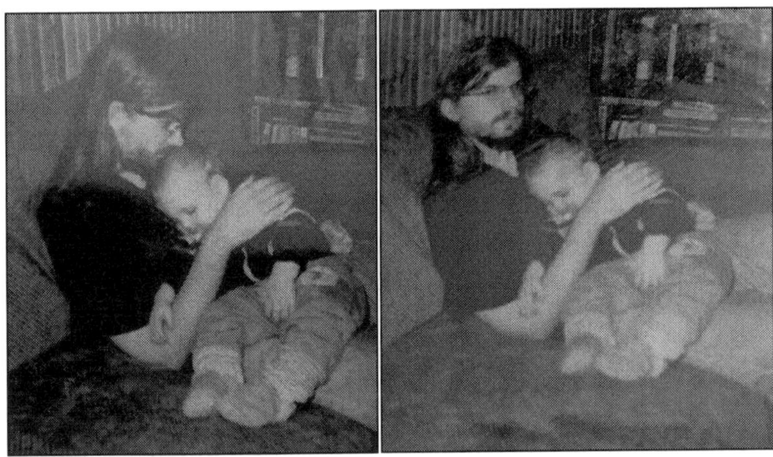

Figure 10: Forest and Simon

Elena was having a lot of trouble in the first year or two. Thinking about it now, she may have had postpartum depression. She also probably was saddened by how some of my attention shifted to Simon. My philosophy is that kids grow up and you have a limited time with them. You have to make the most of it. I didn't do a good job tending to the marriage. She resented that I wanted a child against her original wishes. I've also realized that as much as I enjoyed role-playing the man winning over a significant other, it would wear on me after a handful of years. I would start to wonder why I was always the one giving flowers and never receiving them. I would wonder why I had to plan the dates.

Parenting got so difficult that Elena decided she wanted to move back to California to be with her parents. I agreed and began looking for a job. EA Sports was hiring and wanted to talk to me. I was in LA for GDC when I met them, but between when I set the meeting and arrived, the games industry took a nosedive. It was also shortly after the dot com bubble had burst, so companies were not hiring like they used to. The ones that were, hoped for people who already lived in the area.

Figure 11: Forest and Simon

At MEDITECH, I was just about to be promoted to management when I told them the news. The corporate philosophy extolled "don't fire us and we won't fire you." They asked us to tell them if we were considering a career change. While I didn't have a job lined up, I told them I was looking. After six months of trying to find a new job, while continuing to work at MEDITECH, I was told I was going to be let go in a few months if I didn't recommit. They said I had burned bridges. Meanwhile, they had gotten a transfer from another team to take the position I had been up for, a person who, to this day, I consider the worst manager I have ever worked for.

Elena and I decided to stick it out. As Simon was getting older, things got a little better for her. I "recommitted" but quickly realized I needed to be in another part of the company. Whatever bridges people felt I had burned, it took a decade for me to get another opportunity to manage a team.

My First Divorce

There were many great things about my first marriage. Things I still miss to this day. We had a really solid friendship that lasted far beyond the divorce. Like most couples, we sometimes got into petty arguments. At times, I would be passive aggressive.

During the marriage I struggled with self-worth issues. I had accomplished a lot in the first eighteen years of my life. I had started at MEDITECH in the same group on the same day as a woman who today is an Associate Vice-President. Her first promotion to management was a little after my stumble on the career ladder. It was hard not to compare myself to her. She absolutely deserves her success.

Elena didn't expect me to succeed. She often would discourage me from my efforts at career growth. This really bothered me, and I've often wondered if she was projecting her own self-worth issues onto me, issues that may have been partly due to me. While I didn't know it at the time, this would be a theme for all my long-term partners. All of them have been critical about my attempts to succeed. It bothers me because, for me, a partner is the one person from whom I really want support and encouragement.

During my first marriage, things about which I would have liked encouragement were my website, EastCoastGames.com, my first novel, and my career. I had created EastCoastGames.com in 1998 as a resource for aspiring game developers. It was a first-of-a-kind website. David Perry, creator of *Earthworm Jim*, made a similar site and we had a minor collaboration. Gamasutra was founded a year earlier. I also helped found Compass Rose Games, where I was the co-inventor of a patent for an MMORPG. I also was on the board of the Boston chapter of the Independent Game Developers Association. Near the end of these efforts, I realized that the games industry was not a good place to work for someone with a family, and I soon lost interest.

The first novel I wrote was *Time Keepers*. The first draft was done in 2004. I tried various ways to get a publisher interested but, eventually, gave up. It sat as a file for years. My first draft of *Space Orphans* was finished at the end of 2004. They were written to be in the same universe, but I never wrote novels that connected them. When I couldn't get either published, I tried posting chapters of *Time Keepers* on EastCoastGames.com in 2005.

As Simon got older, I got restless. I played lots of MMORPGs as research for Compass Rose Games. I started with *Asheron's Call*, then I played first the beta and then the release of *Asheron's Call 2*. I was so into *Asheron's Call*, I even attended two in-person Asheron's Call Players Luncheons. I played *Eve Online* briefly, and I did some writing for IGN about *Eve*. I even wrote an *Eve Online* fanfiction. I also tried *PlanetSide* and was in the beta for a little-known game called *World of Warcraft*. By the end of the *World of Warcraft* beta, I was bored with MMORPGs.

In *Asheron's Call*, my original character was called Miyamoto Joan. I played a mid-level character. I joined a monarchy that was very friendly and helpful. I became a solid part of the monarchy and helped newer players. When the developers added housing, our monarch put up some flowers in the guild's home and tagged them as being dedicated to the women of the guild, and included all the women's names, including my own. I felt like such an imposter. I felt like they incorrectly believed I was a woman. I was a woman, but I didn't understand it at the time. I switched to the server Elena was on and began playing as Miyamoto Yoshi. We had a bit of an online falling out: she didn't want me involved in her monarchy, so I found another one and based my character on one of my friends from my prior server. I got a bit higher rank than the prior server.

In 2003, I attended GENCON in Indianapolis. While there, I tried *D&D* and Live Action Role Play (LARP) for the first time. I really enjoyed White Wolf's Camarilla. I played the character they pre-built for me for years. I came up with a costume and makeup for that character and several others I created. Eventually, I started volunteering to help organize work, print a regional newsletter, and create plot for the region.

By the end of 2004, it was clear Elena was unhappy. I was busy writing, and we were both busy gaming. We had drifted apart. She resented the pressure she felt to have a child.

One of the things that bothered her about me was my discomfort in restaurants. I'm still notorious for this. I don't know why, but I used to be uncomfortable in all restaurants. Now, I'm just uncomfortable in fancy restaurants. Basically, any restaurant that wouldn't want a child is a restaurant where I feel unwelcome. This was difficult for Elena because we would go to casual restaurants like Chili's and Olive Garden where I would barely say a word during the meal. To me, an ideal date is an activity like an escape room, laser tag, or rock climbing. If it has to be a meal, I'd prefer it to be a restaurant specializing in foreign food.

Eventually, she asked for a divorce. I was devastated. On 3/3/05, I posted the following on my website:

> *My wife and I are getting separated. Obviously, I have no obligation to post this here. However, I think, at first, I was very much in denial. It will be easier for me to face the facts if everybody knows than if it is a secret. Plus, now I do not have to guess who knows, I can assume everybody does.*
>
> *We are doing what we can to make this a hurtless process. No one person is to blame for this.*

We were living in my maternal grandfather's house. He had passed a little before the divorce. Fortunately, he had lived long enough to meet Simon. Simon does not, however, remember him. Simon remembers the house though. He even has some pictures he took of it.

With my first divorce, we based custody on what my parents did. I had Simon most weekends. He had a clear preference for being with Elena. She also had more availability to care for him.

For child support, I took Rhode Island's formula and added more. Elena had a new car and wasn't going to be able to afford any of it without my help, so I added an amount, as alimony, to cover the full car payment until it was fully paid off. The judge literally hated that we had alimony in the divorce agreement. The lawyer, a woman, said it's why we should have used an attorney. I think she was mostly insulted that we hadn't hired someone who came from her same background, thus making a mockery of the legal system (which, legit, the legal system is something we need to look at with serious derision).

Financially, my biggest sadness was with splitting retirement. I was far younger, but I think it still amounted to $50k.

The Dark Times

My mental and physical health was bad for the next five years. I was too afraid of psychologists to seek one out. I was very depressed. I was never suicidal in this part of my life, but there were a lot of days that just getting out of bed was rough. Sometimes, I'd sleep through most of a weekend.

I felt very fortunate that I had never used drugs or alcohol because it felt like it would have been very easy to use substances to ignore my pain. Ignoring my pain was exactly what I tried to do.

Beyond my emotional issues, I had a few physical issues: the biggest was my allergies. I had postnasal drip that was so bad that the coughing fits would sometimes cause me to gag. After having them for a month, I went to the doctor and he gave me a round of antibiotics. When they didn't work, I returned a month later and he prescribed Claritin. A month later, when Claritin didn't work, he referred me to an allergist.

During this time of unchecked allergies, I was invited to Thanksgiving with some friends. We were supposed to all be there by 4 PM. I didn't set an alarm but ended up sleeping until 4 PM. I contemplated not going, but because I'm an extrovert, I knew I should go. Fortunately, I didn't miss much, and people were happy to have me.

I later suffered from a fungal infection. It took forever for me to realize what it was and get it taken care of.

At one point, I had blood in my ejaculate. It scared me so much I avoided my partner of the time, Cress, for multiple weeks. Ultimately, she convinced me to see my doctor, and even offered to ask her father, a PCP, about it. With the threat of her talking to her father about it, I saw my doctor.

Multiple times, I literally thought I was dying. While I wasn't suicidal, I really didn't mind the thought of dying.

I dove into LARPing, dating, conferences, and dance as forms of escapism. When it was time for the Camarilla to have a conference in our region, I did work to secure a location. The regional leaders were so impressed with my efforts, they asked me to run the 2005 New England Regional Event. There were going to be hundreds of attendees in the weekend-long event. It was the largest event I'd ever been asked to organize. I don't remember if I had hesitation, though I did know I needed a team if I was going to make the event a success. Mostly from a charity auction, we earned $5,000 for the Juvenile Diabetes Research Foundation, and we sent many letters to troops in the Middle East. The Camarilla used a system to incentivize players to volunteer by giving them points that could allow them to make more powerful characters. At the end of the event, I felt burned out on volunteering after having witnessed many people do just enough to earn the maximum points. While I certainly used my points, I didn't limit my work because of points. I found the experience disgusting and, the next year, I left the organization.

I traveled throughout the US to attend gaming conventions. I started regularly attending Boskone and Arisia, two Boston Sci-Fi/Fantasy conventions. I loved that I was able to bring Simon to these local conferences and I began volunteering to help with the programming for kids. I was shocked at how different the kids at these conventions were from the kids Simon went to school with. These were kids that, for the most part, hadn't had their individuality stamped out of them by schools. They had their own ideas and were eager to find ways to express them. It was awesome to see their imaginations and help guide them to success.

During this period of my life, I dated six different partners, all women. Somehow, I had a pattern where I would break up with every other partner and the other half would break up with me. The pattern even corresponded with my first divorce. One of them I broke up with because they threatened to kill themselves, if I didn't get her pregnant.

I was really sad that one of the women broke up with me. Near the end of our whirlwind relationship, we went to a wedding together. She refused to dance with me because I didn't know how to salsa. After she dumped me, I realized I fit her pattern of dating high ranked people from the Camarilla for two weeks and then moving on. Despite the pattern, I decided it was unacceptable to be dumped for dancing inadequacy, so I took salsa lessons for about a year.

I got really close with a woman in the army. She was stationed in Vilseck, Germany. When she had some time to take leave, I traveled to Germany. We explored Nuremburg and Berlin together. I thought we were a great match but when she met Simon, I felt she was jealous of my putting his needs before hers. I felt Simon needed to come first and had to break up with her.

Two of these partners are still good friends of mine to this day. One of them, I met at Firefly, the regional Burning Man event. The other I met at the Fetish Fair Fleamarket in Rhode Island.

I started going to nightclubs in Providence, mostly Club Hell, for their fetish night. At the time, my dance influences were mainly modern, salsa, and the limited amount of hip hop I was exposed to in my youth. One night, at Club Hell, the Boston Babydolls gave a burlesque performance. One of the performers was a woman who hooped. I was amazed at what she could do with a hoop. I was so inspired that I did some searching and discovered the Boston Hoop Troop. I began regularly attending their hoop jams. I soon began making my own hoops.

One day, I brought my son to the Cambridge Commons where the Boston Hoop Troop met weekly. While we were hooping, a man came up to me and yelled at me as if I was threatening him with my hoop. He had a pair of shoes over his shoulder. I purposely moved so that he was as far from Simon as possible. I stopped hooping, hoping that it would calm the guy down. He swung his shoes at me, which caused my glasses to go flying. Some of the others had noticed what was going on and tackled him. We called the police, and he was arrested. I wasn't going to press charges but then I heard from one of the others that the guy had a history of assaulting women. It changed my mind and helped cause him to go to prison.

Club Hell and a local monthly Goth/EDM called DV8 is where I met a group of ravers that spun glow poi. They took me under their wing and helped me to learn poi. I then heard of a spin jam for poi and fire artists in Boston. I began to attend that regularly. I noticed that the styles in the Rhode Island raver scene were very different from the styles of the Boston fire artists. I created my own style by blending my favorite parts of these two styles. The Providence crew decided to run a poi competition. I invited friends from Boston. My friend, Michael, came down and won the contest. I was awarded the Peace Love Unity and Respect (PLUR) award for bringing someone better than me. That night, the Providence crew learned from Michael. This was a real "aha" moment in my life, seeing how exposure to other groups could ramp up learning.

During these years, I made a new best friend. She and I were at a party. The hostess of the party was an employee of the Broad Institute working to crack the genome. The genome has always sounded like a hugely complicated problem. This caused me to think of her as a genius. I would never have believed people if they told me that I would work for the Broad Institute one day too.

I had brought my son to the party, and my soon-to-be best friend had brought a friend's son. She accidentally took Simon's shoes when she left. When I was ready to leave, I couldn't find his shoes and we realized that she probably took them by accident. She returned, we had a laugh, and we've been friends ever since. At one point, her daughter, Ella, and Simon went to the same after-school program. Simon stood up for Ella one time when a kid was picking on her.

One night, at a dance club, we had a charity raffle. I won multiple items, including belly dance classes. I asked the dance school when I could attend, and they told me I wouldn't be able to because it was only for women.

Firefly

Various people I was friends with were planning to attend an event called Firefly in 2005. It sounded fascinating when I started to research it. It was based on Burning Man. I had known of Burning Man for a while but as it was located in a desert and I hate the heat, I doubted I would ever go.

This was a radically transformative event for me that's become the most important of my chosen family's traditions. If you've read my book *Flipping*,[2] you'll remember that there is an event called Lava Love that the characters attend, which is based on Burning Man. Reading how Samantha, the main character, experienced the event will give you some idea of what my first Firefly was like.

Burning Man events are called "burns," and those of us who attend are called "burners." Firefly is the New England regional Burning Man event. All burns are based on the 10 principles of Burning Man. It's very hard to explain a burn to somebody who hasn't attended one. Innuendo, a burner who attends Flipside, made an awesome video for YouTube that explains the principles, which you can view via this link https://bit.ly/3hxNnZq.

Like many volunteer-run events I attend, I became a volunteer for Firefly. While I mainly volunteered for the safety team—rangers—in my early years, I additionally volunteered to help with trail lighting and work weekends. Every Firefly includes a Miss Firefly competition. Contestants, who included people who were assigned male at birth, were required to perform for the crowd and judges. Bribing judges with candy, alcohol, and consensual affection is an honored tradition.

In 2005, one of the contestants, Cress, had brought video equipment to film her involvement. She asked if anybody in the audience was willing to film her. As I knew how to use a camera, I volunteered. She, and the other contestants, were highly entertaining.

I didn't expect much to come of helping Cress, but we chatted a bit and became friends. I bumped into her during a ranger shift and almost lost one of the expensive military spec radios when I took a break to "play ranger" with her. We discovered later that we had actually previously been chatting on a message board together about music composition. We dated for a few months and are still friends to this day.

---

[2] *Flipping*, Stephanie Castle Publications 2020

Cress has a bachelor's degree from Harvard. She had previously dated a guy who I found hugely inspiring due to the size and scope of his art projects. I didn't tell her this at the time, but as I learned more about her, I felt like she was way out of my league. She is so much of an out-of-the-box thinker that I doubted she even knew there was a box. While some of my thinking was outside the box, I was well aware of the box. She made a CD for me of songs she wrote and performed, including a song she wrote about our encounter when I was on shift. While I had been really sad about other partners who had left me, when she decided to stop dating me, I immediately accepted it. I felt she deserved somebody who was at her level. I really enjoyed my time with her and picked up some of her techniques for defusing crises.

Radical self-expression is one of the principles of Burning Man. At Firefly, this meant singing, dancing, fire arts, DJing, digital engineering, art projects, theme camps, cooking, and mixology. I was blown away by the art. I had brought my hoops that first year but, beyond that and a bit of nudity, there was very little that was radical about my self-expression compared to most of the other participants. Several male participants wore Utilikilts, especially members of the rangers. Almost as soon as I got back from the event, I bought my own.

While I've brought more art at later burns, it would be years later that I'd realize that rangering is the main form of art I contribute to Firefly. In my second year at Firefly, I volunteered to be a shift lead for some of the ranger shifts for which I volunteered. A band from Jamaica Plain got their bus stuck on the muddy road to the event while I was on shift. Sometimes, rangering is just about giving a different perspective to participants so they can solve their own problems. In this case, I gave them a suggestion that got them unstuck—literally.

The pinnacle of a burn is when an effigy is burned. At Burning Man, this is an effigy of a man. At Firefly, the effigy is usually of a giant firefly. Before the effigy is burned, fire artists usually perform around it. I had seen fire artists perform in videos, but Firefly 2005 was the first time I saw them perform in real life. I knew how to hoop, but not with fire. I knew how to spin glow poi, but not fire poi. That would all change in a few months, and I later became one of the fire artists to perform in the fire conclave of Firefly 2006.

When I returned to the "default world" after my first Firefly, I felt a melancholy that was hard to shake. I'd gone from a place where people were almost universally friendly to the real world, where people often kept themselves to the minimum level of civility. I'd gone from a place where art was ubiquitous, to a place where art was only allowed inside the lines and was almost universally used for capitalist ends. I'd gone from a place where people could be themselves to a place where people did their best to be what they were expected to be.

I made a multi-year plan to eventually attend Burning Man. While very few burners are snobs about people needing to attend the big burn, I felt an amount of imposter syndrome. Burning Man is a very different event from Firefly and even from Burning Man's past self, but there are a lot of experiences to have there that I can't have elsewhere. As part of my plan, I developed a burner's backpack. I took an existing backpack, added arm rests, EL wire, paint, and spray bottles. I added a pouch in the back for free condoms. The spray bottles were so I could spray myself or others with water. I've brought the backpack to a few events. The project was meant to give me some emotional safety to attend Burning Man. The art helped me feel like I belonged. The spray bottles were a way for me to beat the heat.

Providence GlowBugs

In the Fall of 2005, I attended WildFire Retreat. At the time, I was tempted to attend any event that had fire in the title. I didn't understand it at the time, but WildFire wasn't a burn. WildFire is an event to learn and teach the fire arts. It's also a place where vendors can sell their goods. I learned to eat fire, breathe fire, spin fire, and to fire hoop. I was disappointed at how different the event was from Firefly. I've attended about three WildFires. At my final WildFire, I was teaching hooping when I had an unexpected role reversal: one of the Boston BabyDolls I had seen perform at Club Hell attended my class and learned a tiny bit from me.

Firefly is a place where I'm spiritually recharged. WildFire is a place where I learn and teach. After the third one I attended, I felt there were diminishing returns and I decided to stop spending energy on the event.

I had performed in Boston during the summer solstice for an event with some friends. I was told I needed to wear bright colors. My wardrobe did not contain bright colors, so I went to a craft store and got a yellow t-shirt and some paint. The sun can be very frustrating for me due to my pale skin. I painted a sun on one side of the shirt and on the other I wrote, "Forest VS The Daystar."

At WildFire, I made two friends who had formed the Providence GlowBugs (PGB). They were geographically closer to me than the Boston Hoop Troop, so I gladly joined them. The two founders were vegans, who I worried were not getting enough calories. They inspired me to create a vegan potato salad that I packed with carbohydrates.

I'm generally not a gift person. My primary love language is touch and my secondary is quality time. Usually if I need something, I buy it. I generally prefer experiences to gifts. I also don't like giving gifts. On one of my birthdays, my friends from PGB gave me a purple shirt that had a glow in the dark Big Dipper on one side and said "Forest VS The Big Dipper" on the other side. It also said PGB on one of the sleeves. This is the BEST gift I have ever received. Purple is my favorite color. The thought and creativity that went into this shirt gives me a warm fuzzy feeling to this day. I still wear the shirt, though it's starting to fall apart due to its age.

One time, I went to a party in Amherst with the Providence GlowBugs. I had my son that weekend, so I brought him along. We did fire spinning in a park. Some of the best photos I have of me fire spinning are from this night. After the event, we hung out at a local college. Most people were drinking, and they got worried about my son being there. One of my PGB friends got upset with me when I hugged her. I realized I had misread her signals and felt horribly guilty. Between that and people's concerns about my son, I left the party.

At a WildFire afterparty, I found one of my PGB friends outside. It was cold out, and they had very little on to protect them from the weather. I was worried for her but couldn't get her to say what was happening. Then, she vomited, and I realized she was drunk. I had so little experience with alcohol that I didn't recognize the signs. I tried to bring her inside. As light as she was, she wasn't coherent enough to let me help her. I quickly ran inside and got some more friends. We brought her in and got her warmed up. I felt guilty that I didn't know what was happening sooner.

I became comfortable wearing kilts on weekends and at events. Sometimes, while shopping, strangers would see I was wearing a kilt and ask if I was Scottish. I would always say no and leave them speechless. I've only recently realized that this question was a microaggression against my gender expression. I loved how kilts felt and moved. I also liked that underwear was considered optional for a kilt.

A couple of years after I started wearing kilts, I began experimenting with wearing skirts. As much as I liked kilts, it was limiting what I could pair with them. I ended up buying a skirt online and a skirt at a yard sale. The skirt I bought at a yard sale I once wore on a date at the movies. One of the employees of the movie theater saw the skirt. He pointed at it and laughed. I was deeply shocked and saddened. Because he appeared to have Down Syndrome, I didn't feel like I should say anything.

I wore the skirt I had bought online to my last WildFire. One of my friends from the Providence GlowBugs saw me in it and laughed. I don't know what caused her to laugh but, between that incident and the incident at the movie theater, I decided to stop wearing feminine clothing. I'd continue to wear kilts, but not skirts. I saw her at Firefly in 2019 and mentioned the story. While she didn't remember, she apologized.

Figure 12: Forest in kilt

Green Pirate

When I watched Al Gore's documentary, *An Inconvenient Truth*, I was struck with how worried I was for the environment but also how ill equipped I felt to make a difference. In one of my novels, I wrote the phrase, "Our children should inherit our solutions not our problems." How could I leave such a broken world to my son? Al talked about major systemic issues that, at best, I could write to representatives in order to effect change. I felt there must be efforts somebody like myself could do to help make a difference.

I began doing research and realized there are things individuals can do. We don't have to wait for an act of congress, we can effect our own change. I decided to make a video series. There had been a meme going around at the time saying that as the pirate population decreased, global warming had increased. The main character of my series was a pirate, Captain Greene. He kidnapped Dr. Alder to investigate ways to reduce global warming. Captain Greene's message was clear, that while breeding pirates was a great idea, we needed to make changes to actually stop global warming. Each episode covered a different topic, including electric cars, green electricity, solid state lighting, and energy audits. Simon played the part of Cabin Boy. I played both Captain Greene and Dr. Alder.

The last relationship I had between my two marriages lasted about a year. The woman I was dating thought the Green Pirate series was pointless. Our relationship began to decay as I followed my pirate dreams. It ended with her telling me that "we just didn't have that kind of relationship." It hurt, but we've stayed friends.

Elena was struggling to make ends meet. She had broken up with her boyfriend and was considering moving back to California with Simon. The house I was living in had three bedrooms. I told her she could move in. Each of us would have our own room. She agreed. It worked fairly well, although the amount of damage a few cats can do to wooden floors is phenomenal. But this meant I was able to see more of Simon.

The majority of my friends from this time were best described as hippies. Simon was rarely around them because Elena didn't want him to see nudity at burner events. She didn't believe there was a distinction between nudity and sex. When he had first heard about Burning Man, he wanted to attend but over time, he decided being at an event with a bunch of naked hippies (including me) would make him uncomfortable.

It was awkward being at events that allowed kids but not actually being able to have my son with me. It seemed best for me to date somebody who would fit in at a burn, but the people my age were not at all interested in having kids. It was important to me for Simon to be a part of my life. It felt like it would be impossible to find somebody who wanted kids and would fit into the burner culture. Living with my ex-wife was also a challenge for partners to accept.

I celebrated my 30th birthday with my best friend and our kids. I had invited dozens of people for a laser tag party, but nobody else showed up. I had fun, but I kept having this nagging feeling that nobody else cared. Would anybody attend my funeral? This is also one of the reasons I'm not big on birthdays any longer.

Promotion

Near the end of my first marriage, I was working with my manager to figure out how I could get a leadership position at MEDITECH. My boss was a drummer in his spare time for a small band called Cold Coffee. His boss had been a bassist that had played with a group who would go on to found Aerosmith without him. When my boss told me that I should cut my hair, I accepted it because I knew he was himself a bit of a hippy.

On a trip to San Diego, I got my hair cut. Simon didn't recognize me when he first saw me, which was devastating.

I wasn't promoted to my first corporate leadership position until late 2007, a position that would be considered a Software Engineering Manager position. In order to reduce the chance of people leaving MEDITECH and pay less than the industry average, they deflated positions by calling this position "supervisor development." At MEDITECH, a manager of managers is called a "manager," whereas in the rest of the tech world that role is called a "director." I think I started with three employees. The product my team built, Scanning and Archiving, made $20 million in sales per year. When I left the company six years later, I was making less than $101,000 a year, which included an annual bonus.

A year after I was promoted, I took part in a leadership training course. We were all asked what surprised us about management. Most of my peers were surprised at how much of their job was about conflict management. Some of the technical leaders regretted their decision, which some made for money and others due to pressure from middle management. One of my employees had a heart condition that caused him to need surgery. He was very private and didn't want the team to worry. I had to deflect questions about his absence while worrying about him in solitude. That was something I did not expect.

There was a group of women at MEDITECH who formed a chapter of Mothers Without Borders. I joined because it sounded exactly like the kind of charity I wanted to support. There was a small part of me that hoped I'd also find somebody I could date. I helped us organize multiple charity drives, including a touch-a-truck day. While "husbands" sometimes "volunteered" to help with events, I was the only person who presented as male at our meetings.

During this time, there was a closeted trans woman who worked for me. Neither of us knew the other was trans until long after I had left MEDITECH.

I think that the move to management was part of what caused my year-long relationship to come to an end. The woman I was dating didn't feel like she fit with somebody who led people for money.

The Love of My Life

I can't remember how many of my relationships started on OkCupid. At least half of the women I dated between marriages I met at real life events. I liked OkCupid for its quizzes. I even created a quiz to see what a person's virtue was. At the time, vice quizzes were very popular, and I wanted to flip the narrative. OkCupid had more social media features than it does today. I used it to help promote each episode of the Green Pirate. At the time, OkCupid hadn't tinderized, requiring people to match prior to allowing messaging. One day, I got a sweet message from Nicole saying she hadn't gotten any responses to her messages and that even if I wasn't interested would I please respond.

I checked out her profile. The things that stood out were that she was UU, she lived in a small shoreline town, and she dressed conservatively. She had two kids and was recently separated. While she was liberal enough to be UU, she looked way too conservative to fit into the burner culture in which I was steeped. I didn't want to be yet another person who let her down by not responding. While I didn't think anything would come of it, I wasn't going to rule it out.

The first time I visited her house, she offered me tea. I dislike tea, but I didn't want to say no to her hospitality. It would be several days until I told her why I had accepted the tea and that I don't tend to like it.

I went to the 2008 Boskone science fiction and fantasy convention a week after I met Nicole. While Simon was in the kids programming, I enjoyed hours on the phone with her. I wished she could have attended, but it was too late for her to attend.

I was the first person she dated after she separated from her husband. Between how different we were and that I seemed like a rebound, I did my best to go at her pace.

The biggest fight we ever had was when she asked me if I'd get a vasectomy for her. We were walking together on a hiking trail. She was wearing an R.E.M. t-shirt. I told her no, because if we were to break up it would be unfair for people I dated after if they wanted to have kids. She was deeply hurt because I could imagine a time when we weren't together. We had both been left by our spouse. I very much believed then, and now, that as much as I might want something to be permanent, there are no guarantees. A vasectomy is forever. We soon mended things, though every time I saw that shirt it would send me back to how I felt during that hike, and so, she lovingly retired it for me.

I loved playing with her sons. The moment they met me, they started crying because they had no idea who I was or why I was in their home. Several hours later, we were all playing in boxes. We would later grow to bond over our mutual love for video games.

Nicole and I gave each other mix CDs with love songs. I also made her a few videos to show her how much I loved her. In one of the videos, I had flowers dance around to eventually form a heart.

One day, she asked me to shave my beard. I agreed but told her I'd grow it back. By this point, it had become camouflage for me. It prevented me from seeing what I looked like in the mirror. I thought, especially with the scar on my chin, that I looked creepy without a beard. I don't know who was more freaked out by my face without the beard, but after we took a good look at it, I left. I returned a week later after it began to grow back.

Simon had trouble adapting to Nicole's family. He hadn't had siblings before. To suddenly have young boys around him was a challenge. He got along best with the younger of Nicole's sons. There was one time they accidentally tipped over a paint can on a carpeted staircase at her house. Neither of them thought it was worth telling us about.

Nicole hated doing dishes. She is an amazing cook, and I was happy to do the dishes whenever I visited, even if I didn't stay to eat. One day, while doing the dishes, I overheard Simon tell one of the boys that I didn't love him. I was devastated. I loved Simon. He couldn't see it though because all he saw was that I put him in uncomfortable situations and would lose my temper with him when he got into trouble. Nicole found me crying in the kitchen. It took a while for me to explain what had happened. I think Simon was surprised how much hurt his words had caused.

One time, we went to the drive-in together. One of the boys was doing something that upset Simon and Simon started crying. I pulled over, picked him up, and held him until he felt better. In retrospect, I see that Simon found the new relationship challenging much as I found the early years of my father's relationship with Cindy challenging. I think I could have done a better job of helping Simon to get comfortable with what would eventually become his family. If I ever start another long-term relationship, I hope I'll do better at integrating my kids.

Nicole had met me too late that year to go to Firefly with me. I went without her, wondering if she would fit into my burner life. After returning from the 2008 Firefly, I decided to propose to her. I posted a message to friends on LiveJournal asking for their help. I latched onto the concept of how historically people were expected to get the approval of parents in order to wed. I asked my friends and family to ask Nicole if she would marry me. I recorded them in a video that ended with me, in a kilt, on bended knee, asking her to marry me. This video, and the Green Pirate videos, are still on my YouTube. I made her a DVD with the proposal. As the DVD is circular, I used that symbolic ring. She said, "Yes."

I've rewritten this chapter more than any of the others. I'm finding it hard to express how much I cared for Nicole. Our years together were amazing. I was happy with her in ways I hadn't been with any other partner. She exceeded what home was for me. Home has never been a physical place for me, it's always about being with the people I love. As much hurt as I may have felt when our marriage ended a decade later, I will always love Nicole.

Pon

A month after I proposed, we decided to try and conceive a child together. We didn't expect Nicole would get pregnant quite so soon. As we built our life together, we needed to consolidate. I was living in the house in Pawtucket with Simon and Elena while Nicole was living in East Lyme, Connecticut. At the time, I was working in MEDITECH's Canton office. We put our houses on the market just as the housing bubble burst.

As I would no longer be able to provide a home for Elena, she made the decision to move to San Diego. While custody for Simon was about weekends and school days, we had to adapt to vacations. It broke my heart when he moved. I was driving to work as he and his mother were heading to their new home. I called Nicole, in tears, as I drove. I had gone from seeing him almost every day, to going days without him, to seeing him almost every day, to not seeing him for months at a time. A few weeks after he left, I got a postcard from Simon that said he loved it in San Diego. It was a paradise to him.

My house was the first to be sold. It was bought by a couple who ironically was later foreclosed on, despite the low price they were able to get the house for due to the economy. While I was able to telecommute some days, most days I had to drive for at least four hours. This is when I got the only two moving violations I've ever received.

We decided to have a home birth. While all of our previous kids were born in a hospital, we were very disillusioned with the factory mentality that obstetricians have created. We had a midwife and Nicole gave birth to Pon in May 2009. The birth was a day before Elena's birthday and while I still cared for Elena, I felt it would be unlucky if they shared a birthday. The most beautiful part of the home birth for me was that I caught Pon.

While it physically seemed that Pon was female, almost eleven years later they would inform us that they are non-binary. Pon prefers "they" and "them" pronouns. Pon is their chosen name, we used a different name for them until they changed their name at age eleven.

I love my biological children equally. But I find it easier to get along with Pon. At times, Simon has noticed this and felt I'm unfair to him. Pon and I have the same love language, touch, which always made it easy for the two of us to connect.

We skipped Firefly 2009. We were finally able to sell the house in Niantic. We moved to Middletown, Rhode Island to be closer to Nicole's family. I got along well with my sisters-in-law. The rest of Nicole's family was civil to me, but disappointed when I didn't meet male gender norms. One of her parents had advised her not to marry me.

In early October, we got married in our home. I wore a kilt. Pon slept through the ceremony. We had lasagna and caramel apples for the reception. Rather than a best man, I had my best friend play a game where she randomly recruited attendees to become secret pirates. We also played an icebreaker game where every attendee had the name of someone famous taped on their back. If they were able to guess whose name was on their back, via yes and no questions, they could move the name to their chest. We recorded the wedding and made a tradition of watching both the proposal and wedding on every anniversary.

Progress

For some time at MEDITECH, I coasted by learning as I went. MEDITECH uses proprietary programming languages, which makes it hard to transfer knowledge into and out of the company. The company liked this because it increased retention. The promotion only from within policy meant that no new viewpoints entered the company. Employees entered with an entry-level background. Similar to how I realized that there is value in passing knowledge between dance communities, it was clear that there was value in passing knowledge from other parts of the industry.

Around this time, I read Stephen Covey's *7 Habits of Highly Effective People*. He makes several good points, including how to prioritize time using the four quadrants of Important + Urgent, Important + Non-Urgent, Not Important + Urgent, and Not Important + Non-Urgent.

While urgent tasks have to get done, non-urgent tasks are important and beneficial too. For example, changing a baby's diaper is urgent, it has to be dealt with right away. At times, we can feel overwhelmed by urgent work. But the non-urgent work often can prevent some of the urgent work. For example, the non-urgent task of changing oil will make sure we don't have to deal with an urgent issue like the car engine overheating or leaking. The non-urgent task of relationship building with children can help reduce the number of urgent tasks we have to do to repair relationships that we did not foster. The time spent on non-urgent tasks often leads to new opportunities.

As a leader, I discuss this, the four quadrants, with all employees when we discuss career growth. All of the promotion announcements I have ever written discuss the important and non-urgent work my employee did, like mentoring, architecture work, and managing major successful projects.

The other habit that became important to me was continuous learning. I began reading books on programming techniques, leadership, and psychology. This was around the time the development division created a coding standards committee, which I joined. I also helped develop some continuing education programs. I joined the newly formed development training and education board. I helped create a maintainable code course and helped give a code efficiency course.

I had an employee that I hired into my team from another group named Carl. He grew up in South America. One day, in a one-on-one meeting, he told me that his birth name was Carlos. He had changed his name after he struggled for years trying to get a job in the US. People would see "Carlos" on his resume and not give him an interview. I personally knew that, at times, I had seen Latinx people in the office and assumed they were cleaning staff. I realized my mind was making an awful assumption. I hope that if he had applied as Carlos, I would have still hired him.

I had always had a preference for working on tools. While I liked that medical software helped hospitals, I was ambivalent about writing medical software. I felt that well-developed tools could improve productivity and quality. Even a 1% improvement in either category for such a large company could be like getting multiple employees for free. There was a group in my division that worked on tools for developers. In the greater industry, this group would be considered a Development and Operations (DevOps) group. DevOps is a paradigm created in the early years of this century. Prior to DevOps, development and operations were considered separate groups that were often at odds with each other. Development was about getting new code out as quickly as possible. Operations was about creating a secure and stable infrastructure. Operations wanted things to work slowly, and often did work manually, to make sure there was stability. Operations was frustrated at how fast development wanted to move and that developers often did not take responsibility for their code once they handed it over. Developers felt that operations obstructed their work and whined about their awesome code.

The DevOps group needed a new manager, so I applied for the position. When I joined, they were in the middle of writing a version control system. There are several popular open-source version control systems, but because we always wrote our own software (even email and calendars,) the company had decided to make our own. I avoided changing the group in the first three months. I strictly focused on my learning and mentoring the team. When the three months were over, I sat the team down and asked how much longer it would take us to finish writing the system, how long would it take to implement an open-source system, and how ours would compare to an open-source system. What we realized was that it would take far longer to finish ours and it would have fewer features. While it was tough to let go of all that code, it was the right decision. We were up and running with an open-source system 6 months later. We also experimented with other industry tools and processes that were later adopted by the rest of the company, including Agile, Jenkins, and unit testing.

My Curse

My MEDITECH career was the first time I spent any real time with a person who had transitioned. Near the end of my time at MEDITECH, there was a health challenge in which I participated. As part of the challenge, there were a few organized group walks. I took part in one at the Westwood office where I met Sam.

I've never had gaydar. I've often sworn up and down that someone was straight only to find they were gay and, vice versa. I've had friends who I thought were gay until they started dating. Perhaps the reason I have no ability to detect a person's sexuality is because mine is one of the most flexible sexualities a person can have. I can't truly fathom why others limit themselves to being with a single gender expression.

I do have a superpower, however. If I am within ten feet of another trans woman, I can almost always identify them within seconds. This power doesn't work for non-binary folks or trans men. It also rarely works for trans women who are in the closet. I have theories about why I have this ability. One theory is that I know my kind. Another theory is that it's a safety mechanism. The simplest explanation might be that I've always been interested in women's fashion and, thus, I pay far more attention to women.

This superpower is also a curse. Because I can spot them and see the clues that they were assigned male at birth, I've feared everyone can clock them (i.e., identify them as trans) and could also clock me. When I met Sam, it was obvious to me—painfully obvious to me—that while she presented as a female, she had been assigned male at birth. At first, I wondered if I had known her before she transitioned. When we were walking alone together, I asked a question that you should never ask a trans person, I asked, "Sam, like Samuel?"

I don't remember her reaction, but now, I'm horrified at my behaviour. Whatever her reaction, we got beyond it and had a good conversation. I was glad to hear she was welcomed at MEDITECH. Meeting her actually added reasons for me to not want to transition. The fact I could tell she was trans horrified me. Another scary part was realizing trans people get questions such as, "Sam, like Samuel?"

Post-Feminism

While MEDITECH was moving in a positive direction, I became restless about how slow the change was. I began a job search, and, like last time, I let my boss know. While I felt like I had been burned the last time I did a job search, I also felt the responsibility of my employees needing a succession plan. I knew it was rare for companies to hire frontline outside management. I also knew that there were a lot of DevOps technologies I was inexperienced with but was eager to learn. I was willing to go back to an individual contributor role so I could learn the tools that were at the bleeding edge.

I had a great interview with Carbonite. Elizabeth was the hiring manager for the team. She really liked my view of what DevOps is and was willing to take a risk with me because I knew few of the tools her team used. As expected, I did learn a lot, including CentOS, Ubuntu, Chef, AWS, and Azure. I really enjoyed working for Elizabeth. She had created a stellar team. While working for her, I noticed that she was sometimes mansplained, even by her employees. I noticed other female employees had similar challenges in the male-dominated company.

My mother is a second wave feminist. My impression is that she wears pants because they are comfortable, and women fought hard to express themselves in traditionally male clothing. When I transitioned, my mother asked me if I had ever worn her clothes. It was a sign she felt she would have noticed. Because her clothes were so masculine, I never was interested in them. We also are different sizes. I'm far taller than her.

Whenever I had to buy something at school or for scouts with her money, she would make out a check. Her checks said at the top "Equality for Women" and included the definition of equality. I was super embarrassed by these checks and, at the same time, proud that she stood so publicly for her beliefs. I had grown up hearing that women were equal. I didn't understand that there was more work to do.

Retrospectively, I realized that MEDITECH had been a gender diverse and inclusive oasis. MEDITECH was an exception in the tech realm. Part of the reason MEDITECH had better gender balance is because healthcare tends to attract women more than other tech products, like backup software.

Despite my discomfort with how women were treated at Carbonite, I felt I should stay for a while. I loved most of my peers. My boss had been planning to move to another part of the country when her lease ended. Like many of our team, she would work remotely fulltime after the move. Our VP, who she reported directly to, knew of this plan. At the time her lease ended, she let our VP know and he said she would have to become an individual contributor and that he would hire a manager based in Boston. Obviously, this was unfair. He should have warned her ahead of time. I don't think this would have happened if she had been male.

There is currently a high demand for DevOps practitioners. I get at least one message a week about job opportunities. Until my boss was demoted, I politely declined these inquiries. The week she was demoted, I responded to an inquiry by saying I would meet the external recruiter who had contacted me. I hadn't expected anything to come from my response. It had taken me months of active searching and interviews to get my job at Carbonite. While I wanted to get away from the brogrammer culture I was immersed in, I also didn't want to lose the friends I had made. It also felt very risky for my career to leave so soon.

The company I had been contacted about was Affectiva. I had never heard of them and wasn't even sure how to pronounce their name. I reluctantly began the interview process, thinking to myself that this would be good practice. From my experience at Carbonite, the inclusiveness of the culture was critical to me. The co-founders of the company were both women from the MIT media lab. One of the co-founders was an Egyptian Muslim who, until a year prior to my interview, wore the *hijab*. There were men, including the CEO of the time, who were executives, but there were two women on the executive team. When I was interviewed by the executive in charge of IT and Operations, who was a woman, I asked all the questions I thought were critical to make sure the company was inclusive. I felt comfortable with her answers.

When the company surprised me by making a really compelling offer, I was unsure what to do. I felt like leaving Carbonite so soon would be a black mark on my resume. I'd never worked at a start-up and was very nervous about working for a company that was literally losing money. After researching the risks, and learning terms like "runway," I had follow-up conversations with the CEO and VP of Engineering to get a better feel for how risky joining would be. I also wanted to make sure I'd still have time for family in my life. The industry demand for my skills reduced my concerns about potentially being laid off. I took the job.

Carbonite was civil about the transition. I had an exit interview where I outlined the inclusivity issues that had caused me to consider the job at Affectiva. I'm still in touch with a few of my former colleagues, but sadly lost contact with most of my friends.

The question I never asked when interviewing at Affectiva was, how many women were on the team I'd be joining. The answer would have been none, and I probably would have declined. When I realized that I was joining a group that had no women, I considered quitting. I didn't want a repeat of Carbonite. We were in the middle of moving from Rhode Island to a co-housing community on the eastern edge of Worcester county. Job instability would put the move at risk. The executive team had women, so it seemed possible things could improve. I decided it was best to try and make Affectiva work.

Within Affectiva, as an individual contributor, I began pushing for gender diversity. I asked some hard questions, like why a female scientist had been laid off when men from the same team had been kept on. When I next attended Firefly one of the other members of the volunteer leadership team mentioned that they were working at Facebook. I had read Cheryl Sandberg's *Lean In*, which, at the time, seemed progressive. I asked my friend, as a woman, how she felt about working at Facebook. She told me that they always made sure there were at least two women on a team to avoid tokenism. Facebook had a training program called "Managing Unconscious Bias." The videos and materials for the training were all provided for free to the public. I reviewed the program and felt it was a great start. I chatted with Affectiva's HR and got approval to run the training. The training went well and caused several members of the leadership team to start coming up with ideas on how to make sure our process was inclusive.

While I worked to make the culture more inclusive, there were some issues I ignored. At Carbonite, I had joined a lunch club that was mostly women. We would pick a place to eat and spend time together. I really enjoyed these lunch outings. At Affectiva, there was a similar group that I joined. Women politely declined to join the Affectiva group, which I assumed was a product of dietary preferences and a limited population of women in the company. Over time, as the group began to trust me, I discovered that some of them enjoyed objectifying women (co-workers and waitresses). I regret not speaking up. While I wasn't aware at the time that I was trans, I certainly knew I was feminine, and I didn't want to be excluded. Eventually, I got tired of the misogyny and started eating on my own.

My team finally hired a woman, who sadly was located in our Cairo office. As a startup, employees were often welcomed and encouraged to take on jobs that were outside their job description. I, for example, began doing public speaking for the company. When we started to consider having a public hackathon, I offered to run it. Through various inclusive initiatives, I was able to get an equal number of men and women to participate in the hackathon. We also had racial diversity and religious diversity. We ended up having about 120 participants who created 10 different projects.

One of the participants in the hackathon was a trans woman. Affectiva software is AI that determines demographic and emotion information by analyzing faces through cameras and video. The trans woman was delighted that the software got her gender correct. This was a very humanizing story for the software, which the CEO mentions in interviews from time to time.

While I enjoyed working at Affectiva, after a couple of years, I started considering my next steps. The company was growing slowly, and I wanted to get involved in leadership. I love solving problems, but I prefer solving people problems. I had a chat with the CEO, Rana El Kaliouby, a little while after her promotion. She was making an effort to have one-on-one lunches with all employees. Over Mongolian Hot Pot, I told her I was thinking of leaving. She said that because the VP of Engineering had been promoted to COO, he had less time to spend with the growing team of developers. She said it might be a good possibility for me. She vetted the idea with other members of the team, and I got an offer to be a manager if I was willing to spend time with the developers in our Cairo office.

Clara Oswald

Clara Oswald is the only character I have ever cosplayed. Cosplaying her, in January 2018 at Arisia, wasn't the first time I wore feminine clothing, but it was the first time I was portraying a woman. I imagine you wonder what does Clara Oswald (as portrayed by Jenna Coleman) mean to me? In her run, I was very cautious to *not* say she was my favorite companion (traveling accomplice with the Doctor from *Doctor Who*). As the current companion, there was no distance and ability to see her full story. Also, she's the only modern companion I found attractive (I do find Freema Agyeman attractive but not as Martha). I worried the attraction I felt made it difficult for me to compare her.

Now that we've had more companions, I can firmly state she is my all-time favorite *Doctor Who* companion (sorry Jaime and Zoe). I like Clara's story. I enjoyed the Impossible Girl arc. I also enjoyed the Danny arc and how she left the show.

I loved watching and helping Pon prepare to cosplay Midna from *The Legend of Zelda: Twilight Princess*. I wanted to try cosplay myself, but who could I play? At first, I felt I needed to play to my looks, but what characters do I like with beards? The best I could think of was Thor… but I'm not a huge Marvel fan.

Doctor Who is my favorite show, but I don't find any of the portrayals of the Doctor compelling to cosplay. A lot of women crossplay the Doctor. There are many women who feel confident cosplaying men and who are complimented for it. The opposite is *not* true due to our patriarchal society. Few men are brave enough to cosplay women, and many who do are ridiculed (do a search for "Sailor Bubba" for details). There are also some who actively do it as a parody of themselves. We think, as a society, it's better to be male and we shame men when they appear feminine.

Arisia is generally a safe space. While I'd mostly attended as someone who appeared cis-male, I wasn't too worried about reactions. With all that in mind, I decided to cosplay Clara. Most of the pushback I got was actually from Pon. I like many of the outfits Clara wore. When people ask me what silhouette I'm going for, I refer to Clara as well as Japanese fashion. I really enjoyed shopping for the outfit.

When people ask how I want my makeup to look, I say, "Lauren Mayberry eyes and the rest like Clara." The companion in *Doctor Who* is the audience insertion vehicle. It's hard to relate to an alien who is thousands of years old and lives in a time machine. We're meant to relate to the companion and view the story through their eyes. I enjoyed watching through Clara.

Clara gave me a way to explore my womanhood. This was the first time I used a women's bathroom. I had always had feminine inclinations in the past. I was always jealous of women's clothing. Through this process, I was better able to understand my gender identity.

So, it's not just that I found her attractive. It's not just that I loved her character. It's also that she inspired me. My favorite inspirations have always been women (Joan of Arc, Alice Stokes Paul, Harriot Tubman, Valentina Tereshkova, etc.) but none of them were accessible to me in the way Clara was and is. That's what she means to me.

Cyber Revolution

Cyber Revolution was not the book I set out to write. As was true for many writers, after the 2016 US presidential election, I felt outraged, frustrated, and unempowered. Regardless of his policies, the 45th President, as an individual, is a misogynist, a bully, a liar, an Islamophobe, and a chauvinist. My biggest fear was, and still is, how the election will impact the hundreds of millions in the US who are part of those demographics against which the President discriminates.

As time passed and I continued to worry, I kept hearing story after story of tech companies toadying up to the President-Elect. IBM, who helped the Nazi's build a database of Jewish people, even considered helping Trump to build a Muslim database. These CEOs have put profit ahead of ethics, and it sickens me that I'm part of their industry. They gave excuses, like Tim Cook's excuse that it is best to have a seat at the table. The government of Vichy, France felt the same way about working with Hitler. This is when I realized that I wanted to show how I thought a tech company should act in the face of a government with discriminatory intentions.

The seed of *Cyber Revolution* was to show how a company of similar size and power to those who choose to be collaborators with the new administration could instead choose to protect at-risk demographics. I created the fictional company Fast Futures Machines (FFM), to be a company that would take a stand against the US government.

As I began writing, I wanted to develop a main character that readers could relate to. For years, I've gone out of my way to listen to music by female artists, avoid books and movies that fail the Bechdel test, and work at companies that have diversity. My previous novels all had male characters in the lead role because it was easier for me to write. If I were to do that with *Cyber Revolution*, I'd be creating a book I wouldn't want to read, so I decided to have a woman as the main character. I decided that meeting the Bechdel test wasn't enough, I wanted to exceed it. I wanted gender diversity, but also diversity in other demographics.

I named the main character Rosa Alvarez. I wanted a character who had a biography that would make her empathize with how the administration treats Muslims. At times, I've worried this was a bad choice. People should make a stance against governments that are hurting people, even if they only sympathize with those who are being hurt.

As I added characters, I'd review the current list and do my best to make sure I created a diverse character list. People of multiple ethnicities were included. I also did a lot of research so I could include a blind character, who has become my favorite character in the entire book. I hope I did them justice.

As I wrote the early chapters of *Cyber Revolution*, I realized that having Rosa's career progress, from being an engineer at FFM in 1994 to being their CEO by 2011, would be unrealistic due to the lack of gender equity in corporate America, especially in tech. Companies have made great strides in the last few years. Facebook, for example, has made several effective changes, including a training they've shared with the world called "Managing Unconscious Bias."

Rather than change the timeline, or her character, I decided to have FFM be a fictional pioneer of the work companies, like Facebook, are doing today to improve gender equity. Companies that strive for gender equality are more successful, which meant that having Rosa lead the initiative would also make her rise through FFM more realistic, both because it removed the glass ceiling and gave her a track record of work that made FFM more successful. The early chapters of this book thus became a fictional account of how to improve diversity at an American company.

Within the first few pages that I wrote, I included Martin Niemöller's poem:

> *First they came for the socialists, and I did not speak out—because I was not a socialist.*
> *Then they came for the trade unionists, and I did not speak out—because I was not a trade unionist.*
> *Then they came for the Jews, and I did not speak out—because I was not a Jew.*
> *Then they came for me—and there was no one left to speak for me.*

When I completed the first draft, I decided I wanted to include a quote at the top of each chapter that related to the content in it. As I began searching for appropriate quotes, I began to see a trend. Men are far more frequently quoted than women. I kept Martin Niemöller's quote but challenged myself to find a quote from a woman to start each chapter. I feel it is critical that we tune into women's voices. I succeeded in this challenge and each chapter starts with a quote from a woman like the following from Emma Lazarus's sonnet "The New Colossus":

> *Give me your tired, your poor,*
> *Your huddled masses yearning to breathe free,*
> *The wretched refuse of your teeming shore.*
> *Send these, the homeless, tempest-tost to me,*
> *I lift my lamp beside the golden door!"*

To some extent, Rosa was a wish fulfillment character for me. While I have no desire to become a CEO, I absolutely wanted to be a woman who stood up for people in need.

Women's March

A week after I had portrayed Clara at Arisia, I attended the 2017 Women's March in DC. Nicole wanted to attend, but since Pon was with her, we felt it safer for them to go to the Boston march. My timing was poor, so while I bumped into some friends at the march, I traveled in a bus with women I hadn't met from Waterford to DC at 1 AM. There was a ban on backpacks, so I just brought water, a banana, a plastic poncho, 5 breakfast bars, an external phone battery, and a small first aid kit.

It was forty-eight degrees when the march began. I dressed in layers. I tried to look as cis-male as possible so counter protesters would think twice about bothering any of the women I was with.

There were vendors everywhere. People were selling shirts, hats, bags, and signs. The organisers of the march were giving out free posters. Bathroom lines were long. When I was at the East Market, I needed to use the restroom. There was no line for the men's bathroom but a huge line for the women's. A police officer was enforcing gender segregation. I felt guilty about getting in and out so quickly.

All the police were friendly when I arrived. When I got a few blocks from the start of the march, there was a squad of police on motorcycles, a bus load of police in riot gear, and a police officer with an automatic weapon. I was on the wrong side of the stage to see or hear anything. Some people were listening to the speakers over the C-SPAN radio app. The original estimate had been 200,000 people, but the AP estimates at least 500,000 people. The area where the march was supposed to take place wasn't moving so I walked parallel to it with a large crowd. It was so foggy you couldn't see the top of the Washington Monument. Before lunch, I took a break at L'Enfant Plaza to use the bathrooms. There were huge lines on the first floor. I climbed the stairs and found an open men's bathroom that was filled with women. It was a short wait.

I waited in line for an hour to get a burrito. They had run out of guacamole. Behind me in line was a group of conservative high school students who were visiting for the inauguration on a field trip. They were teasing marchers as they passed by. They said they were appalled that they were bringing children so young "to indoctrinate them." I occasionally corrected them when they made clear errors. Then, a high school girl said she didn't see why women were complaining about equality, I finally lost it and said because women make 15% less than men. One of the other teens said that was "illegal." She said that she had documentation that the statistic was inaccurate, but she couldn't access it because the cell network was jammed. I told her my specific example that as a tech worker, only 15% of my fellow tech workers were women. Eventually, we found some common ground. They were actually Libertarian. I'm glad I engaged them in conversation. They had scared off some adults and were more polite after I talked to them.

Cell signal was sparse at best. The cell towers were overloaded. People used *Firechat* to communicate via a Bluetooth mesh. There were lots of chants that I joined in on including "Women's Rights are Human Rights," "My Body, My Choice," and "The People United Will Never be Divided." Lots of people had signs showing women's organs. Some would have the organs flipping off the reader. Some said, "If I Wanted the Government in my Uterus, I'd Fuck a Senator!" Some showed two female organs followed by an elephant that looked similar and asked, "Which of these three doesn't belong?" There were also lots of signs about keeping hands off of pussies. Some signs said, "My Pussy Bites Back," and "Pussy Riot."

There were signs that said, "President Trump, Divider in Chief." Some said, "Marching to Make Herstory." Many people had "Black Lives Matter" signs. There were also signs that said, "Equality and Respect for All," "Girls Just Want to Have Fundamental Rights." There were variants of Trump's slogan like, "Make America Care Again," "Everyone Makes America Great," "Make America Free Again," "Make America Finland for the First Time," and "Make America Safe Again."

Despite the forecast, it never did rain. I returned tired. My back and feet were sore. The bus was relocated, making it hard to find, especially in the dark. I bumped into one friend from Boston.

Genderfluid

In early 2017, I began buying feminine clothes, not just to wear at conventions but to wear on weekends and vacation. There were already some clothes I wore regularly that were advertised for women but felt to me like either gender could wear them. As I began wearing more overtly feminine clothing people started wondering if I was transgender.

According to records from archive.org, dictionary.com did not provide a definition of transgender until 2016, though it says the origin is the early 1970s. In 2017, I was curious what the definition was. In the short amount of time from then until now, the definition has been updated multiple times. The second definition, which was provided when I looked, said, "noting or relating to a person who does not conform to societal gender norms or roles." Based on that, pretty much anybody who is LGBTQIA+, or a feminist, would fit the category. This definition has been removed. The first definition at the time was, "noting or relating to a person whose gender identity does not correspond to that person's biological sex assigned at birth." That first definition is nearly the same as today's definition. Based on the entry in 2017, I realized I am transgender. I told Nicole almost immediately, but I couched what I said with a statement that I would never transition.

While I had a current definition for transgender, my incorrect understanding of transition was that it required hormone injections. With my fear of needles, and a myriad of other concerns, I didn't think I would ever transition.

For years, I had been telling people they could use male or female pronouns for me. People would almost always use "he" and "him," despite my equal openness to "she" and "her." I found I really enjoyed when people used" she" and "her," but it was very rare.

I started viewing my life as time at work in "boy-mode" and other days in "girl-mode." There were some stealth items that were "for women" that I'd wear at work like my glasses, which came from the women's section, and my socks, like the ones that said "I`m a Girl! What's Your superpower?" As this dichotomy continued, I began to identify as genderfluid.

Figure 13: Forest, Pon, and Simon

Egypt

In the negotiation with Affectiva to become the engineering manager, the company asked me to live for a year in Cairo with my family. While I personally would have enjoyed living in Egypt for a year, I didn't know how the kids or Nicole would feel about it. We had already learned a lot about Egypt and had been able to dismiss some of the myths Americans have about Egypt. It would be tough to leave family for a year and school would be challenging. We realized, however, that we were willing to live there together for the summer. I could stay a little longer and visit regularly afterwards. I made the counteroffer, which was accepted.

As a hiring manager, I revamped recruiting. The team was 11% female when I was promoted, which was below the industry average. I eventually got that up to 36%, more than double the industry average. The most critical things I did were to prioritize candidates of all levels who were of demographics we were lacking. The intern program I developed, first with MIT, and then later with NEU, became a huge part of the success. I would monitor the interns who did well, and I was able to get several of them to join as permanent employees when they graduated.

I made a two week visit to Egypt a couple of months before we moved. It helped me to get my bearings. I learned the most important parts of Arabic well enough to give a person directions to my AirBnB and to eat at a restaurant without a co-worker to translate. The members of the Cairo office were very welcoming. They felt my presence, as an American member of leadership, showed that the home office in Boston truly cared about them. I quickly noticed that there were several disconnects between the offices due to cultural differences. I worked on bridging those gaps, even for teams that didn't report to me.

With the exception of stealth items like my glasses and socks, I packed no feminine clothing for Egypt. While it's very safe for the majority of Americans to visit Egypt, being found guilty of being LGBT earns 10 years in prison.

My family and I landed for our summer in Egypt halfway through Ramadan. We were really excited to see firsthand how the holy month was celebrated within a Muslim majority nation. While 15% of Egypt's population isn't Muslim, the majority of restaurants were closed during the daylight hours when Muslims fasted. This made it a challenge to get settled in and explore the country. We enjoyed sharing *iftar*, the meal to break the fast, and *suhoor*, the meal before sunrise when the fast resumed, with co-workers.

One of my employees invited us to vacation with his family in Marsa Matruh on the Mediterranean Coast, for the holiday feast for *Eid*, which comes after Ramadan. We were expecting that food would be easy to buy on the vacation, especially since *Eid* is a feast. I was warned that we would be roughing it, but with a beach rental that included a kitchen, I didn't understand. It turned out that the only store for supplies was what Nicole would later call an "inconvenience" store. There wasn't much in the way of meals that we could make with the supplies there, and we hadn't known we should pack food. There were no restaurants or food vendors to buy from.

Egyptian stovetops often came with glass covers that people are meant to raise prior to using. Unlike our apartment, the gas had to be turned on manually. Once we were able to get the burner to light, I didn't realize the glass top was a cover that should be lifted, despite us having a cover at our apartment in El Rehab. While Nicole was trying to cook, the glass overheated, which caused it to explode, sending hot shards flying. I can't imagine how scary it was for Nicole. Pon thought that this was a sign that perhaps, for Nicole's sake, we should return to the US. Fortunately, with the help of our friends, we were able to get over this. The beach was wonderful. Pon and I remember fondly how a friend and I tossed Pon back and forth between us in the Mediterranean as we yelled, "Hoopa."

It's hard for an American to understand what a truly old structure is until they've visited the pyramids. The first pyramids we visited were the ones in Giza. It was 115 degrees Fahrenheit when we were there. One of our friends had driven us. It was too hot for Pon, so they waited in the air conditioning with our friend. My youngest stepson joined Pon when we got to the Sphinx. For him, the pyramids were the biggest reason to visit Egypt, perhaps a cooler day would have been better. The camels weren't happy about us riding them.

Nicole and I really enjoyed the people we met in Egypt. We knew there were several misconceptions about the country. When we traveled to Japan years earlier, it helped us to watch guide videos about Japan. There were no equivalent videos about Egypt, so we made a YouTube series, one of which included Pon.

After Nicole returned with the kids to start school, she began to miss me. I felt that it was important for me to stay because I had made a commitment. Several weeks later, Pon began to miss me and wanted me to come home. Pon was struggling without both of us there. I talked to my boss and ended the trip a few weeks early. My decision to stay was one of the things that helped lead to the end of our marriage. While I felt Nicole was more able to cope without me than Pon, I gave the impression that I cared far more for Pon than for Nicole.

To Be or Not To Be

In the summer of 2018, my son asked if he could move in with us. It was unclear at the time what the details of his desire were, but he was obviously uncomfortable living with Elena, Elena's brother, and his uncle's girlfriend. I had somewhat expected, and hoped, that in his early teens he would decide to live with me. I knew Elena could be classified as a helicopter parent, and I expected that, like my teenage years, Simon would want more freedom. After he started high school, I gave up hope that he would want to live with me. Having him move into our small house just before his senior year was a huge adjustment. Nicole was very supportive and welcoming. We had all three boys in the same bedroom, which got a little crazy at times.

I have a non-binary friend who mentioned on their Facebook that their gender therapist had suggested they try hormones. I hadn't thought that non-binary folks had that as an option. Rather than ask why, I did some internet searches. I came across a video with a doctor who discussed the decision to take hormones. Basically, the video recommended that people who were non-binary have a 3-month low dose and see how they feel. The video said that some people who do this will decide to transition. The video also gave some common reasons why people avoid transition, like fear they won't look good, and gave reasons these were unfounded.

After watching the video, I wanted to see what kind of hormones people assigned male at birth were often given. What I discovered was there are several options, many of which did not require injections.

I made a list of pros and cons for transitioning. Next to each item, I included a weight of 1 (low), 2 (medium), and 3 (high). This was my original list:

Pros:
Bathroom 2—I hate men's bathrooms. It would be so much nicer to only use women's or all gender bathrooms.
Social Comfort 3—I relate better with women but portraying male, I have to distance myself (especially in Egypt).
Clothes 2—I love feminine clothes.
Gender label 1—I'd prefer people interact with me as female.

Testosterone 3—My temper is awful, perhaps reducing T would help. It would also stop male pattern baldness.
Porn 3—I hate being addicted to pornography.

Total: 14

Cons:
Temporary loss of sex drive 1.
Could impair Nicole's enjoyment of sex 3.
Cost 1—Considering that I qualify as upper class, I think cost isn't difficult.
Need for hormones 2—I hate taking medication. What if something happens that prevents me from getting hormones, like a conservative government or an apocalypse.
Permanence 3—What if I make the wrong decision.
Feminism 3—Psychologically people are more apt to listen to support from somebody from an outgroup than an ingroup. Thus, a man will get more support for feminism than a woman.
Work 3—I know trans people who have been recently fired (despite the firing being illegal in Massachusetts). Would I be able to get another job as a trans woman? Would I be fired from Affectiva?
Egypt 2—I won't be able to return to Egypt (until I either fully pass or they become more inclusive). Pon and I haven't seen Luxor and Aswan yet!!!
Dept of State 2—Several trans passports were revoked during the Trump administration. I might not be able to get my passport corrected.
Nicole's Family 1—They already had issues with my gender expression, which had always been male when they were around.
Scar on my Chin 1—Without facial hair that scar on my chin makes me look creepy.

Total: 22

The cons outweighed the pros. At this point, it felt best to talk to a neutral party about the subject. As much as I disliked the idea of seeing a therapist, it seemed like the correct course of action. I also thought that a gender therapist could prescribe hormones. Due to my bias against therapists, I presumed the best way to select one was via location. I picked the gender therapist who was closest to my home.

Suicide Plan

Nicole wasn't happy that I was considering transition. While she had been attracted to the man I had presented as, she wasn't attracted to the woman I am. Our physical relationship broke down as I began therapy. My prior marriage had ended a few months after my physical relationship with Elena ended, so I feared the same would happen.

August 20th, 2018 was the first time I saw my therapist. We spent most of the 45 minutes with background information. I let her know about my bias against therapists. I was working from home that day and was wearing a skirt, which was typical for my work from home days. I was upset when I discovered that therapists don't prescribe but felt I should continue to see her.

I read Jenny Boylan's autobiography, *She's Not There*. When I read how Jenny came out to her kids, I cringed. She told the kids that being trans was really rare and not something that would happen to them. Growing up, I thought it was normal to daydream about living as a woman. I assumed all boys did that but would never admit to it. When I took the Combined Gender Identity and Transsexuality Inventory (COGIATI), I scored 260, "classification four, probable transexual." People who are cis are unlikely to even score a classification of two on the COGIATI. A trans person telling kids they aren't trans is very dangerous if they're wrong. A little after I read Jenny's book, I came across an article she wrote about when her daughter came out to her as trans. I was very careful with my kids to let them define their own gender. I suspect when Pon was younger, I did live a little bit vicariously through the gender they were assigned at birth, but I also strongly supported the activities and outfits Pon chose that would be deemed unfeminine.

One day, Pon came to me and said, "I have something important to say, but can we watch *Doctor Who* first?" I knew Pon was worried to tell me whatever was on their mind. I was afraid they were going to tell me they wanted to spend less time with me. When we sat down to watch *Doctor Who*, Pon told me they are bi. I was so relieved. I had already known they had crushes on people of more than one gender. What I realized was that because I never talked about my sexuality to my kids, they didn't feel safe talking to me. Since they had only seen me in relationships with women, they assumed I was a straight (but very feminine) man. I explained to Pon, and later to the other kids, that I'm pan. I also told them that I would always love them. They might sometimes make choices that hurt me, but I'll still love them. I realized I made the same mistake as Jenny.

From that point on, I've done my best to be transparent with my kids about my gender, sexuality, and my mental struggles. I realized it was important to normalize the struggles I've had while keeping the information age appropriate. A year later when Pon came out as non-binary, they didn't even hesitate when they said it. I'm so happy Pon was able to come out like that. Non-binary people, in many ways, have it tougher than trans men and trans women. I fear for the struggles Pon will face, but welcome being an advocate for them.

It was fascinating to me that Jenny hid her femininity from everyone, whereas I only hid mine from work and my in-laws. Only a third of marriages survive a gender transition. Jenny stayed married, although it became a sexless marriage. I know of a woman who transitioned about six years ago, stayed married, but her family (even her kids) use the wrong pronouns, which to me sounds like abuse. I also have a friend whose marriage survived. Between Nicole and I beating the odds of making it, despite being a rebound relationship, and because of the marriages I saw survive, I thought our marriage would survive.

I thought I might lose my job, my parents, and many of my friends due to the transition, but I didn't think I'd lose my marriage. We had both been the one left in our prior marriages, why would she leave me? In retrospect, I know that I had other issues that were causing me to be distant from her. She was hurt, and I had too much hubris to see how hurt she was. I failed at the most important part of a marriage, communication.

During both my marriages, I spent less time with my friends. I had my partner take the role of lover and best friend. When my marriage with Nicole started to fall apart, I realized she was my entire emotional support network. One night, Nicole wouldn't hug me, and it caused me to fear losing her.

The next day, I went to the train station for my regular commute to Boston. I felt like I was a failure as a parent, as an employee, as a manager, as a friend, but most painfully, as a spouse. It seemed like life would only be harder from that point on. Many trans people end up on the streets. One of my non-binary friends had been fired a month earlier for their gender, despite the firing being illegal. I thought about stepping out in front of one of the trains. I knew where to stand so that a train would be going fast enough to end the pain I felt forever. I stood in that chilly air for over an hour. I didn't get on my regular train. I was thinking of all my failures, or as my therapist would later say, my perceived failures. Then I thought about my kids. I didn't know how they would feel about my transitioning, but I knew they would be sad if I died. That set me straight. I couldn't hurt my kids like that. They might not need me as much as they used to, but if they were to lose me…

A few days later, Nicole and I watched *A Star is Born* at the local cinema. I didn't know much about the movie, so I was surprised when Jack committed suicide. I hadn't told anybody what had happened at the train station. When we got in the car to drive home, I told Nicole my story. I don't remember the details of the conversation, but it caused her to mention it to her own therapist, who urged her to have me speak with my therapist. I did, though I felt it was pointless since the feeling had passed. My therapist told me to call her immediately if I ever felt that way again.

A Letter to Nicole

In September 2018, I went on what I thought would be my last trip to Egypt. Two of my co-workers went for the very first time. One of my co-workers, Rebecca, was in charge of HR and Operations. At one point in our trip, she said my feminist views were rare in a man. I wanted to tell Rebecca I wasn't a man, but it was unsafe both due to being in Egypt and because I wasn't ready for work to know.

I came across a photo of Nicole that was uploaded to our family library during my trip. It was part of the prompt that led me to write this letter:

> *Subject: I Love You*
> *Nicole,*
>
> *You looked so happy yesterday. You were radiant. I'm happy for you.*
>
> *This trip has given me time to reflect on our relationship. You've been an important part of my life for over a decade. We made Pon together and I'm so thankful for them. It's hard to imagine my life without you and your sons. We've had such adventures! Thank you for being with me through the craziness.*
>
> *Reading this book about another person's gender transition has been very revelational for me. Jennifer Boylan's wife was very upset for months. Her wife felt betrayed and lied to. They had a very tough time getting through it, and I haven't read how they got past it yet. Their kids (so far) took it well. I fear Pon will feel like I'm stealing something from them if I transition (essentially going through puberty) at the same time as they do.*
>
> *The endocrinologist that Jennifer got HRT from said that a third of patients lose interest in sex becoming asexual, a third flip to like men, and a third stay the same. That was in 1999 and may have changed. I feel that as someone who is already bisexual, I don't have to worry about my interest flipping but I do worry about becoming asexual.*

Many marriages don't survive a gender transition. Some that do have the partners become more like sisters or best friends. Some marriages are able to continue on with sex.

If I believed in a god, I would pray to her that at the very least we always remain friends. Elena and I are on friendly terms, even if we rarely interact. I still feel love for Elena.

Every transition is different. I still don't know how far I'll go. I'm sorry for how much it has hurt you. I'm sorry for how much more pain you'll probably go through. I'm sorry for all the pain you probably have that you haven't shared with me. I wouldn't wish such pain on anyone. I worry how much more it will hurt our family, friends, and work.

I'm not sure I have regrets. Would life have been easier if I transitioned at puberty? Probably. But if that had happened, we wouldn't have Pon, and you wouldn't have asked me to respond to your OkCupid message.

Could I have been more honest with you and upfront? I don't know. I always wanted to experience being a woman, but it never seemed possible (outside of video games) until recently. It feels embarrassing how ignorant I've been on the subject.

Whatever happens, please know that you've made me happy. Writing this email, I've shed more tears than I've lost for months. No matter what the future holds, I'll get through it valuing this amazing decade of fun, family, and adventure I've had with you. Please, let me know what more I can do for you, even if what you need is space. Thank you.

Love,
Forest

Near the end of my September trip, I went to the wedding of one of my employees. It made me feel very nostalgic. There had been so much joy and love in my marriage with Nicole and it felt like it might all come to an end.

In Egypt, there is strong gender segregation. Usually, only men go to the mosque for Friday services. Women who wear the hijab will only remove it around family and other women. Men don't hug women they aren't related to and vice versa. Sometimes, people won't even shake hands with those of the opposite gender. In the US, I always felt awkward hugging guys. In New England, women are allowed to hug everyone, but men showing affection is frowned upon. In Egypt, it's acceptable for men to hold hands, hug, and even sit on each other's laps. I was overwhelmed by the men who wanted to hug me and mostly asked them not to. I was afraid that if I transitioned, they would be upset that they had hugged a woman to whom they weren't related. My love language is touch, so it was difficult when I was alone in Egypt.

Moving Forward

In the weeks that followed, I moved forward with steps to consider transition. I began shaving. Co-workers, who were clean-shaven, complimented me about it. I was saddened by how often I needed to shave in comparison to many men I knew. I wrote in my journal on October 5th, 2018, "I need to look more feminine. Shaving sucks. If I transition, I want electrolysis ASAP." Pon said they missed my beard when it was first gone.

I asked a few LGBT friends and allies in the area for a hairstylist recommendation. I had my hair cut so I could style it on workdays to look masculine but on other days to look feminine. I went to the local Sephora and got a free class on makeup. It was obvious to me that even with makeup, I had lived for decades with testosterone.

On October 6th, I went on a shopping spree. The staff at Charlotte Russe were so nice and welcoming to me. One of the employees kept calling me "sweetheart," and it melted my heart. Their friendliness caused me to forget about my personal rule to never buy bottoms or dresses that had no pockets, causing me to buy my first sweater dress. For a while, I experimented with wearing a burner belt, but I eventually realized it was just a glorified fanny pack, and I should just bite the bullet and get a purse.

On October 7th, I wrote the following to a quarter of my friends on social media:

> *I've known for about two years that I'm transgender (i.e., transgender people have a gender identity or gender expression that differs from their assigned sex). I've created this friends list so I can discuss my issues. If you want to be off this list, let me know. I won't be offended. I will probably get TMI with this list. I put you on this list because you're somebody I trust, somebody who probably already knows, or somebody who is in a group (i.e., burners or LGBT groups) that are accepting. Nicole is on this list. If you want to stay on this list, I need you to not out me to people not on this list. Currently, none of my co-workers know, my kids don't explicitly know I'm transgender (they know I wear clothes made for women), my parents don't know, and my in-laws*

don't know. If you want to talk to somebody about stuff I've said here, make sure they are on this list or ask me first! This list will change over time. I'm coming out to my father tonight... so I'll probably add him after.

Great, with that out of the way, you probably have some questions. Anticipated question #1: Am I going to transition? I don't know yet. When I realized I was transgender, I thought I was gender-fluid. I had zero interest in transitioning because I was ignorant. Also, I've never had major dysphoria (possibly very minor dysphoria). I have a friend who said their therapist suggested trying hormones despite their feelings that they are gender-fluid. This got me curious, when do "experts" recommend transitioning? I watched a video a few months ago of a psychologist who basically said that if you're uncomfortable in your assigned gender you should try hormones for a few months. Any changes caused by the hormones in a short period are reversible.

I talked to Nicole about this and created a weighted list of pros and cons of transitioning. The cons outweighed the pros, but Nicole and I both felt like I needed to get an experienced second opinion, so I started seeing a gender therapist. Most of my con list was concerns for other people (i.e., this is so unfair to Nicole—and it is, btw. This might hurt Affectiva. I can be a more impactful feminist if I'm male, etc. My therapist told me I have to be selfish with this decision. The decision has to be about pros and cons for me. When I take a step back and imagine how I'd advise somebody else, I know I'd say the same thing (and Nicole says it too... even if it hurts her). This greatly reduced the con list, making it so the pros outweigh the cons.

I have not yet decided to transition though. I've decided I want to go on hormones and make a decision after a few months on hormones. The indecision is part of why I'm hesitant to discuss it publicly. I can't safely travel to Egypt while openly transgender. I don't want my parents to feel the loss of their son only to have me decide to stay gender-fluid.

Anticipated question #2: Am I on hormones? Nope, not yet. I'm going to talk to my therapist on Tuesday and try to figure out a good schedule for when to start.

Anticipated question #3: How is Nicole? Umm...she's talking it better than Jenny Boylan's spouse did (Jenny is the author of She's Not There*). Again, Nicole is on this list and I don't want to put words in her mouth. She has a support network and she's working through the pain. I feel VERY guilty for what she's going through. PLEASE be supportive of her.*

Anticipated question #4: Will you divorce? Not now. Members of her support network have said she should run the f--- away before it becomes a total s---show. Part of me wants to punch these people (so don't tell me who you are) and part of me agrees with them.

Simon has had a really tough childhood and we are in absolute agreement that we have to keep things together for his final year of high school. Ideally, we'd like to stay until Pon gets through high school too... but that's like 10 more years, so who knows.

Anticipated question #5: How can I help?

A) Well, most importantly, be careful not to out me.

B) For the past two years, I've said I have no pronoun preference. I will not be upset if you misgender me. I misgender people too. I would, for now, prefer you try female pronouns with me.

C) As Nicole started working with her (in-person) support network, I realized that I've neglected my support network. I feel like I've not been much of a friend to you because I've prioritized work and family. Sorry. I do need emotional support.

D) Shopping and fashion help!

Anticipated question #6: Will you change your name? I have no plans to change my name. Forest is a gender-neutral name. I have put a lot of effort into building a personal brand that is connected with my

> *name and I don't want to start over at age 41. I might change views in the future, but this is my current stance.*
>
> *Please feel free to ask questions here or in direct messages with me.*

The same day that I made that post I came out to my father in person. Nicole, the kids, and I were visiting my father and Cindy on the weekend of the Sandwich Fair. My father lives in Sandwich, NH, so it's a yearly family event for us. All of my parents took it well. I had to wait a few weeks to tell my mother.

I was in "boy mode" (wearing a kilt) for the fair because one of my co-workers also attends the fair. I didn't bump into his family and was annoyed at having to go back and forth between gender expressions.

Gatekeeping

As I got to know my therapist, I realized that she had first seen patients like me many years ago. After coming out to select friends and my parents, I wanted to move forward and start a low dose three-month trial of hormones. I asked my therapist what kind of timeline they thought I should have for starting hormones. She was purposefully vague. Basically, I wanted to get an idea of how long it might take for me to get a letter from her that I could show to an endocrinologist in order to get HRT. She said months to a year.

At prior appointments, I said I have little to no gender dysphoria, which is one of the reasons my therapist thought she was nowhere near being able to recommend hormones. I did some research on dysphoria after the session and discovered I have no dysphoria around my primary sex characteristics (i.e., genitalia) but I absolutely have dysphoria around secondary sex characteristics (especially hair).

I posted my issues to my out-to list on social media. Some friends told me my therapist was whack. Many of them said I should find a new therapist. They also told me I could go to Fenway Health or Planned Parenthood to get a prescription based on the informed consent model. My therapist was operating on outdated standards.

Based on this feedback, I set up an appointment with Planned Parenthood for as soon after my next trip to Egypt as possible. As the Egyptian customs staff often asked me about medication, even ibuprofen, I felt it wouldn't be safe to go to Egypt while on hormones.

Electrolysis

I decided on electrolysis because it's permanent. My first appointment was October 17th, 2018. While laser hair removal could be effective for my skin and hair combination, it's not a permanent solution. Electrolysis isn't pleasant. The root of each hair needs to be zapped one at a time. Due to how hair grows, there is only a third of a chance that a hair that is zapped will never grow back. If the electrologist concentrates on an area, it can start to go numb, so it hurts a little less later in a session. The biggest reason I've never had a tattoo is because I'm afraid of the pain. When I started electrolysis, Nicole and I considered getting tattoos, but ultimately it never happened.

On the 18th, Nicole stayed over at a friend's house. The next morning, when I got off the train on my way to work, Nicole texted that she was sad. She was trying to find a good emoji for sad. I showed the GChat penguin crying over a dropped ice cream cone. She said no, it's way worse than losing an ice cream cone. I called and left a message asking her to call if she wanted to talk.

On social media, she posted that she needed pictures of cute things. One of her friends replied with an emoji saying, "Sorry for your loss." The friend then added, "That was an accidental post, I hope you didn't actually lose anything."

Nicole responded saying, "No, but I like the sentiment. Feels like it, although I didn't actually lose someone/something."

So, I was like, okay, she's sad that she's losing my masculinity (maybe). Then, that night, I got home and asked her if she wanted to talk or hug. We briefly hugged. She said she didn't want to talk about it with me. Her friends were coming over to play games in our community's common house. One of them ordered Indian food for us. Before she left the house, she said that finances were part of the problem. Paying $90 for each hour of electrolysis with two hours a week, we could afford this month but probably not future months. I asked if my messed-up 401k (which was earning us an extra $400 a month) could cover it. It sounded like it would help. I had offered multiple times to go to an hour a week.

Nicole had to go with a friend while I made tapioca pudding for the kids. When the food arrived, I headed over. Another of her friends was there to eat and play. Then, when I went to have dinner, she asked me in front of her friends if I could start a Go Fund Me for electrolysis. I didn't say anything. They all knew I was trans. I was mortified at asking friends and family for money as I'm one of the top 85% of US income earners.

When we sat down to eat, Nicole said I should take care of the kids instead of playing with them. I ate dinner feeling unwanted. She said I should leave after dinner, but I felt like running away before I even started eating. I left as soon as I finished eating and spent some time crying while hitting a punching bag. I walked a bit and swung on a swing set.

She had been talking about making a separate bank account for me so I could budget how I spend it. The idea was she wouldn't have to worry about giant unexpected costs. I thought we might have to separate our finances. I didn't want to move out though. That night, I talked to one of my closest friends. It helped a lot. I had been slowly working to rebuild my friendships.

I drafted an email to Nicole explaining how hurt I had been that night. We had already figured out how much I'd be paying in child support. In the email, I proposed we separate our finances sooner. I wanted a private account so I wouldn't have to argue about money. I never sent the email, it sat in my drafts for over a year. We chatted in the following weeks and things got a bit better.

Chaos

In 2018, there was a ballot question for Massachusetts, asking if the transgender rights bill should remain in effect (yes) or be repealed (no). There was a lot of conservative money being thrown into repealing the bill. On October 28th, there was a trans rights rally at Boston's Government Center. I wore a skirt and was accompanied by several of my friends.

I was very public about wanting people to vote yes on Massachusetts Ballot Question 3, to keep in place the 2016 law that prohibits discrimination based on gender identity in places of public accommodation. I updated my social media pictures to show me (from the neck up) at the rally. The image included the trans flag and "Vote YES on 3." While I was afraid of coming out as trans, a part of me wanted to in order to be in solidarity. My friends knew few trans people and it could have made the issue more real to them.

On October 29th, Nicole spent the day with her mother. When she came home, we met and talked. She said she needed a divorce. Maybe I should have fought for the marriage, but what is there to do if a partner is unwilling? I cried as she told me. She asked me to move out after my trip to Egypt. Simon was about to take the SATs. I asked that we hold off telling the kids until after he took them. To keep the divorce from my work, I asked her not to file until I came out early the next year. After we talked, I blocked Nicole's mother on social media. She's still blocked to this day.

When I told my therapist what had happened, she gave me some good advice. She said that I'm an equal owner of the house, there is no reason I should leave. Leaving could actually make the courts feel like I abandoned the family. While Nicole accepted this for a while, a couple of months later, she threatened to file for divorce ASAP if I didn't move out. I realize things were very strained between us, but it felt like blackmail.

After Simon took the SATs, I told him about the divorce. He didn't seem to take it well, but in retrospect, I think he was mostly worried about me. Nicole and I eventually came up with a bargain so he would continue to live in the home we owned together for the rest of his senior year and I would live elsewhere.

Final Trip to Egypt

During my final trip to Egypt in November 2018, I came across some social media posts that used scare tactics, making it appear that trans people are bathroom predators. There have never been reports in the US of trans people harassing people in bathrooms. However, 70% of trans people have been denied entrance or have been assaulted trying to use a bathroom. People made ads where they portrayed trans people as pedophiles using bathrooms to harass girls. I was shocked not only by the ad, but by all the comments supporting the ad. It felt like the majority of voters might vote no. I came very close to coming out while in Egypt.

My flight from Dubai to Cairo was about to take off when I saw a "Yes on 3" ad on Facebook. Almost all the comments were people saying to "vote no because of perverts."

At a CHVRCHES concert earlier that month, I was in girl mode. I had to use the bathroom twice. The first time was easy because the ladies' room was empty, and I wasn't worried. The second time was during intermission and there was a long line. Everyone that left the bathroom passed those of us in line. I wanted to hide my face to keep from being noticed. I think I would have been at least as uncomfortable in the men's room. Nobody said anything, but I did get a couple of startled looks. I'm a pretty determined individual and that was really hard. I was sure it would be easier on HRT and as I made progress with facial hair removal.

Friday November 9th was rough. Friday is the Muslim holy day, so Egypt weekends are Friday and Saturday instead of Saturday and Sunday. It makes the fact they have TGI Fridays restaurants a bit ironic.

I slept until noon after going to bed around 1 am. I'm more of a night person there, as is most of Egypt. I only got up because Friday prayer was blaring loudly from the local mosque. Arabic often sounds angry. Affectiva's speech classifier, which was trained on English, usually classifies Arabic speech as angry. It made me uncomfortable. I needed to get up and play some music to tune it out.

I had breakfast and watched some Netflix in my apartment. I went to "lunch" around 3 at a nice Syrian restaurant. I went to the local cinema after lunch. I was unsure if I wanted to see *Crazy Rich Asians* or *The Girl Trapped in the Spider Web*. Well, I forgot that *Crazy Rich Asians* was a romcom and decided to see it. I was not in a good emotional state to see it. If you haven't seen it, you should skip ahead as I might spoil it for you.

I was a little uncomfortable with it because I was unsure how Asians felt about it. Is it offensive? Did they like it? I later heard from my friends that Asian Americans liked it but people living in Singapore felt it did a poor job of portraying their demographics.

I thought the movie was funny. I especially liked Rachel's friend from college, Peik, and Peik's family.

I also thought it was sad. I cried. I wondered if people are supposed to cry watching romcoms, or if it was a middle/post breakup thing?

First, there was Astrid's marriage falling apart, which gave the movie a lot of depth I hadn't anticipated. Astrid came from money and married someone who had little. She hid her purchases and wealth so her husband wouldn't feel inferior. She said no to positions that might bother him. He still felt unworthy and started an affair with a woman with whom he felt more comfortable. Part of me wants to shout, "Look, Nicole and I weren't that bad!" Still, money and class played an uncomfortable part in our marriage.

Looking at the relationship between Rachel and Nick I feel I relate a lot with Rachel. My family didn't, to my knowledge, put on airs. I feel I was raised to value people for their deeds as opposed to their class, connections, or wealth. While Nicole's mother never said to me that I wasn't good enough for her, she certainly had said it to Nicole. Thus, I was very uncomfortable with how both Eleanor and Ah Ma treated Rachel.

Near the end of the movie, it looked like Rachel and Nick wouldn't be able to work out their differences. Nick did an awful job at preparing Rachel for his family and did little to support her. Rachel didn't want there to be resentment over their relationship and felt it best to call it off. I'm in a place where I think that was the right decision. So, I don't really like the happy ending.

Don't get me wrong, Nicole and I weren't from such different places as Nick and Rachel. I'm glad we were together for the time we had. I'm so grateful that we have Pon. It's better to have loved and lost than to never have loved at all.

Things were so unclear for me then. Which, in general, I don't mind. I like surprises. I prefer those surprises come from work, friends, and travel. I like having a solid home. I like having a close companion who I can rely on and vice versa.

I was in a different place than when I met Nicole. I'm less than two decades from retirement. I'm heading out of parenting and towards grandparenting. At the time, I thought future relationships would either have to be casual or with people who are at similar points and looking to have adventures after retirement.

I've long planned to work on projects that can't afford me until I retire. Specifically, I'd like to work/volunteer in disaster recovery. I'm especially interested in Burners without Borders, the Red Cross, or possibly a refugee support group like Rescue.org. Travel is a key component for what I want to do.

So, yeah, that was a rough day. But hey, I was excited to be going to Poland at the end of the trip. My work needed somebody to meet with a partner company and had asked me to go.

I didn't shave while in Egypt. I wanted it as a plausible proof that I wasn't transgender. My last flight from Cairo one of the passport control officers pointed out my beard growth was small compared to my passport.

In Poland, I had an AirBnB that was located within the former walls of the Krakow Jewish ghetto, which were built by the Nazis to look like gravestones. I visited the Schindler factory, Birkenau, and Auschwitz.

I appreciate that we don't want to allow atrocities like the Holocaust to occur again. However, when people say, "never again" I inwardly shudder. If we are saying "never again," shall we allow ethnic cleansing, then what about the ethnic cleansing happening today in Syria, and Yemen? Okay, maybe we're burnt out on the Middle East and I certainly don't support another war. Is it the numbers? What about the 1 million displaced by the Central African Republic Civil War (i.e., 1/6th the number of Jews who were killed in WWII)? What about the ethnic cleansing happening in China against Muslims? Okay, maybe we're just talking about western First World countries or even just the US. But wait. Isn't that what we are doing with immigrants in the US? According to the ICE website, we arrested 140k immigrants and removed a quarter million immigrants in 2017. Again, I appreciate and agree with the desire to prevent holocausts, I just don't feel like we actually are.

In Auschwitz, I saw the symbols that prisoners were forced to wear based on what the Nazis had deemed wrong about them. I probably would have had the pink triangle for homosexuals and black triangle for asocials because of my pacifism. The most difficult thing for me to see was the collection of shoes from all the children that had been at the death camp.

Hormones

A few days after my younger stepson's birthday, I began posting on social media some of the things that I appreciated about Nicole. I knew things were rough between us. She was very clear that I was no longer what she wanted as a marriage partner. I hoped I could at least retain our friendship.

Planned Parenthood is awesome. My first appointment was my all-time best interaction as a patient. When I arrived, they handed me a paper that outlined what to expect from an initial appointment. I was asked to write down my pronouns and chosen name so they could avoid dead-naming. The nurse did the regular intake stuff and asked if I wanted an STI screen while I was there. I agreed, because while it seemed unlikely that I'd have sex for a long time (if ever), it would be nice to know. Minutes later, they gave me a clean bill of sexual health.

Next, I met the CNP. She spent time discussing the risks and changes that gender-affirming therapy causes. She gave me a three-page consent form that detailed what feminizing hormone therapy is, what the benefits are, what the risks are, what the side effects are, what alternatives exist, and what else I should know.

She gave me the time to read it. When I finished, I had some questions about the risks to the liver, kidney, and heart disease. I told her about my existing low good cholesterol issue. I asked what percent of people have heart disease due to it. She went on uptodate.com to research my questions. She used a form that determined my baseline risk for heart disease was 2.2% for the next decade. There is very little research on heart disease in transgender women, but often the good cholesterol actually improves. Ultimately, I was satisfied with the risk. She also offered to run a cholesterol test at the same time to be sure.

Before taking blood, she asked me if I had a history of fainting from blood draws. I said, "Yes." She asked what I had eaten—just a banana and some pineapple chunks. She offered me some snacks from the employee snack bin to reduce the chance of fainting. I had some peanut snacks. She gave me several minutes for the food to get into my system before returning to get the blood.

Before I left, they gave me a packet of transgender resources. It included surgeons, PCPs, therapists, and support groups.

The test results came back the next day. Once I got them, she had my pharmacy prepare my prescription. December 1st, 2018, I took my first dose of estradiol and spironolactone. Nicole had expected that the results would take longer. She was very upset when she discovered I had taken my first dose. It felt like our relationship kept bouncing from good to bad. I had been trying to be patient and understanding but that was a final straw for me. It was at this point that I decided that I too wanted a divorce. It didn't make sense how she could be mad about me starting hormones when she had already asked for a divorce.

Holidays

We traditionally spent Christmas and Thanksgiving with Nicole's family. She has more siblings and the family all lives in Newport county. I like Thanksgiving. I can't remember ever being a fan of Christmas. It always feels shallow to me. I'm not good at receiving gifts because I generally don't want stuff. I'm also not good at giving gifts as I have trouble knowing what people want.

After my first divorce, I would begrudgingly bring a fake tree out of the basement for Simon because it was important to him. I don't have any specific interest in Christ. I do like holiday lights, but not enough to own any.

Thanksgiving 2018 went fairly well. I successfully avoided my mother-in-law. It was good to see my nieces, sisters-in-law, and nephew. Nicole and I went for a refreshing walk together.

Christmas, however, was a nightmare. I knew there would be trouble if I dressed feminine, so I had to deal with that discomfort. On top of that, my brother-in-law gave me men's socks for Christmas. When we were about to leave, I took Simon aside and told him that he probably wouldn't see his cousins again. I told him to make the best of his goodbyes. While technically I was invited to Easter, I was only willing to go to Easter if it was very important to Simon. He said it wasn't, so I haven't seen my former in-laws again. I have interacted with one of my former brothers-in-law over the phone and my former sister-in-law over email.

Things continued to deteriorate in my relationship with Nicole. She got upset that I didn't say anything to her for her birthday. I didn't know what to say on the birthday of someone who was divorcing me. I caught myself chewing out two co-workers that day.

At one point, things got so bad between us that we both were literally afraid that the other would be physically violent. The worst thing I think she ever said to me was, "It must be nice becoming a woman after your childbearing years."

In February, I filed for a corrected driver's license. The picture is awful, but I'm so happy to have scored an "F" on my license.

In March, I blocked Nicole on social media. I finally created a separate bank account. We had started to see a divorce mediator. I found it frustrating that I had to miss half a day of work every couple of weeks to go through mediation when we had already used a template to figure things out.

Vacation

I have a timeshare in the Berkshires. I take the family there for a week almost every year. I was both looking forward to the vacation, as it would be a full week in girl mode, and petrified because there were certain things I'd never done as a woman before that I was very afraid to try. It was on the ride to the Berkshires that we had settled on me being called "Umi." When Simon and I had been at the Global Game Jam a few weeks earlier, he caused some confusion by saying, "She's my dad." In some locations, it could literally be dangerous to out me like that.

I cannot say enough good things about my clinician at Planned Parenthood. With her advice and the new double dose of Spironolactone, I only had to go to the bathroom three times after the alteration (which was on par with pre-hormones). The previous night at the old dose, prior to asking her advice, I went to the bathroom at least six times (during one of which I was ambushed by a cat).

When I checked in at the timeshare, they needed to see my license. I still had the old plastic male license with a beard photo. I was a little annoyed about that.

I had planned to go to a small Vietnamese restaurant that we've always loved, but they were permanently closed. Simon found a place in Lee called Salmon Run (which is the name of a game mode in Splatoon so we *had* to try it). When we got there at 6, they were packed and asked if we had reservations. Fortunately, they let us eat at the bar, no waiting. I had a pasta dish with mussels. I was able to get them to use their Fra Diavolo sauce instead of what they usually use. I had wrongly assumed it was dairy free and didn't ask. It was really good though. The kids had Shirley Temple's that came with orange slices and two cherries. Simon had a burger and Pon had chicken tenders. All the food was good. The kids didn't like the fries (but ate them all).

The Green Grocer in Lee closed a couple of years earlier and, this year, even the Price Chopper was out of business, so we went to the Big Y. Figuring out what the three of us want to eat together and the size of this store caused it to be a long trip. When I went to pay, I realized my ATM/Debit Card was missing. I had used it at the restaurant. I paid with my credit card, tried not to panic, and got the kids back to the car. We went back to the restaurant, and, on the way, verified that the Vietnamese restaurant really was closed forever. Salmon Run had my card but needed to see my license to return it. I got my credit card back but was really hating the old license. Fortunately, it stayed in my wallet for the rest of the trip. The staff at Salmon Run were really nice, even gave some advice on what had changed in Lee.

Since I wore a week's worth of feminine clothes and was getting close to coming out at work, I took pictures each day so I could ask which outfits were work appropriate. While some people commit the fashion crime of wearing sweatpants at Affectiva, I preferred business casual. It took me forever to learn business casual for men, so I expected a steep learning curve.

I woke up at 8:30 AM one morning during our trip. Pon came barging into the bathroom saying someone was on the phone with Simon. I told them I'd be done in the bathroom in a few minutes. I threw on a dress so I could see what was happening. Simon said a rude man called asking for "Mr. Handford" and he told him there is no Mr. Handford. I think the timeshare was trying to sell more time. He told them to call back. They called back when I was shaving, and Simon left the phone ringing. The caller gave up. So, that's why I had no pockets that day.

Pon also wore a dress without pockets that day. Their solution: tie a pair of pants around their waist like a belt so they'd have pockets. My solution was my "backpack purse." I was inspired by the purse of the tour guide at Auschwitz. She had the same kind but black. I loved how it was never in her way but still looked good.

When we were about to enter the museum, a male attendant said, "Ma'am, I'm sorry, you will have to carry that by the handle. People aren't allowed to wear any kind of bag on their back within the museum." I was not happy about the prospect of carrying it around in my hand. Mostly, I thought it would be an annoyance. The bigger problem was that it's got so much in it that after three hours of walking with it my arms were exhausted. Apparently, bags hung at the hip from the shoulder are fine because most women, and one man, had bags like that. I couldn't store it anywhere because it had valuable stuff I needed in it. Part of me says, "F@<k the patriarchy," but I didn't see anyone else with a bag like mine… so maybe he didn't know what to do. At least he called me "Ma'am."

I had been very afraid of changing in the locker room after swimming. It was winter though and I couldn't get to our suite without walking outside. I had bought a swim shirt because my chest and arms were still hairy. Pon, who at the time was still using feminine pronouns, changed with me in the women's locker room. I was afraid that I'd get yelled at or that the cops would be called on me. We were fine though. I remember that while waiting for Pon, I did my best to hide my face so people wouldn't realize I was trans or think I was a man.

Coming Out

The first of my coworkers that I came out to was our HR Manager, Rebecca. I came out just after our October trip to Egypt. She was very respectful. I had a friend who had come out at another tech company years earlier, and I offered some messaging resources to Rebecca. I told her that I was planning to go to work dressed as Clara Oswald on Halloween 2018 to see how people reacted. I said that if we were to have a party, it might make things a little smoother. Halloween was a success.

Next, I came out to my direct manager, our COO. He was very respectful and recommended I come out to Rana next. I also came out to a gay member of the company who suggested I have a party to come out to the rest of the company. My original plan was to have an HR presentation, and then, I'd send an email. Hosting a party for me to come out felt uncomfortable. Other teams had held some parties, and then, I realized I could have my team host a party that wouldn't out me until I gave a speech. I let my team know one by one. I got a budget from the COO. Since my parents hadn't been able to celebrate me as a girl, I had an "It's a Girl" theme. We hid the cake and decorations until after my speech.

I posted some pictures and a coming out blog post that night. I had gotten friends to help edit it days earlier. The original version was very standoffish because I was expecting to lose a lot of friends. Fortunately, a trans woman I'm friends with had me tone it down. Here is what I eventually posted:

> *I came out as transgender to ¼ of my Facebook friends in October 2018, via a private friends list. The list was a mix of people from LGBT-friendly communities (UUs, Burners, Geeks, co-housers, etc.). While these were people I was fairly trusting of, I still had some fears. That group was extremely helpful to me in terms of advice and a place to discuss my hurdles. If you want to read those posts, send me a private message.*
>
> *With my mother present, who I had come out to last year, I hosted a diversity celebration at Affectiva on International Women's Day 2019. I gave a speech in which I came out to the entire company, some of whom I talked to ahead of time.*

Now I'm ready to tell the world at large that I'm Forest and use she, her, hers pronouns. You might be thinking, but wait, I like Forest the man. What's wrong with him? He seemed happy and genuine. Well, thanks, I hope you get to know and like Forest the woman.

Have you ever read John Stockdale's quote, "You must never confuse faith that you will prevail in the end—which you can never afford to lose—with the discipline to confront the most brutal facts of your current reality, whatever they might be." Now, John Stockdale was a POW and war hero. I cannot imagine the hell he went through in Vietnam, which included being tortured over fifteen times. I can, however, relate to the quote. For 41 years, my reality was being imprisoned in the gender I was assigned at birth. I made the best of it because I didn't understand the alternatives. I can elaborate in private for people who are curious. When I learned, in the summer of 2018, there were other options, I began a review process that led me to begin gender-affirming hormones in November 2018.

I've started a sci-fi novel that I'm tentatively calling Flipping *which explores living in a world where you can near-instantly change the physical aspects of yourself from clothing to gender. It's been a great way for me to process my feelings. Someday, I might write a nonfiction book, but I feel like my story isn't that different from the ones already in print.*

If you've read this far, thank you. You might be wondering, if I'm changing my gender will I also change my name? Forest is a gender-neutral name (though it is more popular for boys, it is also used for girls). My parents would have named me Forest even if I had been assigned female at birth.

I wanted to let as many people know in person, for the sake of transparency and inclusion. I fear that I may lose some of you over this. If this is a problem for you, I kindly ask you to disconnect from me and move on with your life.

That party was on a Friday. The following week, I returned to work in make-up, a blouse, a skirt, and a blazer.

A few weeks after I transitioned, a male coworker noticed my heels and said he was always impressed with how well drag queens could walk in heels. I took him aside and told him I wasn't offended by what he said. I did, however, want to make something clear. Whenever I've worn men's clothing, I was in drag. I wear women's clothes because I'm a woman and I want to. I relate much more to drag kings than drag queens. He was surprised because he wasn't aware of drag kings.

Forgiveness

In April, I moved to Fitchburg. Simon had been accepted at Fitchburg State University. I found a three-bedroom apartment that was a ten-minute walk from FSU and a six-minute walk from the train station. I had forgotten how much I like living in the city. Now, I can, and do, walk to the hardware store, several restaurants, and the grocery store. I don't need a car to get to work. Simon stayed in my old home with Nicole and the other kids until he graduated in June. She took great care of him, and I realized I underestimated how much she cared for him.

I had started writing my novel *Flipping* in late 2018. I used it as a way to process my feelings about divorce. One day, I went shopping for some sewing supplies in the Mall at Whitney Field, which I had never heard of before. After getting the supplies I needed, I explored the mall. I found a store that said it sold works by, and supporting, Indigenous people (from throughout the world). I probably would not have entered that particular store, but the cashier was playing a guitar along with music that was playing on the store's loudspeaker. Intrigued, I went in and looked around. There was a section with bracelets. I bought a bracelet with a dreamcatcher on it and, immediately, tied it on my wrist after I bought it. The next day at work, I noticed that it was missing. I knew I had not tied it very well because I had been in a rush. I could not find it in my coat sleeve and assumed it was lost forever. That night, I found it in my bed and tied it really tightly onto my wrist. I bought it because it was pretty, purple, and possibly supporting people who needed the money. That night, and every night since, I've remembered my dreams when I wake up. In the past, I would usually remember a dream every couple of weeks. Now, it's at least one dream per night!

One night's dream was of me forgiving Nicole (who at times in the dream looked like Lorelei Gilmore… but hey, it was a dream!) I knew I had been harboring some resentment and anger towards my former partner. I also knew, long before the dream, that for my sake, and our children's sakes, I needed to let it go. I was hoping time and distance would accomplish that. Often, I forgive people after a short amount of time, but this time, it had gotten so extreme that I had blocked my former partner on LinkedIn and Facebook.

The day following the dream, on my train ride to Boston, I researched how to forgive people. I also chatted a bit with a very dear friend who had gone through a divorce that had caused similar issues, which she eventually overcame. With her wisdom, and a lot of introspection, I was able to let go of the anger and resentment. By dinner time, I had internally forgiven her and unblocked her on social media.

It seemed stupid to call and say, "I forgive you." I did not want to upset Nicole if she did not know that I had been hurt. I also did not know how she felt. It was very possible she was angry with me. Still, it felt important, so I called after her work let out. She picked up right away. I stammered a bit, unsure how to say what I had called to say. But I finally got it out. I told Nicole that I had been angry and holding resentment. I told her that I needed to let it go for my sake and for Pon's sake. I forgave her. We talked for almost an hour. It was really a good conversation. I still feel anger from time to time, but it's getting more rare. I think of us as close friends now and feel very blessed that we were able to rebuild a friendship. I unblocked her on social media.

I started writing *Flipping* to work through my pain from that break-up. Originally, it was going to be a tragedy. But, after I had forgiven Nicole, I lost the drive to write that specific story. It felt resentful. I was unsure if my planned story could, or should, change, but I became open to alternatives.

The Transphobic TEDx Talk

YouTube thought I should see Shannon Thrace's TEDx Maastricht Talk entitled, "Getting Real—A Transgender Experience." I was looking for some fluff before bed (and probably should have stopped at the Star Wars Shallow parody). Shannon's was not a video to watch before bed.

Shannon Thrace talks about how her marriage broke down over 18 months. My knee-jerk reaction is that she's pushing the rapid onset gender dysphoria agenda because she's upset about her spouse transitioning. However, I'm open to believing that she truly thinks what she is saying and that there are people who are as she describes.

She says that the internet brainwashed the man she married into becoming transgender. Part of this brainwashing, she said, came from "tranny porn." I'm a sexual being. I've watched my share of porn. The porn I prefer does not have people I can identify as transgender (i.e., there might be transfolk in the porn I watch sometimes, but if they are there they pass for cis). There are genres/categories of porn that focus on transgender people. It's not for me… at all… ever. I know, ironic, I don't like to see porn with people like me… but except for "home videos," cis people watching cis people are not seeing people that are like them either. I mean, raise your hand if you look like a porn star.

Shannon says internet chatrooms for gender non-conforming people further brainwashed her spouse. I guess I can imagine such a thing exists, but I've never been in a chat room like that. I have been to a few transgender meetups, but I found them depressing. Specifically, some people talk about how they had relationships fail, some talk about how they aren't happy with their progress, and some talk about how they are scared to appear as their real gender in public. I totally respect and feel for these people, but I can't sit around listening to them. I also totally respect if you skip chapters where I talk about my speedbumps. It's like, I could pay attention to news about the 45th President… but I'd rather not.

The word "transgender" didn't exist when I was a kid. I thought I just had to be a boy and deal with the fact I'd prefer not to (kind of like what Jo seems to do in Little Women but vice versa). I started to publicly wear female clothing before I met Nicole. A very close friend laughing at me in a skirt at WildFire and a cinema employee laughing at me wearing a skirt to a movie pushed me way the fuck back into the closet.

This was pre-Caitlyn Jenner. It was not safe to be trans. *Boys Don't Cry* is real: the real Brandon Teena was raped and murdered in 1993!

Shannon goes on to say that her spouse had been happy with maleness and enjoyed male things like "backpacking, whiskey, and Johnny Cash" but now refuses to camp because it messes with a make-up routine. I literally shouted bullshit at the screen here. Women can like whiskey, backpacking, and Johnny Cash! I am ecstatic to go camping at Firefly with Pon.

Figure 14: Forest and Pon at Disneyland (left) and Firefly (right)

Shannon says that her spouse required her to act differently. I can believe that. I asked my spouse to use female pronouns, but that's all I remember doing. I never expected my spouse to act differently. I don't see anything wrong with asking the people you care about to use your pronouns. Nicole might feel differently. Also, I did profusely apologize to Nicole about many things, like how I told her two years earlier that I'd never transition. I was mistaken because I misunderstood the transition process (mostly due to media representations).

Shannon goes on to say how depressed her spouse was, struggling to be a woman. Basically, the internet and cultural brainwashing ruined her life and her spouse's life. I'm pretty certain you all know I'm happier than ever. I've had people (including my therapist) say that I appear happier. I didn't ask them. They just volunteered their view.

There are tough times. The night before I saw this TEDx talk, I waxed at home by myself. If my life was a sitcom… well, you would have laughed to see the waxing episode. It was a hilarious event but ultimately successful (except for the armpits). I thought I'd do it again…

but with the exception of my eyebrows being done professionally, I've never repeated the experience.

A tougher time, the Monday before I saw this talk, I got in line at a hot dog cart in Downtown Crossing behind two twenty-something men. One was buying a hot dog and the other was chatting with him. After the purchase, one turned and saw me and said, "Oh shit!" He then started laughing and pointed me out to his friend. I walked past him and ordered my sausage, peppers, and onion. I basically did a reverse bystander intervention by discussing my order with the vendor and ignoring the continued taunts. Ultimately, they walked away laughing, but in retrospect, putting myself between these two people with my back to them may not have been the safest decision.

I think, like anybody who strives to change their appearance, there is a slippery slope, this is true of cis people as well (look at what Michael Jackson did to himself). I'm very conscious of the message I'm sending to my kids. I don't want them to feel they should be removing their hair. If I were to let my hair grow too much, it would look masculine and trigger gender dysphoria. I tried to maintain a balance of hair on my arms. If Pon ever asked me to match their hair for solidarity, I would. There are still hairs I could shave off my arms, but I don't want to. I don't mind being flat-chested, I've never had any interest in top surgery. Will I ever be "happy" with my appearance? Is any woman ever happy with her appearance when we're bombarded with idealized visions of the female body by the media? I'm certainly happy at times. I love when Affectiva software correctly gendered me. The software got my gender correct about 10% of the time a month prior to watching the video. At the time I saw the talk, the software got my gender correct 30% of the time. I'm probably in the training data, which skews my results towards male. A goal of mine is that it gets it correctly 90% of the time (preferably without the science team retraining it by labeling images of me as female… I mean, it would be a sweet gesture, but it wouldn't be giving me the honest feedback I'm using it for).

Shannon goes on to say that people like her are being blocked from speaking their truths. Her truth, by the way, will soon be available in a bookstore. She also says that there are statistics being hidden and modified to push some kind of transgender agenda.

It's clear that Shannon is very hurt. That sucks. I feel for her. It's possible that what she says about her spouse is accurate, even if it's different from my truth. She goes too far though. She refuses to respect her spouse's pronouns. She's arguing that we need to question people who change their pronouns. She argues that we need more critical research. She argues that the public shouldn't block stories like the one she will soon have on sale. From my perspective, she goes too far and maybe it's the pain from her failed marriage that is prompting it, or maybe it's just product marketing.

Where's the Reset Button?

On May 16th, 2019, we met with the lawyer and reviewed the rough draft of the divorce agreement. I have a recurring fear that my co-parent is going to take my child away from me. To some extent, this actually happened with Simon. It's very rare for the courts to take the side of a trans woman. One little lie could make a court believe I'm a monster. Fortunately, Nicole has never done anything to substantiate this fear, but it still persists to this day. That night, I was so afraid that I spent some time crying.

The next day, I had a nagging feeling that something wasn't right. I think the divorce language for Massachusetts is extremely final and permanent. I wanted to make sure one of us wanted this. I was no longer sure I wanted it. I was angry at her for what seemed like forever, certainly longer than ever before. Did we really want it to end? It couldn't go back to what it was, but perhaps it could evolve. Maybe some of my thoughts were because of the sunk cost fallacy. When Nicole and I were at Simon's academic award ceremony, I felt like we should hold hands. I didn't know if she had questioned it since she asked but this seemed like the last chance for us to ask. I could tell there were things I miss. I missed being with my best friend almost every day. I missed having somebody that had my back. I missed helping her when she needed it. I missed cuddling. I missed our adventures together, so many good adventures.

Was it rose colored glasses? Was that the estrogen talking? I just didn't know. I tried calling that night but couldn't get through. I called the next morning. She answered but she was at work. She said we should talk later and said I needed to think about why I was asking.

The next day, we talked for a while. I read to her from my journal about the divorce language and how I had wanted to hold her hand at the ceremony. She mentioned that it's tough for Pon that I moved. She reiterated that she feels I betrayed her by excluding her from planning my transition. I apologized. She said she'd think about if she still wanted the divorce but that she might not change her mind. Eventually, she got back to me and said that, no, she didn't want to stay married to me.

Near the end of May I wrote the following poem as I grappled with my feelings for Nicole. I used a modified version of it in *Flipping*.

Where Has My Friend Gone?

She left me just there.
I remember so well what we were.
Our laughs, our cries, and most of all our adventures.
If I dedicated my life to making a time machine, could I save us?
I miss the hugs.
I miss her touch.
I miss her smell.
Some days, I think I see her.
In a neighborhood—just a stranger,
In a house—just a shadow,
In an auditorium—just a trick of the light,
In a party—just a doppelgänger,
In a crowd—just another of my mind's illusions,
In the eyes of our child...
Was it Karma?
What wrong did I do in a former life?
Is it Fate?
Is there something more destiny has in store?
Is it my wrongs in this life—so many from which to choose?
Or is it just the impermanence which I always see lurking and yet here deny!
I find myself in tears.
When I think of a joke to share—which shan't be funny to any but me,
When I hear something she'd appreciate—that is just static without her,
When I wake alone—when haven't I been alone,
When I watch that show we shared—that we fought over how it should have gone.
When I hear that song,
That one which we danced to,
That one she put on a mixtape,
That one we sang at the top of our lungs driving a bit too fast and a bit too reckless.
Can't we hug?

Can't we hold hands?
Can't we speak as friends?
Then there are the flashes of anger like IM notices,
Never expected,
Never invited,
Never welcome.
Didn't I let that anger go?
It's expectations that lead to pain.
The law that can't be denied.
The law that is oft forgotten.
Where has my friend gone?
Shall I see her again;
Not as a ghost in an auditorium,
Not as a stranger in a neighborhood,
Not as an illusion in a crowd,
Not as a doppelgänger in a party,
Not as a flicker in our child's eyes,
But as a whole being in my arms.
Where has my friend gone?
I miss her so.

Pride Month 2019

Simon graduated at the start of June. His school has a tradition where each student gets a flower, and they are asked to give it to the person they feel helped them the most. He gave his flower to me, and I cried. A middle-aged guy complained to me later saying, "I didn't get a flower."

Figure 15: Grandfather, Simon, Forest, and Grandmother (left to right) at Simon's Graduation Ceremony from Tahanto High School

Pon had come out as bi only a month or two earlier. I'm not really a parade person. It could be I was involved with too many parades from marching band and scouting. I felt it was important to go to Pride Boston in 2018. We got there in time to have lunch before the parade. We waited in the shade but also rotated the family through the spots we were holding so we'd have a good view. I was surprised how commercialized and politicized the parade was.

The last Pride parade I had been to was in Providence over a decade earlier. It was actually a bad experience. A drag queen had thrown something to my son (maybe beads) and got snippy with me because when I helped Simon with it, she thought I was taking it from him.

I had fun dancing when there was music… and when there wasn't. Pon and I got a bunch of swag. A few people, including strangers, said "Happy Pride" to me, and that felt really good.

I got very emotional when I saw the Stonewall veterans and shouted, "Thank You," to them. I cried when I saw the people honoring the trans victims. I'm not afraid for myself, but I'm afraid of the impact on my kids if something ever happened to me.

After the parade had been going past us for a little over an hour, Pon said they were tired. Pon's not the type of person to complain unless there is a problem. They asked to leave soon. Sometimes, these things sort themselves out: so, after a few minutes, I asked if they still wanted to go. They said yes. I think Pon was getting too much sun and heat. We left the parade, and I got the kids hydrated. Simon and I had Italian Ice. Pon had ice cream and a pretzel. We cooled off in the shade. While they were eating, I went to get some selfies at the parade. My teeth were stained red from the Italian Ice so I couldn't get a good one. The best I have is of me looking cross-eyed with my lips sealed.

It's a good thing we left when we did. I had Simon drive and noticed he had gotten sunburned on his right hand. When we got home, I discovered I had sunburn on both of my shoulders. Apparently, my dress had been covering them when I applied sunscreen.

I think we're all glad we went. Simon even asked, "Are we going to do this every year?" I told him I wasn't sure.

Sam

Saturday June 22nd, 2018 started with getting my car inspected. I had no idea how long it would take because I was new to the area and if something was wrong my 2005 Prius might not even pass. The first place I went was a Chevy dealer that said they were too busy, come back in two hours and maybe they'd see me. On my way home, I noticed an independent mechanic that advertised inspections on their signs but had been omitted by Google Maps. I stopped there and was amazed at the speed and service.

I had been invited to a party in my old neighborhood. I didn't feel comfortable there at the time, though I do now. It was mostly in my head. I gave Nicole a heads-up in case she would prefer I stay away. When I arrived, I stopped at the house to give Pon a pride pin that says, "Best Bi," which they had asked me to purchase. Pon asked me to stay to help with a tricky part of *Zelda Twilight Princess*. I was happy to help.

Not a lot of people were at the party yet. I wasn't going to be able to eat there because I had to leave early and most of the meal was going to be meat, I was vegetarian at the time. I checked with Nicole to see if she minded me taking Pon to lunch. We had a blast at a Chinese Buffet in Hudson.

After we ate, I went back to the party. There was a girl, who appeared to be about two, who wanted to talk to me about her toy. We talked a bit and then she said, "Why this," pointing to my skirt "And this?" pointing to my makeup-less face.

I replied, "Because I'm a girl."

She said, "No, you're a boy."

Her parent was horrified and tried to get the girl to gender me female. I wanted to have a long conversation with the girl about gender, but I was too freaked out and walked away.

I usually just wear makeup on days I'm going to work in Boston. It helps me pass a little better but isn't perfect. I also wear makeup on some dates and at really important parties. I had been on the fence about wearing makeup that Saturday because of the party I would be at that night. I only knew one person at the party and expected lots of dancing. I didn't want my face to have trouble sweating and if these strangers wouldn't accept me for who I am, it was better to know right away, so no makeup.

I wandered back to the house to say goodbye to Pon. I needed to leave soon. Pon was outside in a pen with their bunnies. In general, I'm against pets because of the work and some trauma from my youth. The bunnies live in a cage in Pon's bedroom. Their room smelled like hay, which I found unpleasant. The bunnies also always seemed scared. Outside though, they were having a blast. They were eating grass and clover. I got in the pen with them, and they would sniff me and bump into me. It was surprisingly fun. I stayed a little late to enjoy the bunnies and Pon.

My Hip Hop dance instructor had been urging the class to go to a show that his crew was part of. If there hadn't been an after-party with dancing, I wouldn't have gone. I don't care much for choreographed dance, and I've only recently begun to appreciate Hip Hop music.

The first half of the show was okay. I really loved a prison dance routine one group did. I also liked the thought behind a Judy Garland performance and its tribute to Stonewall.

At intermission, I found my dance teacher. He thanked me for coming and ignored me for the rest of the night. I was left wondering, *Is he socially incompetent? Does he not know how to play host? Was he just too busy? Was he freaked out I wasn't wearing makeup (his classes are always after work, so I've always had makeup)? Did he regret inviting me? Did he think my 10 second interaction with him was flirting?* He's so not my type, especially due to his youth.

I posted some highlights of the first half of the show on social media. I wasn't usually online that late in the day. When I was about to exit the app, I noticed a post about my friend and former co-worker Sam having died on Friday. I turned off my phone and said to myself, "It's probably a mistake. I'm going to focus on the rest of the show and enjoy the dance party." I was mostly successful at this, especially since I was in denial.

There was a drummer with a singer who started off the second half. The drummer was great.

Then, an act started with music that I recognized immediately as Billie Eilish. Google Play had been trying to sell me Billie's music for weeks. Usually, their recommendations for me are awful. I got curious one day and watched one of Billie's videos and was awestruck. I soon watched the rest, learned she urges fans to become vegetarian, and I saw a Reacts video of her watching fans make covers of her songs. She was so sweet and humble. As you can imagine, I bought her album. The dancer, Kaylee "Impavido" Millis was amazing and inspiring. The best part of her performance for me was that it was entirely improvised.

After the show, the chairs were cleared, and the after-party began. There wasn't much dancing at first, which is totally typical for a dance event. There were some little kids there, dancing with their parents. I hadn't realized it was an all-ages show and, thus, wouldn't have bought tickets if it was a weekend with Pon.

I really wasn't sure how welcome I would be. There was a lot of ethnic diversity. I was worried though, would I be accepted as a trans woman? Would I be intruding as a white woman? I danced alone for a while. Two to three cyphers formed. I floated between the cyphers, watching from the outside. As our dance teacher has said, Hip Hop isn't about classes. Classes only started as it became popular and people wanted a formal intro to it. We had done a few cyphers at class, but I didn't really feel like I understood how it worked. In the after-party, my dance teacher kept dominating the largest of the cyphers. Maybe I don't understand but he seemed to be showboating and monopolizing the cypher, which just added to my poor impression of him.

When I was dancing alone, one of the women from the prison performance started encouraging me. Until then, I had assumed people were just encouraging friends. It felt awesome. Sometimes, I dance with my eyes closed because I want to forget about other people while I dance.

The smallest of the cyphers was where I spent most of my time. A lot of the people who went in the center were performers from the show. I didn't really expect to dance inside the cypher but a guy who had urged others, one at a time, to take the center motioned for me to take a turn. I literally did the "who me?" look. He nodded, yes you. So, I went in and danced. They encouraged me and cheered me on just as they had for the other dancers. It was awesome.

This is really the type of environment I had been looking for. I had already paid for the following week's class. I wanted to see if I could find a regular place to be part of cyphers. I was especially curious how my teacher would act in class. What I discovered was that, yes, while we danced under a giant rainbow flag, my instructor was uncomfortable with me. I never went to another of his classes.

When the after party ended, I tuned back into social media. While there was no obituary yet, several other friends had posted, and one even included the phone number of Sam's mother. This is when I exited denial and knew it was real. This is when I made my own post.

I was never super close to Sam. This was big to me because she was also a transgender woman. In fact, she was the first transgender woman with whom I had spent any amount of time. Other similarities are that we both worked at MEDITECH, we were both activists (her far more than me), and we both had been regular Firefly participants.

This is the first transgender person I've personally known who died. When I was still in denial, hoping it wasn't true, I especially was afraid to discover if she was a victim of a violent crime or had committed suicide. Rates of both are far higher in our population. Two of my friends posted that it was suicide. I actually stayed in denial about that for days. The obituary didn't say the cause of death and there was no way I would call her mother.

As I got ready to drive home, another transgender woman texted me saying they saw my post and asked if it was true. This may have briefly sent me back into denial and I told her all I knew. I gave her links to some of the posts I had read. Then I told her that I needed to drive, we could talk later if she wanted.

After the texting, I put on some dance music. Something to distract me so I could drive safely from Boston to home. The music mostly did the trick. When I got home, I checked in with some friends to see how they were doing. I went to sleep, afraid of how little I had planned for Sunday to distract me.

I spent Sunday cleaning the apartment top to bottom, packing for Firefly, shopping, and cooking. I was able to pretty much keep myself busy the whole day. Something odd I've discovered is that my internal dialogue for weeks after I heard of her death had been misgendering all trans people I know, including myself. I can't fathom why my mind was doing that. It doesn't seem like a good defense mechanism. I felt like I needed to avoid using pronouns when I talked, until I got back to a normal headspace.

I was able to avoid talking about my weekend at work on Monday. I came close with an intern and was like, "Nope, she doesn't need that."

Sam's death had me asking a lot of questions. On Monday, I got an email from a friend who said it was suicide. Some of what I questioned was:

1) I knew she was having a tough time, why wasn't I there for her?
2) What got her to that point? We are so similar in our backgrounds. She was almost a decade younger than me and always seemed so strong. She transitioned pre-Caitlyn Jenner! Would something ever push me to that place?
3) If it happened to me what would happen to Simon and Pon?
4) How do I protect myself?
5) Who else is in or near that place, and what can I do to help?
6) When was I going to allow myself to cry? Not Saturday. I needed to get home safely. Not Sunday. Too busy prepping for Firefly and ignoring what had happened. Not Monday. I almost lost it at work . . . but I took a breath and held it back.

Suicide can be such a tricky topic to discuss, which means we really should discuss it more! I've only ever ideated on suicide for an hour of my life. It was a dark hour where I was focused on what I felt were my failures (my first marriage, my second marriage, being a stepfather, being a father, etc.). It was the realization of how my death would impact Pon (and to a lesser extent Simon because he is older) that got me through it.

A week later, another trans friend posted on her Facebook, to all her friends, that she had admitted herself to McLean Hospital for suicide ideation. She asked friends to come visit her. McLean is in Belmont. I was in the Boston office that day and discovered that McLean is a short walk from a commuter rail station on the line I usually take. I told her I would visit.

I had never been in a psych ward before. My paternal grandmother died in an asylum before I was born, so I have strong feelings about them. I was really impressed. They have creepy tunnels though. McLean seems to be a good place. They were clearly LGBT friendly. In fact, the staff, especially in that ward, just felt friendly.

My friend and I chatted alone for a while. Sam's death had strongly contributed to her suicidal ideation. Eventually, several other friends, one of them already a mutual friend of ours, joined us.

It was really great to spend time with her and for us to show her she is loved. I probably arrived around 5:30 PM. We stayed until visiting hours ended at 8 PM.

After her friends and I left the hospital, we hung out in the parking lot chatting. One of them had biked to the hospital. I walked with the bicyclist to Star Market so we could both grab something for dinner. I visited her weekly until she was released.

White Privilege

I read an article a friend shared on social media about white privilege. I almost shared it, but the app said I can't share it unless I said something. I wasn't sure what to say. What do I say? I have white privilege? Hell yeah! I benefit from white privilege? Yup. It seemed like there was more to say and I was unready to articulate it.

The article was written by a white woman. She was explaining how no matter what, she could never truly understand what it's like to live in the US as someone who isn't white.

Let me reframe it in a way I can understand—in a way only a transgender person can understand.

I once had a philosophical conversation with my gender therapist. I was like, "How do I respond to people who try to make an analogy of changing gender to changing race? Like, what if I said I want to be Japanese?"

Her response was to say I could move to Japan and absorb the culture. Pon would love that, but I'd never truly be Japanese. I'd never be accepted as Japanese. I'd always be looked at and treated as an outsider no matter how well I matched my clothing and language. My height, skin color, and eyes make it very clear: *not Japanese!*

This goes beyond race. I have the privilege of wealth. When I first joined the full-time workforce in 1998, I was making $26k a year. Today, I can't imagine how I'd survive on $50k a year. Even if I only had to pay for myself, I still can't imagine it. I've made very close friends in Egypt who make *way* less than that. I've seen how they live. Fortunately, it is cheaper to live there. Maybe I could live on $50k there, but not here. Every time I tell a homeless person I don't have cash, it haunts me. If I were to answer honestly to their request for spare change it would be, "I don't want to give you cash because I've been taught that you're going to waste it. I have been taught it's better for me to waste it on myself. From experience, I know that there is a good chance that if I offer to buy you the thing you are asking for, you'll try to convince me to just give you cash because you know I won't approve of how you spend it. I don't have time for this."

There is a really good TED Talk by a trans woman named Paula Stone Williams about male privilege. She talks about how she didn't and couldn't understand until she transitioned. She's right! You can't understand unless you have literally lived as the other. You can't understand being homeless unless you've been homeless. You can't understand being another gender unless you've lived as another gender.

I think people should at some early point in their life try living with the hormones of a different gender for one week. With male to female, the changes would be reversible but from my limited understanding of female to male those changes would be irreversible.

Since I began gender-affirming hormones, I feel differently. I think differently. I've always been female, but I never understood how much testosterone was interfering with my life until I blocked it. Don't misread that. I'm not saying testosterone is bad for everyone: it was bad for me. It didn't match who I was and, thus, created a lot of pain. One of my stepsons said that before I transitioned it was like I hated myself, which caused me to snap at others, including him.

In hindsight, one of the stupid things that held me back from transitioning was that I felt I could be a more impactful feminist while presenting as male. Certainly, men are going to listen more to other men, so allies are needed. One of the reasons it was stupid is because I suspect that knowing I lived as a man, men will listen a little better. Even if they don't, there are male allies that are cis. I don't need to do that job. I need to take care of myself first.

The equity and inclusion issues I tried to help with before, I didn't fully understand. I could sympathize but not empathize. Now, I can empathize. Now, I know what it's like to be cat called. Now, I know what it's like to be judged by your looks before anything else. Now, I know what it feels like to find a male presence physically intimidating. Now, I know what it's like to be the only woman in a room of male technologists.

I had several women who worked for me before my transition. I tried to talk to them about their challenges as women. They generally underplayed them and said everything was fine. Now, I have women who tell me what they struggle with. Now, I'm in a real position to help because they've been able to open up to me and I know how things should be.

Please believe me when I say you cannot understand the other unless you become the other. Listen to people who are different from you with the knowledge that their experience is different from your experience, *and* it is valid. ♥

Firefly 2019

At Firefly, I experimented a bit with what brings me dysphoria. I also examined some of my body image issues. I brought makeup because there was a makeup skill share event, but I missed it in favor of something else. I wore no makeup at Firefly.

When I arrived, I planned to see how long I could go without shaving. Shaving at a "Leave No Trace" event is challenging. I had never shaved at other Fireflies or even other camping trips. I prefer to use a razor from a mail order club. I asked for advice from other Fireflies and settled on using lotion instead of shaving cream. This would allow me to wipe the lotion into my skin and the only trace I would leave in the woods would be the hairs I removed.

I didn't expect to have dysphoria from facial hair because I wouldn't actually be seeing my face. The only mirror I ever saw at Firefly was in one of the porta potties. I did, however, anticipate people misgendering me and pointing out the facial hair. I had shaved Monday morning. Thursday night Pon said that I should shave. I later asked why they had asked me to shave. They said it was mostly because it was confusing their friends.

Some of Pon's friends asked why I had such a deep voice. They assumed that hormones would have raised the pitch. I wish! Testosterone for trans men will lower their voice but estrogen doesn't raise a trans woman's voice. Some of us get surgery. I have no such plans. With effort, I can produce a more feminine sounding voice. At Firefly, and with my kids, I'm usually too relaxed to bother. I just talk how I naturally talk. I did give their friends some demonstrations of a more feminine voice. I also realized one of my cis-female friends has a deep voice, almost as deep as mine naturally is. I suspect she gets misgendered on the phone but didn't want to upset her by asking.

I waited until Friday morning to shave. I don't like shaving at night. The cream worked okay, but I couldn't really clean the razor. Monday after getting home when I used that razor again, I cut myself twice before tossing it. Hopefully, I won't have facial hair next Firefly (which will possibly be in 2021 since 2020 was cancelled due to COVID-19). If I do shave at Firefly 2021, I might use a disposable razor instead.

Another thing I tried was going topless. Many people at Firefly, of all genders, go topless. One of the reasons I used to avoid buying dresses was because of chest hair and because of my lack of breasts. Ironically,

I now prefer dresses as I think they complement my figure better than skirts.

At Firefly, you encounter all body types. It was really helpful for me to bump into a few cisgender women who were topless and had smaller breasts than me. I got two photos of me topless at the photo booth.

The only person who asked me to put on a shirt was Pon. I just scowled at them and said, "No." I told Pon I wasn't trying to embarrass them, but I wasn't going to put on a shirt. I later discovered that it wasn't embarrassment that motivated Pon but fear I'd be hurt by somebody who is transphobic. I've let Pon know that Firefly is a very safe space, and it was extremely unlikely anybody would even say something transphobic.

Pon and I have had a lot of conversations that I expect more often happen between female siblings than between parent and child. This was still before Pon came out as non-binary. When I first bought bras, Pon was like, "You don't need those."

"Yes, I do," I'd reply.

"No, you don't."

"Yes, I do."

We even talked about who is bigger. Pon's point is that, proportionally, they were bigger. I told them it doesn't really matter, that, ultimately, they'd be bigger, not knowing at the time they were non-binary and would become dysphoric about their chest.

I didn't feel comfortable early in the event going in the steam bath. Topless was one thing, but fully nude was another. Fortunately, the heat made me less interested in going.

The heat, however, did cause me to want to take a dip in the stream. There is an area of the stream that makes a fairly large pool. It was so hot, and I was getting dirty.

I wasn't the only transgender person to bathe while there. When I arrived, there was someone who was either trans masculine or non-binary. They (or he) hadn't had bottom surgery and was nude. If they could do it, so could I! I took off all my clothes and got into the freezing water. Nobody stared. Nobody pointed. Nobody laughed at me. I went again Thursday just before a thunderstorm was due to hit.

I think this event had several healing effects for me. An event of 1,300 people, I'd guess at least 50 of us were transgender. L'FUCC,

Camp Lamp, and Library Camp had the highest concentration of transgender folks out of the camps at which I spent time.

Dating

In early 2018, I went on a handful of dates. One of the dates was with a man who took me to a seafood restaurant (this was before I was vegetarian). He had come up with the idea. He had offered to meet me at the train station. He opened the door for me. He even paid for the meal, despite being between jobs. I loved it. I don't think I'd like it all the time, but it was wonderful that night.

Unfortunately, dating that guy didn't work out. Through various examples, he showed me that he didn't respect me. First, when we spoke on the phone, he said I had a deep voice but that was all right because he was bi. I'm a woman! It doesn't matter to me if he is bi. Second, despite me being a hiring manager for the type of role he was looking for, he disregarded much of my advice. Third, he pressured me into inviting him into my apartment by arriving far too early for our final date.

I also have gone on a few dates with a non-binary person who, at the time, was presenting as female. I kept finding myself unsure of how to act. Do I open the door? Do I pay for the meal? Do I drive? I even told them about my concerns and they reassured me that I was doing fine. I had a great time, and I enjoyed many other dates with them.

They had been afraid to come out to me because they saw how much I reveled in my femininity. They thought that by discarding their femininity, it would upset me. It didn't upset me, and I'm glad I was able to see them develop into a more true vision of themself.

I can't speak for cis people, but I have the impression cis-hetero folk often follow their gender's stereotype for how to date. Men are expected to court and chase (unless a woman says no). Women are expected to be wooed and won. Men are expected to propose. Men are expected to give flowers. Don't get me started on what women are expected to do in the bedroom!

I started working on better stating my needs. I continue thinking about what I do out of habit, what I do to fit cultural norms, and what I do because I enjoy it (like traveling with a partner and having adventures). I hope that you, the reader, also take time to consider for yourself what you need, what you want, and what you are willing to give. Oh, and please don't ever think of limiting what you give to what you feel you get. Scarcity mentality is a lose-lose.

Internal Dialogue

After I started taking Estradiol, I found myself regularly having the following internal conversation:

My Impractical Self (IS) would start by saying when I'd see a baby, "Oh, look at that baby. Isn't he cute? Wouldn't it be nice to have another kid?"

My Practical Self (PS) would respond, "That must be the estrogen talking."

IS would cajole, "Come on, you wanted kids before estrogen too."

"Grandkids, I'll probably have grandkids… someday."

IS saw the opening and said, "Probably…"

"Shut up."

IS would continue, "Grandkids are at least a decade away."

PS would point out the obvious, "I can't even have kids, shut up!"

"You can adopt."

"Uhh, I'm basically single. How about no?"

IS would say, "You've always wanted to adopt. There are so many kids who need a home, especially older kids. Then, you don't even have to change diapers."

PS would scoff, "I don't mind changing diapers."

After a pause IS would say, "Because you want kids."

"What? *No!* Grandkids? Yeah. I want grandkids in a decade or two. If my kids want their own kids."

"Sure."

PS would insist, "I can't fill my loneliness by having more kids! I need to be happy with myself first."

"…so, talk again when you're 'happy'"?

"Kids would ruin my 12-year retirement plan!"

IS would exclaim, "Maybe it's a crappy plan! Who even plans over a decade out? You love spontaneity, remember!"

"I also value security."

"Freak!"

"Really, name calling?" PS would say, "How about we table this so I can concentrate on work and validate that this is just the estrogen talking."

IS would always have the last word, "It's not ok, but fine. Let's see what your friends say."

When I shared this on social media in 2018, most of my friends agreed it was the estrogen talking. However, there were also suggestions I consider fostering. It's absolutely something I'm open to doing as Pon gets more self-sufficient.

Surgery Options

I get asked more often than I expect about my surgical plans and status. Dear cis people, I don't currently mind this discussion, but many transgender people would prefer not to have it. I have never asked a person what genitals they have, and unless you are planning on having sex with a person, please do not ask (unless they give you a personal exception). You might also get a pass if you're immediate family who is worried about your family member having surgery.

I know, you are curious. I'm curious too. Think about it like this though. Imagine you are a horse but for some odd reason you have a horn on your head. You know you're a horse but that damn thing on your head keeps confusing people. Sometimes, you are asked, if you don't identify as a unicorn, why didn't you have that horn removed? Maybe it's because the surgeon doesn't return your calls, maybe it's because you can't afford it, maybe it's because your insurance won't cover it, maybe it's because there is gatekeeping for who can have the surgery, maybe it's because you're afraid of the risks and side effects, or maybe it's because sometimes you like having it, like when you need to stab a human. When another animal talks to you about it, they are reminding you of that stupid thing on your head that you have been trying to ignore. If it's another horse that mentions it, then you suspect that horse thinks of you as a unicorn and it makes you feel like an imposter.

I've seen a lot of articles recently where people call a transgender woman's penis a "female penis"—because they are female. I agree with the concept, but for me, personally, that term makes me feel squicky. I do love it when a trans girl under the age of five responds to a misgendering by saying, "I'm a girl with a penis." You go girl!

There are various surgeries available to transgender folks. For trans women, like me, there is top surgery (to amplify breasts). My breasts are fine as is. I have no plans to have implants. Technically this procedure matches what cis women sometimes call a 'boob job.'

Transgender men (like Chaz Bono) and non-binary folks who were assigned female at birth also have an option for top surgery. This is actually the opposite of what trans women get. It's similar to a double mastectomy, but there tends to be molding to shape a more masculine physique. It's my understanding that trans men are more likely to get top surgery than trans women. I'm told binding hurts, is hot, and has risks.

For trans women, there are actually multiple bottom surgeries available. There is the bilateral orchiectomy which is the removal of testicles. This is a low risk and fairly affordable surgery (~$5k). With Blue Cross mine cost $1.5k at UMass Memorial. The outdated real life experience requirement from the WPATH/Benjamin guidelines used to require a person to wait after having changed their legal identity and lived as their gender for at least a year. It was a form of gatekeeping. Many surgeons have replaced this with informed consent. Blue Cross had the following three gatekeeping requirements:

- a letter from my hormone's prescriber with an MD saying I'd been on hormones for at least a year.
- a letter from a therapist with a master's degree that I saw regularly who feels the surgery is important for me.
- a letter from a therapist with a master's degree that I saw in an evaluative capacity that says the surgery is important for me.

I wanted surgery as soon as I could get it. I literally could have paid cash for it and bypassed the insurance, though it would have emptied my savings. I didn't mind waiting, especially as I began tuition payments for Simon. The biggest obstacle, at first, was that I literally couldn't get a hospital to return my calls. Boston Medical supposedly performs this surgery regularly but took months to call me back. My PCP called Boston Medical and had no luck either. Finally, I was able to connect with my surgeon through UMass Memorial, where my PCP works.

The reason I wanted this was because I was taking the max dosage of Spironolactone, 400 mg twice a day. There are risks and side effects with Spironolactone. I was also super paranoid about missing a dose or two (which happened only a handful of times). I was afraid of detransitioning but even just experiencing testosterone again would be problematic.

An alternative to a bilateral orchiectomy is a scrotectomy. I'm unclear why people would do this as it makes it difficult to later have vaginoplasty. It's riskier than a bilateral orchiectomy, I'm not sure what the cost is.

The other bottom surgery for transgender women is vaginoplasty. If a bilateral orchiectomy had not previously been performed, it will be included. Recovery from vaginoplasty takes longer. It's an in-patient surgery that costs about $30,000. It's cheaper in Thailand, but there are a lot of risks having it done there. In general, this is a riskier surgery. Some people suffer side effects for the rest of their lives.

I don't currently get dysphoria from my genitals, so I don't have a pressing need to get vaginoplasty. I do, however, want to get it in the next eleven years. When I "retire" in eleven years, my plan is to do disaster recovery work. Some of the places I would do this work might get upset if they discovered I have male parts. My life could be at risk in these parts of the world.

If you are compelled to ask a transgender person about their surgical status, it's best to ask something like, "Are you no-op, pre-op, or post-op?" Again, you really shouldn't ask unless you plan to have sex with the person or need to give them medical care down there. Think of it this way. How would you react to someone asking, "What's in your pants?" Multiply any disgust you can imagine from that by ten.

There is also a surgery to shave the Adam's apple, making it less apparent. My Adam's apple isn't very noticeable.

There is a surgery to make a voice sound more feminine called laryngoplasty. While I would like to sound more feminine, I'd rather do it through speech therapy. I don't want a surgery involving my neck!

Finally, there is facial feminization surgery. This one creeps me out the most. I have some information about what it is, but I can't stomach writing the details. Basically, it makes it, so a face looks more feminine. Do some internet searches if you want details.

Satan's Hip Hop Class

I stopped attending class at my old dance school because I felt that my teacher is transphobic. I take Hip Hop classes as a way to learn new moves that I can incorporate into my existing repertoire for freestyle dancing.

After a wonderful meal at Veggie Galaxy, I discovered that Satan is a dance instructor, and his class is Hell. I'm not going to say his real name, or the studio's name because, while I hated the class, it is clear that Satan has a devoted following of worshipers (aka, masochists) who get value out of his class.

Before the class, I was already out of sorts. When I arrived at the studio, I got in line to fill out a waiver. The employee told each cisgender-looking woman in front of me that the women's room was behind them to the right. They told each cis man that the men's room was upstairs. When it was my turn they said, "The women's room is to the right, the gender-neutral room is upstairs, and the men's room is upstairs." I didn't know it at the time, but that was a microaggression. I was wearing my jacket with a she/her pin. I had makeup on. I was wearing a pink workout top and a sports bra that was obvious if she had looked at me. I was not thrilled to be reminded that I failed to pass as female. This would not have been an issue if they either listed all bathroom options to everyone (which is probably their policy) or if they asked each of us for our pronouns and gave us the corresponding location.

I proceeded to the women's room to shockingly discover the first section was a locker room where multiple cis women were changing in the open. I absolutely panicked, "Oh no, they are going to call the cops. Don't look, just find the bathroom stalls." After the locker area, I discovered the bathroom stalls. Both stalls were occupied and there was somebody in a state of undress at the edge of the locker area who might be waiting but I wouldn't look to confirm. I kept my eyes staring at the sinks, because the alternative was the occupied showers to my left, the locker room behind me, or the bathroom stalls, which had large gaps between the door and the frame. The first stall emptied and the woman at the edge of the locker room went in. Finally, the second stall emptied, and I locked myself in. While in the stall, I thought to myself, *Perhaps I should have used the gender-neutral room*. When I was done, I quickly left, avoiding looking at anybody. I made it out safely.

In later weeks, I returned to this locker room but prepared for the experience. I've never had anybody complain that I was there.

I had been in a women's locker room in the Berkshires. In previous visits to the Berkshires, I had been in the men's locker room of their sports complex. I had a good idea what to expect. I had been mentally preparing for over a month. Pon was with me in that locker room as we were going swimming together.

Satan greeted us for class cheerfully and briefly asked for new people to raise our hands. He asked us to stay towards the back because the warm-up was choreographed, and it was best for us to see veterans in the front. I knew there would be push-ups, because it was mentioned in the class description. While I think push-ups are pointless in a dance warm up, I had decided to try the class anyway. I also expected stretching and sit-ups. Of the 1.5-hour class, 30 minutes were devoted to a warmup that was a mix between a Richard Simmons workout and what I understand of Basic Training PT. Satan told us that it's okay if we struggle but all of us needed to fight. He demanded that we verbally shout things like "up" and "down" during sit-ups and push-ups.

After we completed the regular push-ups, Satan singled out a new guy who had bent his knees during the push-ups. He required all of us to do all ten push-ups again because he had done it wrong. Satan said, "You're not cheating me, you're just cheating yourself." This was the first, and hopefully last, time in my life I've been told to do one-handed push-ups.

During the class I had various thoughts including, *I paid $15 cash for this* (because Hell doesn't accept credit cards). *I am literally going to die! I will be incapable of playing cricket tomorrow with my co-workers. I will have to work from home tomorrow! I think I am about to pass out! Never again! Can I escape with my life? Oh, I can sweat there too?* and *Why don't I have earplugs in my backpack?*' I now have earplugs in my backpack.

When the warm-up ended, we had a one-minute break. I took a look at the other classmates. It's a big class, possibly fifty people. While I probably was the oldest person in the room, it wasn't by more than a few years. One of the male students was wearing a shirt that had some logo I didn't recognize that said, "boot camp."

Satan announced that today we would be learning the first two to three parts of the choreography to Janet Jackson's video, "If." As he showed us each move, he had us say a corresponding word for the move like, "left," "right," "slap," and "lift." While I found this embarrassing, I suspect he is correct that it can be a useful way to memorize each movement.

I love Janet Jackson. I was a fan back when I was a tween. Having her music literally playing at what I suspect was 130 decibels is extremely unpleasant. I didn't need earplugs for the CHVRCHES concert, the Amanda Palmer concert, Boston Decompression, or Firefly but, at all of those events, I had them just in case. This music was literally being played louder than music at all those events. My ears still hurt 24 hours later. I didn't notice anyone else covering their ears. This is the only complaint I emailed the studio about. It's irresponsible to allow classes with sound levels that loud unless they provide ear protection. Everything else in this chapter is about me being in a class that isn't for me.

I hate choreography, possibly due to my Modern Dance roots. In general, Hip Hop isn't meant to be choreographed. Also, Janet Jackson's "If" isn't Hip Hop! "If" is Pop, with a blend of Trip Hop, Rock, and, of course, dance-pop. It is hard to find gems from choreography that I can incorporate into my freestyle repertoire. Also, I'm slow at learning choreography. His veterans at the front of the class, one who had been taking Satan's classes for three years, all knew the song's moves already. I have no idea how many classes they worked on it. Near the end of the class, he said he likes to teach choreography to show students how quickly it can be learned. That's probably a great goal for people who care about choreography.

He ended the class by saying he was leaving for LA the following week and his last class, which we were all invited to, would be Saturday. This was a relief in that I'd never take his class, even by mistake, again. I also wouldn't feel like I missed out if I hadn't had time. It also may have been why attendance was so high. Perhaps these workout masochist followers were there to see him before he left. While it probably was a good workout, it was absolutely not what I wanted in a dance class. I did like one bit of advice he had, that we should all stretch in the shower before bed, or we would regret it the next day.

I found another Hip Hop class, at the same studio to try the following week. The description did not mention push-ups. I brought earplugs but didn't need them. A student hurt her knee early in the class and class was cancelled while they waited for an ambulance. I went to later classes. While the class was gentler, it was also too focused on choreography, so I stopped going.

TERFdom

While I like what Caroline Criado-Perez said in her "99% Invisible" interview, I discovered, as I started to read her book, *Invisible Women*, that she completely omits intersex and non-binary people. I made excuses for her to do this, like they are a small percentage of the population and women are almost 50%. Then, a friend asked me how I was liking the book because her view of the author was that Criado-Perez was "TERFy." TERF stands for trans-exclusionary radical feminist. Well, it turns out the author is a TERF and is also racist. I absolutely cannot support a book about bias by someone who has so much bias. There is an open letter from The CUSU Women's Campaign you can find on the internet asking for the author to not be allowed to speak at the "Women of the World" festival. The letter outlines both her transphobia and her racism.

Thank you to my friend, Emily, for helping to enlighten me. I was sad, at first, to discover this. I was turned off from JK Rowling over the summer of 2019 when I discovered she is a TERF. I was hoping that Emily was operating on outdated information but, based on a blog post she made 5 years ago and still hosts titled "Becoming a Woman: Trans Women and Male Violence," Criado-Perez is still a TERF, despite acting like a friend to trans folk.

If Criado-Perez were to have apologized since, I could let it go. But she hasn't. Sure, we (trans women) were born in a position of power. I hated it though. I hated seeing other women oppressed. I also hated how being assigned male at birth put me into a box. I alone should define me. What about trans girls who transition as kids? I can't believe somebody who transitioned at three would ever have enjoyed male privilege. Some of these TERFs literally think I'm part of the patriarchy. Rather than fight each other, how about we work to end misogyny and get truly inclusive equal rights!

A book I firmly recommend is *Excluded: Making Feminist and Queer Movements More Inclusive* by Julia Serano. I read this book in Library Camp at Firefly. It talks about how lesbian and dyke communities used to exclude trans women but would include trans men! For example, Mitchfest was a music festival that only allowed "womyn born womyn." It makes no sense to include trans men in a women's space and exclude trans women! Some conservatives deny TERFs exist by saying that they aren't trans exclusionary because they include trans men. Trans men are men. That's misgendering them!

I equate TERFs to racists among the suffragettes, like Elizabeth Cady Stanton. Some of the suffragists justified their actions by saying it would be too complicated to include black women in the movement. Some were just plain racist, and I cannot excuse that, Stanton being one of them. There were some, however, who were not racist and fought for inclusion.

I'm sure there are ways it can be said that I am making a false analogy. Regardless of how much male privilege I may still be profiting from, I certainly have white privilege.

In 2015, Glamour awarded Caitlyn Jenner their "Woman of the Year" award. Many articles were written criticizing this decision. A man whose wife posthumously won the award returned his wife's award because of how insulted he felt about Jenner's award. Is this TERFdom and transphobia, or do they have a legitimate argument?

Every time I'm at a women's only event, or am even invited to one, I have some amount of imposter syndrome. I knew I was an imposter when I was male presenting and being with boys. In computer science, we often face imposter syndrome when we struggle with a problem that we "should know how to solve." Do I belong? Are people uncomfortable with me? Should I leave? I don't know of a single transgender person who hasn't felt imposter syndrome. After safety, it can be the second most important reason to strive to pass as cisgender.

Yes, I benefited from male privilege. I wasn't told as a child to be polite and sit like a lady. These things are damaging to girls and I strive to raise my kids to be who they want to be, as long as they don't hurt others.

As a child, I was told to be manly and take risks. This causes transgender people damage. It also makes it a struggle for us to be ourselves.

When I was a teen, I was very ambitious. I thought about becoming President and being the CEO of a tech company. I was the CEO of two tech companies that failed and a co-founder of several companies, including a non-profit that was a success. As time went on, I learned how broken our government is and how little the President can actually accomplish, despite the ridiculous amount of effort the job requires to be a good President.

I still like leadership. I spent much of my youth learning to lead and as a teen having youth leadership roles. I also spend tons of time leading volunteer organizations. It took me nine years to get my first professional leadership title. I had done mentoring and training, but despite asking several times for a management role, I didn't get one until 2007.

I like solving problems, especially human problems. Recruiting great people, mentoring them, and helping them achieve their goals is what I enjoy most about work. It's not always easy: sometimes, I have to give feedback that can be upsetting to hear, especially if it's not delivered well.

I no longer want executive positions, unless they are in a very small company. I'd feel uncomfortable leading a group larger than 100 because I would have trouble knowing all of the team. I dislike the idea of having employees I don't know, at least in passing. Maybe I'm wrong, I regularly serve as Officer of the Day (OOD) for Firefly Rangers. It's a 24-hour shift where I'm basically responsible for everything happening within the Rangers for 24 hours. Reporting to the OOD is the shift lead, who manages a 6-hour period of time. Reporting to the shift lead are the non-supervisory roles for the Rangers and sometimes a trainee for the supervisor role. The Rangers help make Firefly a safe event through peaceful communication. From time to time, Rangers are in danger, and during that 24 hours, that danger is ultimately my responsibility. While I spend time with all the shift leads, and some of the people who report to them, there are literally some Rangers who are on during my shift that I don't know by name. I've also been on the Board of Directors for Firefly and, when we had a liaison system, I was the liaison to the Ranger team. The Board also has 24 hour on-call shifts and needs to make decisions like when to eject a participant and how to pay for the thing the event suddenly needs that we could never have expected.

Would I have had those volunteer positions if I were assigned female at birth? I'm pretty sure I would. I can't remember the Board ever just having men on it. The Ranger Lead for several years was a woman who we all deeply admire. I hope the same is true for management. My paternal grandmother was a small business leader, and that was a long time before I was born.

Like most women, I have never once in my career asked for more money. I have never negotiated for more money. In fact, at times when

I have asked for promotions, I have specified to the person I reported to (or would report to) that they wouldn't even have to pay me more.

So, sure, maybe I have benefited, and still benefit, from male privilege. Does that mean I should be excluded from female spaces? I don't think so. Does that mean transgender women shouldn't get awards for women? I'm not sure, maybe gendered awards are stupid but, at the same time, it's ridiculous how little our society recognizes women. We need to fix this and excluding transgender women from the fight is not going to help.

When I am mistreated as a woman, I'm likely to say something, because I know how I should be treated. If I see other women mistreated, be they my CEO, the next Vice President, my female employees, my mother, or even Criado-Perez, I'm likely to say something, even if they don't want my help. Despite the awful things Criado-Perez says about trans women, I would stick up for her human rights. Maybe the knowledge and power I have to help women only comes from having lived like a man, but isn't that knowledge and power helpful to us women? I say yes.

As for Criado-Perez's book, I was in the sample section. I will read no more of it and I will never pay money for it. I cannot accept a book about bias by a TERF and a racist.

Happy Birthday

We delayed the divorce by a couple of months so that we'd reach our ten-year anniversary before the divorce was final. The 10-year anniversary mark makes it so a former spouse can collect the maximum amount of social security. As I didn't want the divorce and the social security only impacted Nicole, I agreed to the delay. Ironically, the delay caused the court date to be on my birthday.

To limit associations between the divorce court and my birthday, I made my birthday information private in as many places as possible. I missed a few but didn't get the usual flood of birthday greetings on social media. I did tell a few of the people who brought it up why I wasn't celebrating in 2019.

That morning, Nicole and I met at her house. She drove us there. I silently cried a little on the way. I also called her "Honey" when we had a green light, not realizing she was turning left.

We ended up being the second case. The judge did not have any concerns, unlike the judge in my first divorce. He did, however, misgender me multiple times. The divorce documents purposely omitted gendered terms like husband and wife. I wanted to correct him but didn't want to sabotage the proceedings or get held in contempt of court. I did have contempt for that court. I had been afraid that I wouldn't make it through the hearing. As we left the courtroom, I struggled to keep from crying. I just wanted to make it outside. I rushed out and then started crying in front of the courthouse. Nicole held me and did her best to comfort me. It took me several minutes to recover.

After court, she took me to brunch for my birthday. Nicole had wanted to correct the judge as well. She said it helped her to think of what he said in the past tense. Same sex marriage was legal in Massachusetts when we were married, but it wasn't in Rhode Island which is where we had been married. It's unclear if that was part of the misgendering.

We talked until 2 PM. We realized we were probably at our best while working to have and raise kids. As Pon grew up, we had a harder time connecting. I wonder if I need a common cause to sustain a relationship. When I got home, I made a brownie sundae. I explored Coolidge park and cried some more there. On the train ride to work the following day, I cried thinking of our anniversary, which was half a month away. The divorce wasn't final until the middle of January 2019.

Are you LGBT?

This is a pay it forward chapter for people wondering if they are LGBT (though mostly trans/non-binary). Feel free to skip if this isn't you, though you may want to share the info.

Context

When one of my children recently came out to me, they were nervous about it. In fact, they came out to my co-parent first. Thankfully, I have a great friendship with both of my co-parents, so we can share things like this. I was somewhat surprised they were more hesitant to come out to me. While I didn't talk to the kids about my sexuality, I do talk a lot about gender.

Literally weeks later, I had someone I'd been dating come out to me as being non-binary. They were also nervous about coming out to me. I asked them why, and to paraphrase: it was basically because I'm so enthusiastic about my femininity that they were worried I'd react poorly to an opposite view.

Are You Really?

I've always known I was feminine. I didn't always know I could transition. Just because I follow the most common narrative for trans people, it doesn't mean other narratives aren't real. I literally only learned last year that The Matrix was about being transgender. It is so obvious now but not so much when it came out. The movie alluded to a term I also learned last year: "egg," a person who is trans but has been protected by themselves, or others, from knowing the truth. It's safe in an egg. Taking the red pill has risks and consequences that you cannot understand until you've "experienced the Matrix."

Cis and hetero are the default. In the movie *Love Simon*, the main character had this wonderful fantasy that all kids would have to come out with their sexual preference, not just non-hetero people. I have the same fantasy about gender identity. Have you and the people around you always assumed you are a given gender because of what someone said when you were born? "What are your pronouns" is a valid question to ask people in your life, especially yourself. I will, however, warn you that there are some trans people who feel they pass and would feel horrified if you asked them this.

LGBT stories are rare, in part because we often have to hide, but also because we are a subset of the population. Many of us don't want to talk because it brings up trauma. Just because most people aren't CEOs doesn't mean you can't be a CEO.

"Maybe" is a valid answer. Maybe you are not straight, maybe you are not cis. If you're unsure I urge you to explore but realize I'm very privileged (due to my skin color, the area where I live, and my wealth) and my exploration was far safer than the norm.

Can you Come Out/Transition?

This is where I struggled. I thought the answer was no because of ignorance stemming from problematic media representations. I only realized I might be able to transition when I saw a video talking about how trans women can safely experiment with a low hormone dose, which is completely reversible, to see the impact over a short period of time. I've learned that's not as true for people using hormones to make them more masculine, but still can be worth exploring. Personally, I have a lot tougher time identifying trans men, possibly because I'm not one but possibly because the path can be more immediately successful.

What the video mostly focused on were all the excuses people make to avoid transitioning. Ironically, I watched it because I was curious why a non-binary friend of mine had a therapist suggest they try hormone treatment. Once I saw it and did some more research, I realized I could at least try hormones. If they didn't work, I could back out.

After this revelation, I went into full Rory Gilmore mode and made a weighted spreadsheet of all the pros and cons of the decision. Originally, the cons outweighed the pros by 66%. Through gender therapy, I realized some of the faults with the list and it eventually had the pros outweigh the cons by 78%.

The Point

When I hear somebody say, "It's too late for me to transition" or "I can't do that," it makes me cringe. If you would rather have a different gender representation (or sexuality) than please explore it! You only live once (as far as I know) make the most of it.

Sexual Discrimination

For many years, I had dreamed of working at Google. I liked that some of the executives were members of the Burning Man community. The efforts that Google did publicly to improve inclusion were appealing to me. Unlike Amazon, it was unclear to me how any of Google's products and policies were destructive. While many of my friends saw some of what is bad in Google, I had a confirmation bias that blinded me from it.

In September of 2019, a recruiter from Google reached out to me about an engineering director position. I wasn't sure I wanted to leave Affectiva, but it sounded like a great opportunity. At the time, I believed that Google was diverse and ethical, so I agreed to chat with the recruiter.

On October 3rd, 2019, I had a technical interview with Jacob, a manager in the Accelerate Storage SRE team at the NYC office. As with most names in this book, Jacob is a fictitious name for this individual. There is a belief in many tech companies that advancement should be through meritocracy. There is a paradoxical expectation in some companies that the leadership should still have up-to-date technical skills. Some companies take this expectation to absurd lengths where an engineering leader should be more skilled than their employees. I personally want to hire people who are smarter than me. Let me handle the conflicts, scheduling, and external communication, while my team does the technical work. There is a belief that nobody will follow a leader who is rusty. This causes some leaders to do everything they can to appear like they are still competent even if technology has gone through great changes since they last did technical work. While some leaders, like myself, are able to make time to do technical tasks, the amount of time we have for technical work is, by definition, smaller than that of our employees. While I only spent about 25% of my time at Affectiva doing technical work, Google expected that to be a director (i.e., a manager of managers) I should be technically competent.

Jacob said, "Let's say that we have a population of hamsters. We know the genetic parents for each hamster. Write a function that given two input hamsters will tell us if they are genetically related or not."

While I did find the question challenging, I also found it offensive. The question was to determine if two hamsters are related. This requires discussion of sex and gender. It also requires the candidate to act as if gender is binary, which it is not. Asking a transgender or non-binary person this is deeply offensive and certainly hurt my ability to solve the question. I'm not sure if Jacob was doing this to discriminate against me. It's possible that he did not know I am transgender and why the question is offensive. I hope they have the question removed, and have interviewers take sensitivity training. The question also has religious issues as the 'Adam and Eve' scenario must be considered where there are only two hamsters in the original generation.

Yet another issue with the question is the choice of hamsters, which are very similar to their rodent cousins, gerbils. Of all the animals to pick, either could evoke the homophobic stereotype of gay men who engage in gerbilling. Thus, it could appear that the species was picked to imply I am a gay man and do this (neither of which are true).

Another issue is that Jacob really wanted me to use tree traversal, which is far less efficient than my original plan of storing and comparing the first generation of ancestors. Based on some of the videos about Google interviews, I was given the impression that code performance is critical. I compared the two approaches and found that tree traversal is 6.5 times slower than storing and comparing the first generation. A copy of both versions of the code is in the git history of https://bit.ly/3pufnlR. I don't know why he did this but, based on the videos about the importance of performance and his feedback that the code wasn't good, it does paint a picture of discrimination.

Jacob has made it clear that I am unwelcome at Google. While I know there are some transgender people at Google, as well as some allies, Google is clearly not the inclusive company it claims to be.

I wrote an email to the recruiter after he told me I was rejected because Jacob felt my code "wasn't good." I explained the discriminatory nature of the interview in the hopes the team would see what was wrong with this interview and why it needs to change. I hope that future transgender and non-binary candidates are treated with compassion.

If the recruiter had replied with an apology, and said they would look into making improvements, I would have dropped the issue. After several business days went past with no response, I filed a report to Alphabet, the parent company of Google, via their EthicsPoint website. The website was made to receive reports like mine about instances of discrimination.

A month went by and I hadn't heard from Google, despite their website saying they respond within a week. I'd mentioned what had happened to another trans woman in tech to see if she agreed with me. She made two excellent points: first, that there are better tree traversal questions. For example, you could just have a binary tree. You could also traverse lineage of things that are not biological like languages. Her second point was that regardless of being trans, the interview was sexist.

At this point, I lost all faith I ever had in the company. I suddenly realized that they have a monopoly on several products, and I had become dependent on Google. From that point on, I've slowly migrated off as many products as possible including Chrome, Hangouts, Search, and Google Play.

I decided to file an inquiry with the EEOC, but I was worried that Google might decide to delete my accounts causing me to lose what data I still have in the cloud. I also worried that I might be blacklisted by my industry. Many companies refuse to hire whistleblowers. The EEOC converted the inquiry into a formal charge. Unfortunately, because the interview was over the phone and my resume did not include any gender indication at the time, the EEOC decided they might have trouble proving that Jacob knew I was a trans woman. It didn't matter that it had come up in the original interview with the recruiter and was clear on my LinkedIn profile.

It was a tough decision to publish this. There are only a handful of people that know about my experience with Google prior to my writing this chapter.

ISO: The Perfect Life Partner

At a party I went to in October 2019, I caught up with one of my closest friends. We compared dating notes and my friend asked what I'm looking for. After verbally articulating my wishes, I thought it would also be useful to write them down.

First, I'm not in any rush to get into another long-term relationship. Some of my searching has been half-hearted. I hadn't even opened a dating app that month. I enjoyed several recent dates.

I wanted to heal a bit. I was working to strengthen some friendships. I also wanted to stabilize so I had a solid understanding of who I am as opposed to how I define myself within a relationship.

My top priority, at the time, was to replace my car. The whole episode of my car dying helped me to realize how tricky it can be living without another adult (not counting my son). If I were still living in my old neighborhood, I could probably borrow a car as needed. Living in Fitchburg has reduced my driving, but I still need a car to get to appointments and drop off Pon at Nicole's. Long term, it would be nice to have community (which doesn't require a romantic relationship). This could mean living in a city with competent public transportation, which I do.

Another reason I hadn't wanted to rush is because I was still changing. There was an initial clearing of my mustache hair that week. My cheeks were pretty much fully clear of hair. I still had a lot of hair on my neck.

I saw my provider on Saturday via a Lyft ride and went to a final estrogen prescription that will get my levels to match that of cisgender women.

I still hadn't had any surgery, which is funny because someone I had reconnected with that month said, "Congratulations on your surgery." I considered correcting him but didn't think I could have done it without fits of laughter. When I was at the Hip Hop cipher in Cambridge one week (with a coworker), one of the guys we met asked me, "Do you have a penis?"

I replied, "Do *not* ask me that." He dropped it so he could try flirting with my co-worker again.

I feel like this is a job description:

Requirements:

- Will absolutely not discuss sex with me until at least a day after our first date. The guys who tell me about their genitals on OkCupid in under 5 messages have no chance with me.
- Must have respect for who I am. I don't expect a person to be perfect, we all have things to learn. I will not stand for multiple incidents of disrespect.
- Must accept that my children are an important part of my life. Must honor my time with them and, if you enter their lives, treat them with the respect I will expect them to treat you with.
- No expectation to become financially dependent on me.
- An understanding that, in 12 years, I plan to retire in order to do disaster recovery charity work in far-off places under poor conditions. No need to go with me, just respect and support my plans.
- Acceptance that I will not have another biological child.

Nice to Haves:

- Interest in cuddling (this isn't code for sex). Cuddling on the couch, cuddling in bed, etc.
- Desire to go dancing.
- Adventure partner (i.e., travel, burns, escape rooms, Laser Tag, etc.).
- Someone to chat with.
- A sense of humor.
- An ability to accept and understand I have some baggage.
- You can critique my creativity, but please do it constructively and support my works.

Does that really describe what I want? Probably more in the nice to haves. I miss cuddling. I miss having an adult (who isn't my child) to talk to. I miss having young kids around. If I was in a relationship with someone who has no kids, I would be interested in adopting an older child, especially one who could go to college when neither Pon nor Simon are in college.

When I had created this list, I had gone a year and a half without sex. My libido bottomed out when I started hormones. It's still about 1/10th of what it used to be. For the most part, I like this because previously I bordered on sex addiction. My libido seemed all consuming. Now, it's just an occasional itch that I can ignore if I want to. I've also become far more sapio-sexual, whereas, before hormones, I was very visual.

Sheryl Sandberg's Myth of the Catty Woman

In 2016, Sheryl Sandberg had an opinion piece published in the New York Times about "the myth of the catty woman." At the end of October 2018, a friend shared the article and asked what my thoughts were on it.

I agree with the findings, except I would note that Americans, in general, have unhealthy beliefs about competition that don't exist in other parts of the world. In *The New Psychology of Leadership: Identity, Influence, and Power* the authors spoke of how Americans want to see a single winner in a competition. There is no room for ties, which is another reason soccer fails as a sport here. It's unclear if their research accounted for differences in gender, but based on the statistics they showed, I think the research was true regardless of gender.

I do feel men are far more competitive, but Americans are taught to accept and expect that, whereas we expect females to be "nice." The competitiveness men have is one of the things that drove me crazy when I was portraying as male. It felt like every guy I met would have a conversation like this:

Guy, "So, what do you like to do?"

I'd reply, "Well, I enjoy rock climbing."

"Oh. Me too. In fact, I climbed Everest once. What's the highest you've climbed?"

I'd roll my eyes, "I don't know."

It's like when two guys meet, they have to size each other up and create a hierarchy. Who cares? What does "better" even mean?

In Stephen Covey's *7 Habits of Highly Effective People*, a part that's always stuck with me is what he says about synergy. With synergy $1 + 1 > 2$ whereas without synergy $1 + 1 < 2$. I could go on for a while about synergy, but the point for this discussion is that American men often fail at synergy because they make everything a competition. While I believe there is room for healthy competition, like a well-run hackathon where the objective is for everyone to learn, many competitions are unhealthy. Our culture even ridicules men who don't mind coming in anywhere but first.

I've worked with guys who put themselves above anybody else. Guys who have asked me to help them only to take any credit for themselves and never even thank me. I do my best to distance myself from these types of people.

I have a colleague. She and I sometimes get annoyed at each other and, at least once, she's thrown me under the proverbial bus. It's possible I've done the same. As annoyed as we can get at each other, we still really care about each other. We once had, what I felt was, intense digital communication for over a week and, finally, I asked her, in person, if she was upset with me. She clarified things and I got over it. We both are very supportive of each other, and I absolutely value her presence in my life.

The podcast I listen to the most is "Verity!" that identifies as "Six Smart Women Discussing Doctor Who." I mostly listen from oldest to newest. In the first year of their podcast, they got a lot of feedback that the women seemed very aggressive to each other and should seek counseling. It's clear to me that while they disagree and tease each other, they also have really strong friendships. In 2012, when they began the show, it was very rare to find a place to hear women debating each other, which I think led to this inaccurate perception. Clearly, another part of the perception was the expectation that women are kind.

One of my major concerns with transitioning was that feminists perceived as male are more effective than feminists perceived as female. I didn't want to reduce my ability to be an impactful feminist. It's always seen more favorably to support people in an outgroup versus an ingroup. The article touches on this, and the psychology book I mentioned earlier shows the tests they did that prove the theory. To have people from different groups support each other, the authors discovered they needed to expand their definition of the in-group. If you think of yourself as a baseball fan, you can accept baseball fans in New York as being part of your in-group. If you think of yourself as a Red Sox fan and that New Yorker as a Yankees fan, you'll have a bias against them.

The article also mentioned how minorities distance themselves from their own kind. At sci-fi cons, I've seen this to be true of certain minorities. It's as if when the dominant group sees the minority group gathering, they get scared there will be an uprising and literally the dominant privileged group feels excluded.

For me, I love spending time with my trans-feminine friends, but only one-on-one. Trans gatherings make me uncomfortable due to a mix of imposter syndrome, survivors' guilt, and fear that I'll always be as easily clocked (identified as trans) as they appear to me.

In summary, we have a long way to go to accept women who are assertive. I think this is worse in the US than some other countries. This hurts our ability to synergize across in-groups, which literally impacts our GDP and standard of living. I won't say, "Be gender-blind," because, just like color-blindness (aka, All Lives Matter) is a cover for racism, gender-blindness would cover sexism. We have to realize, respect, and accept each other's differences while striving to treat all of humanity as having value.

Earrings

When I first publicly transitioned, I got lots of advice. Some advice was helpful, some less so. I was pleasantly surprised by how supportive people were. One recurring suggestion was that I get my ears pierced.

There were two reasons I didn't take this advice. First, ouch! Second, it felt like I'd just be doing it because people told me to. I wasn't onboard with the idea, so I refused.

Months later, after struggling to find jewelry that works for me, I decided to get my ears pierced. Part of the decision was because people stopped mentioning it, so it was clearly my idea at this point. Part of it was that necklaces don't work for me and there are very few bracelets that interest me.

The kids and I went to Claire's. Actually, Simon avoided Claire's and waited in other parts of the mall. Yes, I know, probably not the best place to get pierced. It worked out this time, and I don't want more piercings.

I realized with the help of friends, and research, that despite what Claire's says, I really should wait 6 weeks to change from the starter earrings. That first week was awful. My ears were aching all the time. There were several times that I almost gave up. It got easier after that first week. Only about four people noticed that I got pierced, ironically one of them was a friend I hadn't seen for a couple of months.

After four weeks, I switched the earrings but continued to wear them 24/7. I made the switch when Pon was around, and they were very helpful.

It was hard to find details on piercing care after the first change. From what little I could find, I decided I needed them to stay in for two weeks, and then, I could finally sleep without them. So, after eight weeks, I had the best sleep since the piercings. When I woke up, I had trouble getting an earring into the left ear, I still have this problem over a year later. I switched to the right ear and it worked fine. I could get an earring into the left ear, but the back seemed to have resealed in the night.

I had Pon look at it. They were like, "What did you do? It's bleeding!" I told them the details and we realized that because I mostly sleep on my right side, the right side was fine, because it had been treated so roughly. The left side was treated so gingerly it wasn't ready to go overnight. Pon said I should give up on the left ear.

Well, after all that work, I was not going to give up. One earring was not going to do it. I did research. I cleaned the left piercing with alcohol. I soaked it in water. I stretched the ear. I put triple antibiotic cream on the piercing and earring. I was prepared to force it through a membrane in the back of the ear, but it went in fine. I guessed, at least with that ear, I needed to keep it in at least a couple more weeks. What an underestimation that was!

Trans Scripts Part 1

I saw *Trans Scripts Part 1: The Women* in November 2018. It felt a bit like group therapy for me. At points, I wanted to chime in but remembered it's a play. They picked stories of seven trans women to play. The cast was a mix of trans and cis actors and actresses. They put it on as part of Transgender Awareness week. The Transgender Day of Remembrance was the following Sunday.

The stories were all at least a decade old. That was problematic in that some of the terminology has evolved since that period of time.

What I related to most was the parts of their stories where they struggled being in the closet, and some almost committed suicide. I also love that they touched on the Stonewall riot.

The audience was almost entirely cisgender. There was a Q&A after. The moderator seemed to assume we, the audience, were all cisgender and asked what we felt we could do to help trans people. I brought up one of my biggest concerns after transitioning was that my kids lost their father. I mentioned how it helped that when I asked Simon if he missed having a father he said, "I love you just the way you are."

Pon's answer was far more nuanced, they said, "I don't understand the question. I never had a dad."

The cis actors were asked how they felt playing trans women. While she didn't use the phrase, one described her experience with imposter syndrome. Another said she was alarmed when she researched a trans actress who said cis people should never play trans folk. In this case, the cis people are not being paid, they are learning about us, and the play wouldn't have happened as there are not seven trans women available to act for free multiple nights in Fitchburg.

A thing I learned that night was that some trans women couldn't get through the gatekeepers of that era in order to get hormones. They used birth control pills, which had similar effects. There were also places selling hormones under the counter and some pharmacies that didn't require prescriptions. The gatekeeping conversation was timely as it coincided with the gatekeeping that I encountered to get my passport.

If you go to see this play, bear in mind that most of us don't use or like the word "transexual" (I personally hate it and have never identified as transexual, though it is now technically true), the stories are from before the word "transgender" existed.

Transgender Day of Remembrance

As of this writing, November 20th, 2019 was the most recent annual Transgender Day of Remembrance (TDoR). The following is the list from Wikipedia of names of known transgender people murdered *in the US* since the 2018 TDoR:

Brianna "BB" Hill (aka. Breonna Be'Be), 30, a trans woman of color
Itali Marlowe, 29, a trans woman of color
Elisha Chanel Stanley, 46, a trans woman of color
Bee Love Slater, 23, a trans woman of color
Bailey Reeves, 17, a trans woman of color
Jordan Cofer, 22, a trans man
Pebbles LaDime Doe, 24, a trans woman of color
Kiki Fantroy, 21, a trans woman of color
Tracy Single (née Williams), 22, a trans woman of color
Denali Berries Stuckey, 29, a trans woman of color
Brooklyn Lindsey, 32, a trans woman of color
Zoe Spears, 23, a trans woman of color
Chanel Scurlock, 23, a trans woman of color
Johana Medina Leon, 25, a trans woman from El Salvador seeking asylum in the United States, died in Immigration and Customs Enforcement (ICE) custody
Chynal Lindsey, 26, a trans woman of color
Paris Cameron, 20, a trans woman of color
Michelle "Tamika" Washington, 40, a trans woman of color and longtime transgender rights advocate
Muhlaysia Booker, 23, a trans woman of color
Claire Legato, 21, a trans woman of color
Ashanti Carmon, 27, a trans woman of color
Jazzaline Ware, age unknown, a trans woman of color
Ellie Marie Washtock, 38, a non-binary person
Dana Martin, 31, a trans woman of color
Kelly Stough, 36, a trans woman of color
Tydie Dansbury, 37, a trans woman of color

As you can see, there are trends in this list. It's also well known that the list is incomplete. Many deaths are misreported.

That year, more than any other, I became aware of the fact that while I am minutely at risk, the chances of me being murdered are unlikely, as I'm white. I also know my high income protects me.

I have endured discrimination, harassment, and transphobia, but not one incident has been physically violent. Caitlyn Jenner has done a lot for the trans community. It was much harder and more dangerous to transition prior to when Caitlyn came out. At the same time, her $100 million net worth protects her from things that even my $1/4 million net worth cannot protect me from. Having her as a role model for transgender women is excellent. Thinking that the lives of most transgender people is in any way similar to hers is dangerous.

For that TDoR, I heard a speech by one of my newer friends. In their speech, they pointed out the remarkably high percentage of the deaths that were trans women of color. They went on to state that gender nonconformity (i.e., all of LGBTQIA+) is a threat to the patriarchy. If we are able to determine our own gender and sexuality, it undermines male domination.

Another thing they pointed out was that not only are we at risk, but our friends and family are at risk. Early in my transition, the kids were still calling me "Dad." I thought it actually might be safer for them to do that, so I wasn't outed, but when I was presenting as female, it confused people. People heard my kids use "she" and "her" to refer to me, but they also heard "Dad." Not only was it confusing but I realized, in the wrong neighborhood, it could be dangerous.

One day when Pon was visiting me at work, a co-worker referred to me as "Pon's Dad" when talking to Pon. Pon is used to dealing with the confusion and, sometimes, when I'm not around, it's easier, and safer, for them to call me their father, which I support. When my coworker told me what happened, because I was in another part of the office at the time, she told me she used "Dad" since that's what Caitlyn Jenner does. Well, I'm not Caitlyn Jenner.

I have mixed feelings about Caitlyn Jenner. I was glad prior to transition to hear that people at Affectiva respected her. They would sometimes bring her up in conversation. While I've run cross country, I was never interested in any of the track and field sports that occur in the spring. While I like to watch some of the Winter Olympics, I have no interest in the Summer Olympics. Not only was I unfamiliar with who

Caitlyn was, I sometimes got her confused with Chelsea Manning. Chelsea Manning is the trans woman who was in the US Army and became a major contributor to WikiLeaks. If I were to pick one of the two to have dinner with, I'd easily pick Chelsea Manning. I admire what she did for my country.

When my coworkers brought up Caitlyn, I would often say something that made it obvious I often got the two confused. The thing I value the most about Caitlyn is that she made us mainstream. She paved the road for trans folk to transition more safely. Caitlyn's image caused many liberal states to create protections for us. For these things, our community is grateful.

Unlike Caitlyn, my kids call me "Umi," which is Arabic for "Mom." We picked that name as a family to remain respectful to their birth mothers. I do not want to replace their biological mothers. I honor and respect their role in our children's lives and do the best to make it clear I'm not intending to threaten their role as mothers.

While it is good that we take this day to remember those who we lost, it would be far better if we stopped the violence. Of the countries in the world, the US is ranked as being tied for 47th when it comes to safest nations for LGBTQIA+ people. We can do better. We should do better. We must do better.

Sex As A Woman

I went a year and a half without sex. I believe this is the longest I've gone without sex since my first time when I was a teen. While I dated fairly continuously since my separation, none of the people I dated really clicked for me as more than kissing friends. Nicole advises girls that sex for the first time is a big deal emotionally.

While I've kissed some of the people I'd recently dated, it never felt right to go further. Some of the things that have caused reluctance on my part include gender dysphoria, relationship baggage, body issues, a lowered libido since I began hormones, and uncertainty about how sex would even work for me now.

A new love interest came into my life in October 2019. We met on a social media dating app at almost the moment I first tried that app. I kept forgetting about the app. I'd go a few weeks before I'd remember to check for messages from her. I'd catch up with what she had written and respond. I also apologized for not being competent with that app. Eventually, we realized it would be easier to text. We began texting several times a day.

She and a guy on Bumble were pursuing me when school bullying became catastrophic for one of my kids. I told both of my love interests that I needed space to handle what was happening with my kid. They both understood. I kept texting her though. Eventually, she invited me to see her speak at the Transgender Day of Remembrance. We hung out so late that Sunday night that I got home around 2 AM. The following workday was mentally challenging.

I hosted Thanksgiving for the first time in 2019. I didn't think she would be able to attend, but I invited her anyway. It turned out she was able to go. I drove her up after work on the Wednesday before turkey day. We got home late, and I was exhausted. After doing some turkey prep, we headed to bed. We kissed and cuddled, but I thought we would just go to sleep. We tried sleeping and failed. We had some hot foreplay and then succeeded in sleeping.

I needed to drive her back Thanksgiving night so she could work Black Friday. We took a 35-minute nap together because I was so sleep deprived that I knew it would be unsafe to drive her home without a nap. She lives 1.5 hours south of me. After the nap, we started kissing.

I was really nervous about sex. I hadn't had sex since I started gender-affirming hormones. My body works… differently. Between relationship baggage, inexperience with my changed body, internalized transphobia, and imposter syndrome, I was an emotional basket case.

After we had the safe sex talk—because that's what I do with *every* partner for the first time—I discussed what I knew of my limits and boundaries. Pre-hormones, I had very few limits and boundaries. Now, I feel like I'm covered in landmines!

She was very respectful and sensitive to my boundaries. I've slowly shed some limits as I got more comfortable with the changes I've been through. That night, we found boundaries I hadn't even anticipated, and she respected those as well.

Despite all the fears and limits it was *amazing*. We spent two hours having foreplay and sex. Exploring each other's bodies and learning how we work together. I don't remember ever enjoying sex this much before. Sex with male hormones always felt like a pressured race to orgasm that was followed by exhaustion. Role-playing male in my past during sex had also been emotionally taxing. That night, there were multiple points when my back was arching. I can't remember moments like that with male hormones.

I'm glad I waited to find the right person. We really clicked, and I had hoped we would be together for a long time. Ultimately the relationship lasted four months. It's hard to say how much each component (my partner, how long I had waited, new relationship energy, and female hormones) factored into my enjoyment, but I am looking forward to finding out over the years that follow.

First Year of Hormones

At the one-year mark, I took note of what I'd noticed since I started gender-affirming hormones. It's hard to say how long I've done electrolysis as I paused it so I could afford Pon's tuition.

I could see physical differences. The first year is always the most noticeable. Changes will continue over the next four years, but they will be slow and subtle (except when it relates to surgery and electrolysis).

The physical differences I noticed in no particular order include:

- Reversal of male pattern baldness—it probably won't get much better than where it is now. It's still thin in the front on the top, but much better than before.
- Softer skin—this is one of the things I noticed in the first couple of months.
- Less oily—I used to have oily skin and hair. I literally stained shirts and sheets. I had to shower daily to keep it in check. Simon is paranoid about leaning against walls because his mother told him he'd stain walls like she said I used to stain walls.
- Breast development—they are small, but bigger than a small percentage of cis women. If they grow more, great, if not, that's fine too.
- Smell—I smell different. It might partly be a shift in products, but there is a definite change.
- Body hair—I think some of my hair is whiter than it used to be. It's hard to tell for sure because I shave and trim. This might just be confirmation bias.
- Hips widened—they won't ever match a cis woman. I only noticed this because I woke up with sore hips a few nights. I can't see the difference: I just know what the pain indicates.
- Less beer belly—this might partly be due to going vegetarian. I have unintentionally lost some weight, and I'm keeping a close eye on it to make sure I don't lose too much. This and breast development are part of "fat redistribution." In theory, my butt might have

gotten bigger, I have no way to tell. People do say I look more curvy though!

Other Changes:

- Crying—I think on average I cry once daily. Usually for sad things but, sometimes, for beautiful things, occasionally from onions, LOL. I really like this change. I always felt like my emotions were muted with testosterone. I hated it. I wanted to feel. The only way I knew to consistently get myself to cry before was to watch my copy of *Iron Jawed Angels*. I still love that movie, but don't need to watch it for that reason anymore (which is good since I don't have a DVD player).
- Laughing—I laugh more often. Sometimes, it's when I'm alone, and I think of something funny. Sometimes, it's because something is funny and I'm enjoying it.
- Temper—I have far less of a temper. Pon said this is the biggest non-physical change they noticed. Pon said I used to yell a lot and they would tune me out. Pon feels I'm a better parent than before.
- Happiness—I am happier. I was living a lie, and now, I can be myself. I was at a party one night where I only knew the hostess. One of the women was explaining to a cis guy how he was failing to think like a woman. She called out the names of the cis women in the room and my name and said we're examples of how women think. It was an odd conversation, induced by some amount of alcohol, but it felt so good to be counted as a woman by a cis woman who had only met me a few hours earlier.
- Libido/Sex/etc.—I talked about this in other chapters so no point rehashing.

Montreal

When I initially filed for a corrected passport, I was denied. After several calls to the State Department, I discovered that they had denied it because the letter from my nurse practitioner wasn't acceptable to them. They required a signature from an MD. When I got my passport, I had such a case of wanderlust that I immediately planned a trip. I decided to go to Montreal. I invited both my kids, but because it was winter, they both thought I was crazy and declined.

I had several reasons why I went to Canada. I wanted to prove I still could travel on my own. Things went well until the Montreal Science Center. I kept wishing I had other people to explore it with.

I was expecting Canada to be a magic place where trans people are accepted. I know we have better rights there. Everywhere I went, from my hotel to the restaurants where I made choices bad for my stomach, to the Museum of Science, I kept being called "Sir" (when we spoke English—I only spoke French while shopping and at some restaurants). I was wondering, since they learn French first, maybe they don't see "Sir" as gendered. After paying a 20% tip, I asked my very polite waiter at the most expensive French restaurant I went to if he calls everyone "Sir." Very embarrassed, he said in a thick French accent, "It is a very delicate thing. I try to determine which gender people are with a close look and use 'Madame' or 'Sir' accordingly." I dropped the question and booked it out of there. Apparently, he hadn't noticed my pin saying "She/Her," the dress I was wearing, or the trans symbol painted on the back of my jacket. I never felt in danger, harassed, or mistreated. I don't think I ever even felt afraid. I did feel disappointed.

That night I got extremely sick. While I usually avoid dairy, I wanted to take in the local cuisine, so I used lactase in order to eat dairy. Unfortunately, I ate far more dairy than lactase could handle. I can't remember ever being that sick before, and it lasted almost 24 hours. Pon was having a difficult time with Nicole's family and asked for me to pick them up. I wanted so badly to get to Pon, and I could barely walk across my hotel suite. After I called to extend the stay and texted Nicole that I had to wait, I fell apart. I cried for a long time. I felt so alone. I felt like I had completely lost control. I wished I had brought somebody: Nicole, Pon, or my partner of the time. I felt so stupid. It became clear that I need a bigger support system than I was used to, and I'd made less progress extending it than I would like.

When I finally got to Pon, they said they would never let me travel to Canada alone again. They went on to say that had they been there, they would have prevented me from getting sick. Pon is partially correct. While they wouldn't have been able to stop me from having dairy, I never would have taken them to that fancy French restaurant. We would have gone to the ramen restaurant and had a blast.

Mount Watatic

Simon asked if we had any plans for the first weekend of 2020 because he wanted to work Saturday. I checked and said, “No.” That Friday, I panicked. What was I going to do that weekend? I had just finished the fourth draft of *Flipping*, so I needed a break from that. Money was tight because of Pon’s final tuition payment, Simon’s spring semester meal plan (half of which because of COVID-19 was wasted), Simon’s tuition, and the prepaid AirBnB for Arisia. If money wasn’t tight, I’d probably go roller skating… or something indoors.

I knew I needed some exercise. I also needed to clear my head. A distraction would be really nice. I was processing some relationship baggage and feeling guilty about how it unfairly impacted my partner. She stayed with me and the kids during New Year’s but was back working on that weekend.

So, climb a mountain! I was up late the prior night. Simon got out at midnight from work, and I had picked him up, so he didn’t waste an hour’s wage on Lyft. While waiting for his shift to end, I was rewatching *Euphoria*. I accidentally skipped an episode, so I was literally in between two episodes when I drove to get him. I also had some research relating to LGBT topics that I did. Ultimately, I went to bed at 3:45 AM. I slept until noon. In other words, I had limited daylight left. I decided on Mount Watatic because it was close, and (not counting a nap at the top) I was able to climb and descend it in the fall within 1.5 hours. I also knew the trail, so even with the snow cover, fog, and rain, I wasn’t worried about getting lost. It was short enough that even with the bad conditions, I could probably finish it in the 3.5 hours of daylight left.

I dressed really well, in water-proof layers. I packed enough food, water, and extra clothes so if I slipped and got injured, I could survive a night. I didn’t have good shoes to choose between. It was either shoes that handled wet conditions well but had no ankle support or shoes that had ankle support but would risk my feet getting cold. I chose warm feet over ankle support. In retrospect, it was the right decision but shoes that do both would have been better.

I didn’t have the time to shave before the hike. My pants layers were all from pre-transition, as were the shoes. I figured it would be safer to be misgendered than raped… so yeah. The last time I had hiked this mountain, the parking lot was full and lots of cars were parked along the road. I wore a dress that day because it made me feel good. That dress had been a little more restrictive of my breathing than I had expected, causing me to stop four times on the way up to catch my breath. In January, despite worse conditions, I only stopped twice on the way up.

As is probably already clear, I was worried not just about my safety due to the conditions but also due to how people might act if they encountered me. When I parked, there was a guy in white fatigues who had a backpack that must have weighed at least 60 pounds, which he tossed onto his back as if it was as light as a jacket. He was… muscled. He was attractive, but way too young to interest me. It was clear that he was either going beyond the summit for an overnight or he was training. He left before me and never passed me on the way back, so I suspect he camped over the NH border.

The only woman I encountered was several steps behind a man (I suspect they were a couple, but they could have been friends, or even siblings). There are a lot of stories that make it sound dangerous for a woman to hike alone, especially with so few other people (i.e., witnesses). However, once I was back in my home, I did some research, and the statistics show women are as safe (or unsafe) hiking as we are in other public spaces. So please don't read this and get paranoid. Remember, I'm still new to being an obvious member of a more at-risk demographic (trans female).

Most of the guys I encountered were solo. There was a guy with ski poles who passed me twice, he was climbing the mountain for at least the second time.

What freaked me out was a slippery and steep area that I was traversing when two guys began to catch up with me. They were poorly outfitted, which made me suspect they weren't experienced hikers. To add to that, they kept slipping in places I had navigated without issue. They were conversing about how awful their work was. The conversation had a lot of expletives and sounded very aggressive. While these guys weren't good at keeping themselves from slipping, they were catching up with me. I took a short break, which reduced the gap between us. I pushed myself more than I probably should have, but ultimately, they passed me, completely ignoring me. Since they passed me from behind, they probably assumed I was male.

The real danger was the slippery conditions. There were several inches of wet snow. I fell twice on the way up but caught myself both times. My first fall was 7 minutes in, and I considered turning back. At the 15-minute mark, as the trail was getting rougher, I considered it again. I wasn't sure I could get to the top. Going down, especially in those conditions, is harder. I only had so much daylight. I pressed on.

I had taken the fast, but difficult, route up, as I wanted to make good time. My plan had been to take the gentler, but longer, route back. As I got used to the conditions, I did a better job of foot placement and routing. It was a surprising amount of mental work. When I got to a landmark, I knew I'd get excited—and distracted—which would cause me to slip and remind me that I needed to either pause or look at the ground.

I took off my coat early on the hike up. When I got beyond the tree line, the visibility was awful. There are two peaks, and the trail lets out on the slightly lower peak. There are several ways to get to the higher peak, but that peak wasn't visible. I had to guess at which path to take: there are no trail markers past the tree line. I finally found my way, in part because I saw the guys I had encountered earlier returning from the summit.

I reached the summit in 1 hour and 6 minutes. The summit was really cold. It was drizzling, and the wind was strong. I put my coat back on, took a couple of quick pictures, and headed back down. This is where my plan to take the gentler route fell apart. I had never taken that other route before in either direction. The last trail sign at a split was confusing. It pointed left for the parking lot and right for several other things that I didn't want. Google maps was equally unhelpful. There were three trails and the map only showed two. I went left, and soon discovered I was on the path I had taken up—not a path I wanted to use for a return trip. I considered going back, but the risk of getting lost with only a couple of hours of daylight left, I decided to take the tough trail.

On the way down, I fell on my back once and I fell on my side (hip) once. I also had several controlled falls (i.e., purposely sliding to or from a tree). Ultimately, I'm really glad I did the hike and didn't turn around. It had been a few years since I last climbed a mountain in the winter. It took me two hours and five minutes. I wish I hadn't been so rushed. It would have been a better view if it weren't for the fog and rain.

When I got back home, Simon said, "I thought when you said you were climbing a mountain today, it was a metaphor."

I asked, "A metaphor for what?"

He shrugged, "I don't know."

The Bathroom of My Nightmares

I dreamt one night that I was starting a new year at school. It felt like high school. It wasn't a school I've been to in real life but looked a lot like a high school. In the dream, I went to the male restroom. I got into a stall and then had a panic attack because I realized I was in the wrong bathroom. I got out as quickly as possible but accidentally forgot my bag in the stall, the one farthest from the entrance. I contemplated asking someone to go in and get it for me. That seemed even more embarrassing, so I went in and got it as quickly as possible, hoping nobody noticed me. On my way out of the bathroom, I caught a glimpse of myself in the mirror. I saw myself with a very short beard and mustache. The mustache, however, was partly shaved off. It looked ridiculous. I suddenly realized I had gotten interrupted shaving that morning and hadn't had time for make-up.

I went to my first class and did everything I could to hide the facial hair. I sat in the back of the room (which isn't like me at all). When the class ended, I feigned illness and went home.

This home wasn't like an apartment I've ever been in either. I was completely panicked about who might have seen me and why I went into the wrong bathroom. I shaved, but I couldn't get rid of the fear that the hair would grow back, and someone would see it. I was scared to return to school. This is when I woke up.

Possible Interpretations

I haven't had a dream about being in school for at least a decade. I'm not sure where that came from.

I remember when I was younger, I had recurring dreams that I went to work naked. When I was closer to school age, it was the same dream but in school. The feelings of discomfort in those dreams were very similar to this dream. It was a feeling of being in a place where I wasn't prepared, and it was inappropriate.

When I first publicly transitioned, I had a fear of going into the wrong bathroom out of habit. A couple of times, I found myself walking to the wrong bathroom. I think it helped that Affectiva moved to a new building and I was barely aware of the men's bathroom location and never knew the key code.

On December 26th, I was driving north with Pon through Connecticut after dropping off my girlfriend of the time. I was still recovering from French food when I needed to stop for a bathroom break. I got to one of the Connecticut rest areas. It was open, but the women's room was locked off as a guy cleaned it. I knew how far the next rest area was—too far. I also wanted to get Pon home. We were exhausted. I used the men's bathroom. There was a family inside. Nobody said anything to me. This might have inspired the dream. I've thought about that incident frequently and generally think gendered bathrooms are stupid.

The night after the dream, I had an appointment scheduled with my electrologist. She had to reschedule to later in the month because a friend died, and she wanted to attend the service. Last year, I had to pause electrolysis for a while. I was close to having my upper lip initially cleared. I couldn't, at that time, actually grow as much hair as was in the dream. In the dream, there was a sense of futility about my facial hair. Perhaps, I was just frustrated with the slow progress.

Security

January 16th, I was at the Affectiva office at Exchange Place in Boston in order to take part in an in-person interview of a candidate. I had to pick Pon up from school in Framingham by 5 PM. I usually worked from home on days I needed to pick Pon up because the drive was shorter. I try to get them around 4 to leave a large margin for error.

My last meeting was set to end exactly at 2:45. My plan was to leave immediately. I was parked at Alewife station, so I needed to walk to the Downtown Crossing station and take the Red Line Subway to Alewife. Once at Alewife, I would drive to Framingham. Maps advised me that I would arrive at 4:30. An accident on route 2, 128 south, or I-90 West could easily make me late. Not only would that be bad because I'd be fined for arriving late, but it also might cause Pon to be anxious. This was the first time for me picking them up after being in the office. Pon knew I would be a little later than normal. I was nervous though.

When my last meeting ended, I remembered I had scheduled to install a firewall in the Waltham office the following week. Just as I was leaving, I grabbed the firewall, so I'd be able to bring it from home to Waltham.

On my way to the elevator, I realized the firewall was heavy. I started worrying it would slow me down getting to Downtown Crossing.

When I got through the security gates on the first floor, I heard a voice call from behind me, "Ma'am?" I turned. It was the security agent at the gate. He said, "Sorry, Sir." In other words, he was apologizing for correctly gendering me and then he misgendered me when he saw my face. I grimaced. I didn't have time to educate him. I was wearing a skirt, leggings, and my purple jacket with the She/Her button in the front. I also had makeup on and thought that at least my looks would cause me to pass (as female).

He further apologized for not catching me before I passed through the gate. He asked for the form required to take boxes out of the building. This is one of the ridiculous security measures that the building feels they need to take. I had completely forgotten about it and had never taken a box out before. The firewall, btw, is small enough that I could fit it in a suitcase and not be stopped.

I explained that I forgot and was in a rush. He said I needed to go to the front desk and fill out the form. I told him I didn't have time and suggested I just leave it with him and have him return it. He said "No," and that I needed to go to the front desk.

I went to the front desk and was again misgendered. They asked about the form. I explained that I had forgotten about it and was in a rush. They asked for my building ID and company. I handed over my ID and said, "I'm with Affectiva." They asked if I had a monitor, I told them it was a firewall. They asked what a firewall was, I explained it's a commercial grade router. They made a phone call. They talked a bit and put it on speaker phone. It was the office manager, Rebecca, on the other end. Security misgendered me again, and she thankfully corrected them. I was correctly gendered from that point on. I explained to Rebecca what was happening, and she told security to let me through. I then walked to Downtown Crossing, 15 minutes behind schedule.

I was very flustered through this whole process. I was upset about being misgendered, about forgetting about the box policy, about wasting Rebecca's time, and about potentially being late for Pon.

Fortunately, traffic was lighter than Maps had anticipated, and I arrived at 4:20.

I had a dream that night. Bear with me. I know it will sound unrelated, but I'll explain how this fits with the misgendering at the end.

In the dream, I was hanging out with a guy while we waited for some friends. We were in a room with a pool table. He pulled a gun on me and raped me. I didn't resist because he had a gun, although I probably could have disarmed him in real life.

After raping me, he made me clean up. He threatened to kill me if I ever said anything. When the people we were waiting for arrived, I went with them to help prepare a group meal. As soon as I was alone with the group, and he wasn't there, I told them what had happened. I asked the other women if they had experienced something similar. Three of them nervously acknowledged that they had. The whole group was shocked, but as we waited for him to return, I had a sinking feeling they wouldn't help me stand up to him.

This is when I woke up. It was about 4 AM and my heart was racing. I did some meditative breathing to relax. At first, I was like, *Where had that dream come from?* I've had dreams of rape before (although I think the rapists in prior dreams were never male). I've been fortunate that I've never been raped in real life.

What I realized is the dream was really about losing control. Usually, accidental misgendering doesn't bother me. I had an epiphany that the issue with security was that I was being misgendered by authority figures. I was being misgendered in a situation where I had less power than those who were misgendering me.

When Nicole and I went to court, the judge had misgendered me. I wanted to correct him but didn't because I wanted the hearing over and I was afraid that he'd hold me in contempt of court (and I certainly have a lot of contempt for court).

I've long had a fear of being pulled over by the police and being misgendered. I have a similar fear of the TSA and border security.

The building security had also misgendered me after Affectiva's Emotion AI Summit, when my hair and makeup had been done professionally.

I think the dream was really just about losing control. Like how I lost control of how I'm gendered. I can brush off accidental misgendering by people who know me, people on the phone, the reception staff at my allergist, and retail workers, but when a person has power over me, nope, it sucks.

Going forward, every time I left and entered the building, I saw security and remembered that they think I'm a man. Yuck, that sucks!

Too Much of a Good Thing

On a Thursday in late February 2020, I had put on two Estradiol 0.1 mg patches. Thursday night at 9 PM, after seeing an email from my provider from Planned Parenthood that she was able to reverse a BCBS decision to deny coverage for more than one patch at a time. I woke up on Friday morning and discovered that my back surrounding my right scapula was extremely sore. I assumed I had just slept in an odd position. I did some stretching and exercise in the morning and throughout the day to try and reduce the pain. I also did some self-massage with my hands for the areas I could reach. After a few hours of pain, I took an ibuprofen. The pain was okay until dinner time. I took a second ibuprofen around 7 PM. When Simon and I dropped off Pon at Nicole's house, I mentioned the back pain. After I explained the pain to Nicole, she did a little massage work on it, which made it feel better. Simon and I got home around 10:15.

I wanted to stay up, but I was planning to go on a hike on Saturday morning, so I got ready for bed. I began the exercises my chiropractor recommends. As I got into position for the first exercise (a wall slide), the room began to spin. The room spun counterclockwise about 45 degrees and then immediately reset to normal, then spun counterclockwise again to 45, *ad nauseam*, literally. After the spinning had repeated about seven times, I lowered myself to the floor and closed my eyes. When I first re-opened my eyes, the room was still spinning, but to a lesser degree and more slowly. Eventually, after experimenting with my eyes open and closed, the room went back to normal. I have had brief minor bouts of dizziness in the past, sometimes due to wax buildup in my ears. After I got back on my feet, I had minor nausea. I went to the kitchen and grabbed a pot so I would be prepared if I vomited in bed. After putting the pot next to my pillow, I began changing for bed.

When I had visited, Nicole had asked me if I had changed anything in my routine to cause the pain, and, at first, I came up blank. After the dizziness, I realized I had a bubble bath on Thursday, but the internet confirmed that was probably not the source. Then, I remembered I had changed doses. When I had first been prescribed two patches, at the start of February, I followed that dosing for a week, and then, I ran out and switched back to one patch because of the insurance issues. I dug up the prescription information and both the printed and online documents for

Estradiol said dizziness and nausea are potential side effects. One source said it was a sign of overdose. All sources seemed to agree I should reach out to a clinician (though the urgency varied by source). I went to the bathroom and had another minor bout of nausea and dizziness. I removed one of the patches. With the intention of going to bed (and emailing Planned Parenthood the next morning), I walked from the bathroom to my bedroom when the dizziness happened again. I leaned against the wall and lowered myself to the floor. I called out to my son to call 911. He explained that his mother (I loved that he called me that) had collapsed.

While waiting for the EMTs to arrive, I had Simon get my phone and I called Nicole to let her know what was happening and to check in with Simon if she didn't hear from me. Pon was with her at the time.

After the call, I felt an urge to have a bowel movement and possibly vomit. I went to the bathroom and had a bowel movement.

I was worried about a case of trans discrimination that I had read about where a group of EMTs refused to see a trans patient. The EMTs arrived as I was finishing in the bathroom. When I came out, I could tell they were confused about my gender, so I just said, "I'm trans." They got my pronouns wrong a couple of times but always self-corrected and apologized.

The EMTs said I was very pale. My son confirmed that I was paler than usual. They took my blood pressure and pulse oxygen level as they had me describe what had happened. As we talked, I was starting to feel better. They said my vitals were normal and ran a blood sugar test. They asked if I wanted to go to the hospital and said color seemed to be returning to my face. They said the hospital was packed due to a stomach virus, I could go and wait to be seen and potentially catch the stomach bug or I could stay. I decided to stay home. They told me to drink a 50/50 mix of Gatorade and water that Simon made as we continued to talk. They also asked me to wait 30 minutes before going to bed and call if anything went wrong.

I wrote to Planned Parenthood while I drank the mix and waited the 30 minutes. I finally got to bed at 12:45. My provider called on Saturday. She thought my electrolytes were off because of the Spironolactone, and she asked me to lower my dose from 400 mg a day to 300 mg. My sodium had been at 134, just one unit below the reference range, during my last visit. As she had instructed, I had immediately changed the dose and drank Gatorade for a week, the same week I had first doubled my Estradiol. The Gatorade was causing headaches and I happily ended its consumption that first week as she had recommended. Her theory is that my sodium is still too low. Fortunately, the bilateral orchiectomy scheduled a few weeks later would mean I never need Spironolactone again (unless some day I develop high blood pressure).

She asked me to have my PCP run some lab work, especially an electrolyte panel and an EKG, tests which they aren't equipped to run. She cautioned that because I am now asymptomatic, the tests may be inconclusive. She said that if the dizziness returns, I should get to the ER (via me not driving). In other words, I should have taken the ambulance ride. A few weeks later, the hospital called to inform me they were canceling all elective surgeries because of COVID-19, including mine.

EmpEmp.org

My experience with Google made me realize that as good as a company might appear to be, protections are needed for candidates and employees. Employers do not want us talking about our salaries because it gives us the power to ask for more money. In the US, however, it is illegal to prevent employees from sharing their salary information, as per the National Labor Relations Act that was made into law in 1935. As Erica Baker has shown us in her time at Google, sharing this information improves lives.

While the law protects us, it can still be a risk when your data is not anonymous. Websites, including salary.com, H1B Visa Salary Database, and Glassdoor, allow us to see and post salaries anonymously, but critical information is missing. Hispanic women currently make 46% less than white men and 31% less than white women. These websites don't include demographic information that would enable people to determine if they are making less money than their white cisgender hetero male counterparts.

What do we do? Share our information! Push for existing tools to add demographic data and look into options to create our own tools.

Wealth Inequality

Executive compensation can be found in SEC 10-K filings but is often misleading. For example, in 2018, Mark Zuckerburg's salary was $1. Comparing a Facebook employee salary to Zuckerburg's would falsely make an employee believe they are well-compensated. A better tool is Sec Form 4's insider trading, which shows the billions of dollars he makes from stock sales.

Being able to see executive compensation, how much an executive's shares are worth, and how much the executive is making in stock sales, paints a clearer picture, especially when you factor in that salary is taxed at a higher rate than the capital gains tax applied to the sale of stock.

Continuing with Zuckerburg as an example, in a year he earned $1.8 billion in stock sales. The least paid software engineer in Facebook's Boston office with an H1B Visa makes $105k a year. For every $1 that employee made, Zuckerburg made $17,142 in stock sales. Is that fair?

Employer Ratings

Websites like Glassdoor allow people to rate employers. While you can rate on a large number of generic things, issues specific to women and minorities can't be specified in discrete data fields that are summarized. For example, imagine if these websites could let you specify your gender in your profile and when you rate a company ask:

> Have you ever felt discriminated against (Yes/No)?
> If yes, was management part of the discrimination (Yes/No)?
> Have you ever felt harassed (Yes/No)?
> If yes, was it by management (Yes/No)?
> If you are listed as female in your profile, do you feel like you are required to do your normal job and office housework while men do not (Yes/No)?
> Do you feel like an outsider (Yes/No)?

With this kind of information, the page for the company could then say the percentages of people that feel that way.

Solution

Create a non-profit to build open-source software that makes it clear to candidates and employees if pay inequality exists at a given company. Allow employees to share information about how inclusive their employer is. Provide employees a safe space to discuss issues without having management eavesdrop. Empower employees to petition *en masse* and to vote to strike. Clarify to employees how much more C-Suite employees are getting than they are. Illustrate to employees how much profit and how much of the company's income they get compared to what stockholders get.

How You Can Help

I feel like asking, at this time, amid so much instability and insecurity due to COVID-19, but I'm unlikely to get much response. At the same time, it feels like we are at a historical tipping point. The 1% are still using capitalism and politicians to protect their positions while the middle class and poor struggle.

Early in 2020, I completed a rough draft of a business plan for this non-profit. In the summer, I helped launch EmpEmp.org. I tried recruiting people one at a time, but it was challenging to get in touch with people during the pandemic.

My biggest need is somebody with marketing experience. I can also use the help of programmers, artists, UX designers, QA, and proofreaders. I'm sure there are many other skills that could be put to work. If you have time you could dedicate to this endeavor, please contact me. If you don't think you can personally help but want to support the effort, please spread the word.

Remembering Pronouns

A co-worker at Affectiva once asked me if I knew a trick to remember people's genders. He said sometimes he realizes when he thinks of me, he does so with a male association. A lot of trans folks switch jobs when they transition. It didn't bother me when people at Affectiva misgendered me, except for conference calls with external participants who were meeting me for the first time. It was frustrating hearing a co-worker use male pronouns for me with people who were meeting me for the first time.

I actually misgender myself sometimes. For example, when I need to motivate myself, sometimes I'll think, *Come on, man*, *Dude, let's do this*, or *Come on, guy*. My parents misgender me frequently, but I know there is no malice in it. They love me.

At MEDITECH, there was a trans woman who worked for me for several years. She and I transitioned around the same time. I internally misgender her from time to time (sorry if you're reading this).

Funny enough, I sometimes misgender cis people. In fact, there was one time I misgendered my co-parent's boyfriend. I have no idea what caused me to do it, but Nicole laughed and asked me not to misgender him.

An option I frequently use is whenever I have new people enter my life, I try to not gender them unless they gender themselves. Once they have gendered themselves, then I try to think of them as X until they tell me otherwise.

The thing is, similar to sexuality, gender is a social construct. I don't care about people's sexuality unless I'm interested in dating them. This is why I never talked about my sexuality prior to transition. Unless a person wanted to date me, it didn't matter. Gender gives us a way to classify people that often causes us to assign stereotypes. Oh, that's a guy, he makes the money. Oh, that's a gal, she raises the family. Obviously, these stereotypes are problematic.

I'm not sure that helped. I'm certainly not offended if you misgender me in your head. In person, as long as you aren't intentionally misgendering me, it doesn't bother me.

Mother's Day 2020

How does Mother's Day feel for a mother who is transgender? For me, in 2020, I felt invisible. I've made sure Pon talked to their other mother. I dropped several hints with my stepsons in the hope they will do something for her today. I told my son to reach out to his mom.

I was doing a Google search for "Trans Mom" in late 2019 when I came across an article called, "What This Trans Mom Wishes You Knew." On the surface, it sounded like a similar story to me, but the author's relationship with her former partner is very different from mine. I consider Nicole a close friend and our divorce was amicable.

There's also a quote in the article from her therapist saying, "Would your kids be better off with an alive trans mom or a dead dad?" The author had struggled with suicidal thoughts for years before transition. Again, this didn't happen to me, the only time I considered suicide was when I knew I would transition and was afraid I'd lose everything.

What I was really looking for was how other transgender parents feel about being called "trans mom" or "trans dad." Somebody I only recently met said it to Pon and I was unsure how I felt about it. It's pretty obvious I'm trans, and I consider it part of my public identity, but will that always be true? Someday, in the far future, will I pass so well I can let go of it? Will I need to hide that I'm trans for safety reasons?

On the flip side, I didn't want to be called Pon's or Simon's mom either because I felt that it was unfair for their biological mothers. I really value their contributions as mothers to my kids and don't want them to feel I'm encroaching on their role. So, for example, when I would call Pon's school I identified myself as Pon's parent (I don't ever say I'm their mom. I think it but I don't say it). I have a huge network of trans friends, but I think only one of them is a trans mother.

Nicole used the phrase "trans mom" to describe me for a while but, eventually, she settled on, "Pon's other mother, Forest." I really appreciated this and similarly usually call her Pon's mother, Pon's other mother, or my co-parent.

I spent the day with my stepmother, who was in the hospital due to lung cancer. Several people wished me a Happy Mother's Day and I very much appreciated it. My mother sent me a card with a check so I could buy flowers. She added me to her checking account a long time ago in case something happens to her. I was delighted to see she updated the checks to preface my name with "Ms."

As women, we often try to take less space. Between imposter syndrome and wanting to be respectful of mothers assigned female at birth, even here in a women's space, I try to minimize the amount of space I take.

Someone recently suggested introducing a Parents' Day. I love this idea as a way to be inclusive of intersex and non-binary people.

Last year, I wanted to hold Mother's Day sacred for my two co-parents. I don't want to celebrate Father's Day for myself: it doesn't make sense. I frequently describe myself as a single mother of two. In fact, I use that description so often my phone auto-suggested the entirety of it as I typed. Two years ago, I still celebrated Father's Day, but it was complicated. I wonder how I will feel next year and a decade from now.

Body Image Issues

I have someone close to me who struggles with body image issues. I realize that I'm a role model to some of the people in my life (including this one). I've been very transparent about my own body image issues, and I think it contributes to the body image issues of others. My fears are mostly wrapped up in imposter syndrome and a fear of being misgendered. I can't fix this overnight but, from this point forward, I'm going to display the following ideals and, hopefully, someday, I will truly believe them:

- I am tall and beautiful.
- I have facial hair and, while as a lipstick feminist, I will continue to remove it, I am beautiful.
- I have a deep voice and I am a woman.
- My legs and armpits are hairy and, while at times I may shave them, I am beautiful.
- The hair above my forehead is thin and I am beautiful.
- I do not need to look like women who are in the media to be beautiful.

I'm making this my mantra and whenever that voice in my head says, "I'm too tall," I will reply, "I am tall and beautiful." When that voice says, "The hair on my head is too thin," I will reply, "I am beautiful."

Figure 16: Forest

Larry

A cis friend who I dated for a few months, posted a music video featuring a group of trans people on his social media profile. In the comments section, he asked me what I thought of the song. I watched the video while feeling like I was expending energy so he could feel like a good ally. I found the video a bit confusing, but I liked the song. I made a comment to him that it was beautiful (please don't search for this. I don't think he understands why this was a problem). At the same time, I felt like saying that this wasn't how to be an ally, but I didn't want to shame him on his social media, and I didn't want to engage via a direct message.

The next morning, I woke up to a text from Larry about Aimee Stephens (the trans woman who was fired due to transgender discrimination that led to the recent supreme court ruling). His message felt patronizing.

I did a Duck Duck Go search for "Things an Ally Shouldn't Do" and came upon an article by Jamie Utt that referenced Mia McKenzie's book *Black Girl Dangerous*. They discussed how "ally" is not a noun, it's a status. They repeated a concept I've heard before, that allies often respond to criticism from those they say they're allied with by saying, "But I'm an ally." This is also related to "white women's tears," which as a white woman I'm very sensitive to avoid, and I have worried that my "I Cry" YouTube video could be problematic.

Next, I dropped into a Discord server for Boston area trans folk, planning to pose the question to my trans community, asking how they feel about cis people sharing trans stories with them. As I caught up with messages on the server, I realized the answer was self-evident, and I didn't need to stir up trauma my peers have felt due to cis people.

I replied to Larry's message saying, "I feel like you're being patronizing towards me. I feel like you consider me a charity case."

He replied, "I'm an ally. That was a mass message. Jesus, get a grip!"

I hadn't known it was a mass message, so I felt slightly bad. I blocked him, as I'm done with his drama. I know he has other trans friends that would have also gotten that message. In general, I hate mass messages. If I want to read about the things you care about, I want it to be opt-in. I want to go to your profile and read your stuff. It's very rare that I find mass messages appropriate.

Larry used to date a trans man prior to dating me. He was closeted when they were dating. When he came out to Larry, Larry felt a need to support him. Larry told me he was happy his partner found his authentic self and so whenever he was with his partner, Larry would use he/him pronouns, even in public, thus outing his partner multiple times. Larry's partner told him how awful and unsafe it was to be outed by Larry. I met Larry after this relationship had self-destructed. He told me this story in confidence and that he had come to realize he was making his former partner's gender about himself and that was wrong. When Larry told me this, we were dating, and I was already out publicly. I wasn't afraid he might make a mistake with me, but I did worry about him making a mistake with my friends and family. I think Larry has probably become better about this, but he has a lot more work to do in order to be a good ally.

If you want to be a good ally, you need to be a good listener. It's okay to talk about the issues of those with whom you are an ally, but ideally, you are quoting them or giving them a microphone. Allyship is about acknowledging our privilege and using that privilege to amplify the voices of those without our privilege.

Be careful about talking to those you are allied with about the issues they face. As was the case with Larry that morning, it can come across as condescending. It also has the potential of retraumatizing people. I feel bad for all the trans people Larry is friends with who got that message. I shouldn't have to tell him it was problematic, and he shouldn't have defended himself by saying he's an ally. If somebody asked me how I feel about the President's latest attacks on trans people, or about the murder of a trans woman, I'm going to have to relive how I feel about these events. Ask me how I'm feeling, but please don't repeat bad news for trans people that I may (or may not) be aware of.

I am sure I personally make lots of mistakes when trying to be an ally. I apologize to those who I've hurt with those mistakes. It's on me to try to learn how not to make those mistakes.

Larry eventually e-mailed an apology. He hoped that we might try and be friends again. He mentioned that he and his family have been enjoying a video game to which Simon had introduced them. I told him I'm open to trying to get coffee and potentially revisit friendship after the pandemic ends.

Loved and Lost

Love is like fire,
Before the fire, there is all-consuming darkness.
You cannot appreciate the light without that precursory darkness.
Then. a match is struck, and the contrast of light is startling.
A match is fragile.
If not cared for, it will go out, but there are other matches.
Some matches refuse to light.
Some matches burst forth as if they had been held back waiting for just that moment.

A match has a limited lifespan.
It must quickly be applied to tinder.
Like a match, sometimes tinder refuses to burn.
Recent history may have dampened it to the point the tinder cannot light.
Once a match is applied to the right tinder there is more to do.

Kindling is the next phase.
Much like the prior phase, only the right kindling will work.
Slow growth makes it hard to remember back when that spark entered your life.

Is firewood the final phase?
It's a huge step.
Matches, tinder, kindling, all seemed to need so much work.
Some logs of firewood can burn for hours.
Care is still needed.
Take the fire for granted and it will go out or consume your world.

The fire of love can burn so bright that I can be lost in we.
You can be lost in we.
Everything else can become impossible to see.
This is where the metaphor falls apart for me.

Fire is conditional.
A fire's conditions are heat, fuel, and oxygen.
My love has no conditions.

That tinder a month ago.
That match a year ago.
That bonfire a decade ago.

All those loves still burn in my heart.
I cannot pretend otherwise.
Sometimes memories of past fires cause me to neglect the new.

I look at my matchbook and cannot decide what to do.
I miss many of those fires deeply.
Does my heart have room for more?
How many more matches?
How much more tinder, kindling, and firewood?
Who will get burned?
Can it ever be sustained?

Hey Little Lady

My son and I were going to climb Mount Watatic together in July. Instead, he told me he couldn't go because he hadn't slept well, which is code for watching *anime* all night. The first few minutes on the trail, I felt jumpy. Due to the pandemic, I wasn't used to the sounds of nature (frogs, chipmunks, mosquitoes, birds, etc.) I saw a gorgeous snake that got away from me as quickly as possible. At most, 10% of the other hikers were wearing masks.

At one point, a guy going down the mountain passed me while I was going up. In a "hey, little lady" tone he said, "Be careful up there. It's slippery, and I cut my knee."

He showed me his knee that was skinned and lightly bleeding. He was wearing a red shirt, jean shorts, no mask, and had no bag with him. I thanked him and briefly considered looking for a band-aid in my backpack for him. I was unsure if I had one and decided I'd rather not spend more time with this guy. I've climbed up the mountain in snow, ice, and rain. I was happy to move on.

Later, a family passed me. It was the one time that I sat down on my way up. There was a father and son leading the way. They didn't even look at me. About 50 feet behind them was a girl about 13 years old. She stopped, gave me this huge smile, waved, and said, "Hello." I waved back.

When I reached the summit, it was too hot and sunny for me. All the groups of people were without masks, but they did have distance between each other. Several of the people were snacking.

Sexual Racism

A post about sexual racism created a debate in a forum I'm in. Here's my take. I agree that dating people based on their color is racist and remember in my teens believing I only found white people attractive. I don't know when I got over that belief but after my first divorce, I dated a Black woman and later a Latina. I suspect I still have some racist beliefs and tendencies and hope to continue to find them and deprogram them.

Literally, the day before I saw the online debate, I was watching an episode of Queen Sugar, where one of the main characters (Ralph Angel) had dinner with a Vietnamese family a member of which he was dating (Trinh). The food looked amazing, as does the Cajun food that's often featured in episodes. I caught myself fantasizing about dating somebody who was Vietnamese because of their food.

The person who shared this to the group I'm on included an analogy to trans folk. Since I transitioned, I've discovered how few cis people want to date trans people. A few years ago, a study was run in Canada that discovered only 18% of cisgender (Canadians) would date transgender people. On OkCupid, there is a question asking, "Will you date somebody who is transgender?" Most people have answered this question as a way to filter people.

When I first started using OkCupid after I transitioned, I simply updated my photos and set my gender to "Trans Woman." I would match with somebody and quickly realize they thought I was a cis woman. I added to the very top, "I'm outgoing, adventurous, and a trans woman. If you cannot respect trans women, I'm not for you." I think that improved things, but I still got people (mostly men) who hadn't read my profile. Thus, I made it a point to bring it up early in a conversation after matching with someone. While this is what I do, I totally understand why other trans folks don't include that they are trans in their profile.

This dating tax I have to pay as a trans person is a lot of work. Often people who have answered that they won't date trans people will "like me." It happened so often I finally decided to like one back and ask them about the inconsistency. They said they hadn't realized I was trans and apologized. I've even had a person match me just so they could say transphobic things to me (to paraphrase they said, "Stop dressing like a woman and be a man for your kids.")

Many of the marriages that survive a transition become sexless. One trans woman I know is still loved by her Catholic wife, but her kids and wife still treat her as a man even though she transitioned years ago.

Another problem I face as a trans woman is "chasers": a cis person who might consider themselves "trans-amorous." Larry probably falls into this category. Sometimes, these are bi-curious men that feel it's safe to test the waters of same sex relationships with trans women. But we aren't men, so this is fundamentally wrong! There are many that fetishize us (trans porn is mostly bought by cis men). There are also those who treat us well in public, but then, make slurs about us in private. I know a trans woman in a long-term relationship with a cis guy who considers himself straight but, occasionally, calls her gay for liking him.

I don't want somebody to date me just because I'm trans. While my being trans is a notable characteristic so is that I'm a parent, an author, a programmer, an engineering manager, a burner, and so on. I'm a package deal, and I come with baggage.

Back to the thought I had about Queen Sugar, I shouldn't date somebody just because I like the food for which their culture is known. I certainly wouldn't want somebody to date me because they thought I'd make English or French food. That would be a disaster since I can't eat French food and I can't stand English food.

Personally, I'm avoiding dating at the moment. Part of me thinks I'm undateable. With the pandemic, my surgery, remote school for Pon, and settling into a new job, it just feels like dating isn't in the cards right now.

How do you feel? If you're white, do you only want to date white people? If you're cis, do you only want to date cis people?

The Future

The thing with a memoir is that as long as the author is alive there may be more to the story! I certainly hope there will be more to my story! I have no idea how long I'll live, but I hope it will be long enough to be a grandmother (if my kids decide to have children).

As Hunter Schafer has pointed out in an interview about *Euphoria*, with the exception of *Euphoria*, most trans characters are only shown during their transitions and in struggles with their transness. Some obvious examples are the very problematic portrayal of Max from *The L Word*, Brandon in *Boys Don't Cry*, Nomi in *Sense8*, and Sam in my novel *Flipping*. The exceptions I can think of are all very recent; Jules from *Euphoria* (as played by Hunter), multiple characters in *The L Word: Generation Q*, and multiple characters in the Netflix version of *Tales of the City*.

Just as fiction has this problem, non-fiction has this issue too. The most famous trans person is famous for what she did prior to transition. I think the stories of people like Hunter Schafer, Brian Michael Smith, and Wendy Carlos are more important as they became famous after transition and their fame is not about their gender identity.

Other Publications from Castle Carrington Publishing Group

Other Life Stories Available from TransGender Publishing

Publishing Transgender Life Stories and Non-fiction

https://transgenderpublishing.ca/

Triple Trans: One Woman's Journey to Freedom (2021)
Rose Barkhimer

For me, *Triple Trans* means:
Transgender, the knowledge that one has been born with the incorrect physical body,
Transverse myelitis, a neurological affliction that was a catalyst in my decision to change gender and,
Transition, the process of change.

It is my hope that *Triple Trans* finds its way to at least one individual who is wrestling with the conundrum that is gender dysphoria and that my story helps them to understand their own journey. I also hope that my story will explain to the general public the experiences of one transgender individual and demonstrate that, despite our differences, we are all human beings struggling with life's journey.
(https://transgenderpublishing.ca/triple-trans-one-womans-journey-to-freedom/).

Journey of a Lifetime (2021)
Karen M. Vaughn

For all of her life, Karen has struggled with gender dysphoria and her true identity. Frightened, confused, and tired of living a lie, she embarks on a journey—one that will change her life, her marriage, and the world she thought she knew. This is her story of coming to terms with who she really is, her struggles to find her way, and the life-altering changes that came along with her journey.
(https://transgenderpublishing.ca/journey-of-a-lifetime/)

Before My Warranty Runs Out: Human, Transgender and Environmental Rights Advocate (2021)

Joanna (Sister Mary Elizabeth) Clark and Margot Wilson

Joanna (Sister Mary Elizabeth) Clark is an elder trans woman and advocate. During the 1980s and 1990s she was an LGBTQ+ activist and speaker. She was the first person to serve as a man in the US navy and as a woman in the US army. Later, as Sister Mary Elizabeth, she was the driving force behind the AIDS Education and Global Information System (AEGIS) database. These days, her focus is primarily on environmental activism. *Before My Warranty Runs Out* is a personal narrative that recounts Joanna's life experiences.
(https://transgenderpublishing.ca/before-my-warranty-runs-out/)

TRANScestors: Navigating LGBTQ+ Aging, Illness and End of Life Decisions (2020)

Volume I: Generations of Hope

Edited by Jude Patton and Margot Wilson

This volume (and the ones that follow) have been in the works for some time. What finally emerges after many months of assiduous advertising, recruiting, editing, and organizing is a volume of intimate, nuanced, and heartfelt stories that reflect the wide diversity in the ways in which trans, non-binary, and Two-Spirit people have come to recognize, signify, embody, and celebrate their difference as their authentic selves. Moreover, with an increasing emphasis on the experiences of trans youth, elders constitute a routinely overlooked, disregarded, and/or silenced segment of the community. In response, this volume documents the myriad ways in which trans elders are coming to terms with the real-life challenges of aging, illness, and end of life decision-making.

TRANScestors is planned as a series of edited volumes that address the issues of LGBTQ+ aging, illness, and end of life decision-making and will be published by TransGender Publishing. Additional volumes include: Volume II: Generations of Change, Volume III: Generations of Pride, and Volume III: Generations of Challenge.
(https://transgenderpublishing.ca/life-trips/)

TRANScestors: Navigating LGBTQ+ Aging, Illness and End of Life Decisions (2020)
Volume II: Generations of Change
Edited by Jude Patton and Margot Wilson

Generations of Change is the second volume in the TRANScestors series. These stories are, by turn, heartfelt, revealing, inspiring, sad, joyful, humorous, irreverent, and incredibly varied. And yet, strong, common themes of courage, persistence, honesty, resilience, and authenticity emerge clearly through the detailed recounting of the individual lives lived. Each author details those specific circumstances that have led them to the places and situations in which they find themselves today. On the whole, these are places of comfort, confidence, revelation, and affirmation. The wide range of attitudes, expressions, and worldviews held by the LGBTQ+ elders presented here challenge us all to carefully consider and adjust our perspectives on our own aging processes and, ultimately, on finding our own places in the world.
(https://transgenderpublishing.ca/live-trips-vol-ii-generations-of-change/)

We are God's Children Too (2020)
Rona Matlow

At the heart of Jewish experience is narrative. Around the dinner table, we tell stories of our families, recalling the quality of a grandmother's cooking, the kindness (or stinginess) of a particular uncle, the ways in which traditions have developed and shifted in our families. In synagogues and Jewish schools, we read the Torah, which is filled with stories of our religious patriarchs and matriarchs. And then there are the stories of Diaspora–the history of Jewish communities existing in exile for over two millennia. There are family stories and history books dedicated to our many wanderings. All of these stories help Jewish people connect to their heritage and lineage. What of the queer Jew? Even as more and more Jewish communities emphasize inclusivity and find a place for queer congregants, Jewish stories do not. The Bible offers no queer lessons, leaving queer Jews split in two; a Jewish heritage and a queer present. Enter Rabbah Rona Matlow, with hir queer *midrashim*. *Midrashim* are stories which approach Biblical texts from new perspectives, often exploring areas of confusion or possible contradiction within the Bible. Unlike Torah, they are not presented as factual, but as possibilities. Fictions which might yet be possible alternate histories. *Midrashim* bridge gaps. Rona's queer *midrashim* bridge the gap between the contemporary queer Jew and the (seemingly cisgender and straight) Bible, offering a way for us to see ourselves in our Jewish tradition.
(https://transgenderpublishing.ca/we-are-gods-children-too/)

Transgender Heart: Life Stories from the Inside Out (2020)

Bodhi Thompson Gardner

Transgender Heart is a collection of short stories that trace the heart-journey of a small farm kid, youth, and adult, from rural Saskatchewan, across the binary landscapes of life. A deeply grateful soul emerges, while exploring all the hidden nuances of the people, places, and things that held them together. Hidden comforts are revealed from the inside out, an inner harvesting of an authentic self. Their true self searching for somewhere to belong, finds love, acceptance, and authentic connection in the most intriguing and unusual spaces. Black hockey skates not only enrich their game but authenticate their heart. Spaces of unconditional love come from four-legged wild beasts, two-legged mentors, matriarchs, warriors, and elders. An RCMP officer who saw their struggle and offered a hand instead of handcuffs, gifts of nature, and family support abound: however, the biggest surprise of all is their most cherished treasure, the one thing that kept them alive for over 50 years. Transgender Heart highlights the courage and tenacity of the human spirit to rise up!
(https://transgenderpublishing.ca/transgender-heart/)

QdQh: Queen of Diamonds, Queen of Hearts, The Life and Journey of Michelle Nastasis, the First Known Transgender Professional Poker Player (2020)

Michelle Nastasis

QdQh: Queen of Diamonds, Queen of Hearts is the life story of Michelle Nastasis, the First Known Transgender Professional Poker Player.™ Michelle is courageous whether going head-to-head with the best poker players in the world, speaking out on television for LGBTQ+ rights, or marching in parades to celebrate being transgender. She is calm, cool, collected, and absolutely fearless. Possessed of fierce intelligence, Michelle is a beacon for younger transgender people. She shoots straight from the hip. She's blunt, loud, sarcastic, and occasionally irreverent. So, sit back and enjoy the ride.
(https://transgenderpublishing.ca/misunderstood/)

Dancing the Dialectic: True Tales of a Transgender Trailblazer, Second Edition (2020)

Rupert Raj

Rupert Raj is a trailblazing, Eurasian-Canadian, trans activist, and former psychotherapist, who transitioned from female to male in 1971 as a transsexual teenager. Dancing the dialectic between gender dysphoria and gender euphoria, cynical despair and realistic hope, righteous rage and loving kindness, this Gender Worker tells us all about his lifelong fight for the rights

of transgender, intersex, and two-spirit people—and his later-life role as a Rainbow Warrior working to free Mother Earth's enslaved animals.
(https://transgenderpublishing.ca/dancing-the-dialectic-true-tales-of-a-transgender-trailblazer-second-edition/)

Glimmerings: Trans Elders Tell Their Stories (2019)
Margot Wilson and Aaron Devor (editors)

Tell us your story. A story about growing up before the age of global communication, at a time when the Internet and worldwide connectivity were still visions of the future; when inflexible, dichotomous categories of male and female, men and women, existed; when heterosexuality was the only sanctioned form of romantic attraction or sexual conduct; and when any expression of interest outside of these strict prescriptions was severely censured. Tell us your story about living in a time when those whose preferences, perspectives, and behaviours contravened the prevailing paradigms and prohibitions, when you had to negotiate dark, prejudicial places where fear, shame, guilt, despair, isolation, and a little bit of hope. Contributing authors include: Stephanie Castle, Joanna Clark, Ms. Bob Davis, Dallas Denny, Jamison Green, Ariadne Kane, Corey Keith, Lili, Ty Nolan, Jude Patton, Virginia Prince, Rupert Raj, Gayle Roberts, Susanna Valenti, and Dawn Angela Wensley.
(https://transgenderpublishing.ca/glimmerings-recognition-authenticity-and-gender-variance/)

My Untrue Past: The Coming of Age of a Trans Man (2019)
Alex Bakker

Born the youngest daughter in a small-town family in the Netherlands, Alex Bakker underwent gender reaffirming transition when he was twenty-eight years old. A new beginning, in the right body, he literally put everything that reminded him of his old life into boxes, never to be opened again. More than fifteen years later, he has finally gathered the courage to face his past. In *My Untrue Past*, Alex goes in search of the painful truth. What does it mean to be betrayed by your body, to be immensely jealous of boys, and to decide that everything needs to be different?
(https://transgenderpublishing.ca/my-untrue-past-available-now/)

Girl in the Dream: Stephanie (Sydney) Castle Heal, a Transgender Life (2018)
Margot E. Wilson

Girl in the Dream is the life story of Stephanie (Sydney) Castle Heal, an advocate, activist and elder in the Canadian transgender community. The outcome of an almost four-year collaboration of storytelling, recording, analysis, and writing, *Girl in the Dream* is a first-person narrative that depicts in intimate detail Stephanie's transgender journey. An enthusiastic and accomplished *raconteuse*, Stephanie tells her story with the verve, passion, and expressiveness of a veteran storyteller.
(https://transgenderpublishing.ca/girl-in-the-dream/)

Feelings: A Transsexual's Explanation of a Baffling Condition, Second Edition (2018)
Stephanie Castle
Edited and Introduction by Margot E. Wilson

Feelings is written in a style that reveals Stephanie Castle as a woman of great confidence, conviction and humour. It reflects her attitudes toward life in general and transgender issues in particular, and definitively emulates the intricacies of her personality and character. *Feelings* provides a very personal view into one transgender woman's journey, a metamorphosis that is as vital, authentic and significant today as it was when she wrote it. A complementary volume to *Girl in the Dream*, *Feelings* provides a comprehensive and in-depth view into the nature of the transgender experience based on the intimate, challenging, and often poignant experiences and perspectives of one singularly remarkable woman.
(https://transgenderpublishing.ca/feelings/)

Pushing the Boundaries!
How to Get More Out of Life
Peter Jennings

Pushing The Boundaries! How To Get More Out Of Make Life features profiles of 32 people from around the world (many of whom are well-known and featuring many Canadians) who reveal how they triumph in life. We're talking people who have overcome uneasiness about taking risks, like daredevil Nik Wallenda; doctor-of-change, Patch Adams; intersex supermodel, Hanne Gaby Odielle; international clothing designer, Tommy

Hilfiger. Also included are Canadians like Marina Nemat, who defied certain execution in her teens at Evin prison in Tehran; McDonald's of Canada Chair, George Cohon, who persevered through 14 years to break into the Russian market; Rick Hansen, who pushed himself around the world in a wheelchair to raise awareness of people with disabilities; Katie Taylor who's broken the glass ceiling by becoming the first female Chair of a major Canadian Bank; Donald Ziraldo, who put Inniskillin Winery on the map by making Icewine into an immensely popular beverage worldwide; etc. As Jack Canfield, renowned co-author of the *Chicken Soup For The Soul*® series says in the book's Foreword, "Having the conviction to reach beyond your fears and take chances means you're ready to achieve lasting success." (https://castlecarringtonpublishing.ca/pushing-the-boundaries/)

Until I Smile at You (2020)
How one girl's heartbreak electrified Frank Sinatra's fame!
Peter Jennings with Tom Sandler

It's 1936. Take Ina Ray Hutton, the "Blonde Bombshell of Rhythm," add 22-year-old Ruth Lowe, who become Ina Ray's pianist. Ruth marries music publicist Harold Cohen, but he dies in the midst of debilitating surgery. Ruth is devastated, full of heartache, a grief-stricken widow far too early. Consumed by anguish, she pours her heartache into a lamenting anthem that becomes an internationally famous song—"I'll Never Smile Again"—destined to electrify the career of 25-year-old vocalist Francis Albert Sinatra. Ruth next composes what becomes Sinatra's theme song, "Put Your Dreams Away." And then, Act Two begins for Ruth Lowe: she withdraws from the limelight to become a caring wife, loving mother, society doyenne, and friend to many. Amazingly, this superstar has escaped the investigation and adoration that her life so richly deserves—until now. (https://castlecarringtonpublishing.ca/until-i-smile-at-you/)

Ruth's Wonderful Song: A Story for Kids (2021)
Peter Jennings

Ruth's Wonderful Song is a true story of a young woman who loved to play her bright yellow piano. She wrote a wonderful song that people are still listening to more than 80 years after she wrote it. Tom, Ruth's son, tells the story of how Ruth wrote her wonderful song and what happened next. (https://castlecarringtonpublishing.ca/ruths-wonderful-song/)

Trans Fiction Available from Stephanie Castle Publications
Publishing Transgender Fiction

https://stephaniecastle.ca/new-releases/

A Lion in Waiting (2021)
H.W. Coyle

While serving as an observer with the British Expeditionary Force in 1940, Ian Wylie survives a massacre of prisoners. In its aftermath, he resolves to find a way of sitting out the rest of the war, safe from both the Germans and his responsibilities. At first, he finds sanctuary on a small farm owned by a teacher, Andrea Morel, who harbours him until an incident leaves her no choice but to send Ian away. With no wish to return to England and the war, Ian assumes the identity of Andrea's sister, Diane Lambert, and accepts an offer to teach at a Catholic girls' school in Normandy. His efforts to turn his back on the war are frustrated by a local businessman who enlists Ian's aid in passing intelligence on German activities in Normandy to the Allies as well as by a group of schoolgirls who take it upon themselves to fight for the liberation of France. (https://stephaniecastle.ca/a-lion-in-waiting/)

The Legend of Alfhildr (2020)
HW. Coyle and Jennifer Ellis

For generations, a legend spoke of a young Viking girl who led a Saxon-Dane army against a usurper. The story was passed from storyteller to storyteller, who freely embellished the feats of Alfhildr as they sought to entertain and enthrall their audiences in the great halls of their lords and masters. Some claimed she had been raised by a wolf, others that she was a witch. The truth was vastly different.

But before she became a legend, Alfhildr was a flesh and blood person with a family, a past, and a secret. With the passing of time, all but the legend was lost from living memory until an archeologist stumbles upon something he has not been expecting. Bit by bit, Professor Bannon and his students come to realize that the legend once thought to be little more than a myth could be grounded in history. He also begins to suspect one of the students participating in the dig has a secret that links her to both the discoveries they are making and the legend.
(https://stephaniecastle.ca/legend of alfhildr/)

Flipping (2020)
It cost him nothing, but it cost her everything.
Forest J. Handford

Born on a space station, Samir Zeka was raised Muslim, observes a Halal diet, fasts during Ramadan, and prays 5 times every day. An introvert, he mostly stuck to his work, his home, his family, and his church community, until the day he decided to push beyond his comfort zone and attend a party that would forever change his life. Intending to look his best for the party, Samir searched his neural link "mesh" for random looks until he came across one that suited him. After some fine-tuning, he "flipped" to the persona of Samantha, a late 30s East Asian, cat-eared woman with shoulder-length purple hair. At the party, Samantha meets Anna, someone who will change Samantha's perceptions of herself and transform both of their lives. (https://stephaniecastle.ca/flipping/)

The Elysian Project: A Story of Betrayal and Payback (2019)
D. Axt

The Elysian Project is an expertly written, fast paced action thriller with a twist. It follows US marine scout sniper, Brent Chandler, his surviving teammate, Lyle, and his adopted father (the Gunny), as they go after those responsible for betraying Brent's sniper team during a military operation in Haditha, Iraq. Chandler's betrayal didn't just change the lives of his U.S. Marine sniper team forever. It set him on a path of unimaginable discovery. His quest for the truth and revenge quickly goes awry, drawing the attention of billionaire Stanley Tivador and the DOJ-FBI cabal he controls. The chase is on, from northern Minnesota's Superior National Forest to the Canary Islands. With help from the Gunny, his crotchety, retired Marine father, and Staiski, his friend and former sniper teammate, Chandler uncovers a terrorist plot of carnage inconceivable in magnitude and in lives lost. With seconds remaining, they risk everything to stop The Elysian Project. (https://stephaniecastle.ca/the-elysian-project/)

Partnership: A Novel about Friendship, Love, Family and Gender Transition (2019)
Stephanie Castle
Edited and preface by Margot Wilson

What happens when a lawyer, the son of a prominent Vancouver family, and a baker, the son of a devoted Catholic family who moved from Italy to Montreal following WWII, team up while going through gender reassignment? This humorous, yet serious, depiction of two families coping with gender dysphoria and the challenges of keeping family relationships intact addresses both legal and religious issues. The depiction and commentary on a range of human personalities in the hands of the author are both perceptive and entertaining. The underlying accuracy of this fictional story depends on the author's personal experience as a transgender woman and as a counselor in the transgender community in Vancouver. (https://stephaniecastle.ca/partnership/)

Far Side of the Moon: A Novel about the Life of a Trans Child (2019)
Stephanie Castle
Edited and preface by Margot Wilson

In Far Side of the Moon, Marjorie Burton and her husband, Jack, demonstrate all the attributes needed to help their child, Jenna, through a successful male to female gender transition. For children raised in an era when the condition of gender dysphoria was unknown, when anything unusual or unexplained was written off as a sexual aberration, it is small wonder that children, like the author, kept their feelings hidden out of shame and fear. Fortunately, that is not what happens with Jenna.
(https://stephaniecastle.ca/far-side-of-the-moon-a-novel-about-the-life-of-a-trans-child/)

Now Available from
Perceptions Press
Publishing innovative, avant-garde (and occasionally provocative) transgender fiction and non-fiction
https://perceptionspress.ca/

Trans Deus (2020)
Paul Van Der Spiegel
Will2Love Series Book 1

In the beginning was the Verb,
the Verb was with God, the Verb was God.
In her was life,
that life was the light for all people.
The Verb was made trans woman.
and she lived amongst us, full of grace and truth.
Her light shone in the darkness,
and the consumer-military-technocracy
comprehended it not.
We cast our votes on TV remotes,
crucified her live on Channel Five. (https://perceptionspress.ca/trans-deus/)

7 Minutes (2021)
Paul Van Der Spiegel
Will2Love Series Book 2

At the point of death,
lost to all we've known,
adrift from those we've loved,
what stories do we tell
ourselves?

7 Minutes is the story of a death—charting the progress from cardiac arrest, the brain's release of its massive reserve of endorphins, through the unravelling of personality, memory, and identity as the brain's consciousness-generating areas are hit by a tidal wave of opioid neuropeptides that are simultaneously being starved of oxygen.

Self-told narratives unfold and are re-contextualised, fears awaken, desires awaken, time is warped and regresses as the mind is trapped inside a dead husk, unable to communicate, lost to those it has loved and been loved by.

Those who have experienced so-called 'near death' experiences have described bright lights, meeting loved ones: but no-one has returned from behind that light to describe the process of dying. And so, we are left with either a gospel of redemption and condemnation, or its opposite, a gospel of cosmic resignation and the final extinction of personality. One day, perhaps not too far away, we shall know—or, then again, perhaps not.

7 Minutes is the collage of stories and half-truths that our protagonists' collapsing neural networks narrate as the brain asphyxiates—light and dark, fact and fiction, actuality and narrative—until the final arrival at the truth of an earthly existence. *7 Minutes* is a head fuck. But after you've read it, I hope you can celebrate being alive. (https://perceptionspress.ca/7-minutes/)

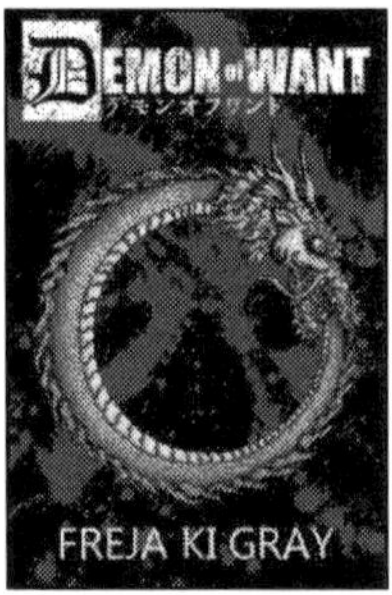

Demon of Want (2020)
Freja Ki Gray

Izumi Yamakawa, a directionless twenty-something, is a part-time employee of the Oh Joy Toy Store. When she witnesses her manager die in a horrific merchandising accident, she discovers that he was a member of a Japanese demon hunting organization and had been eyeing her for recruitment due to her family lineage. Now Izumi, along with her trans girlfriend Maria, and a boisterous sword-for-hire, Rhea, get caught up investigating the various monsters and demons running the Oh Joy Toy company. Demon of Want is an eclectic blend of tongue in cheek urban fantasy, over the top violence, and gratuitous sex.
(https://perceptionspress.ca/demon-of-want/)

Can't Her Bury Tales: A Transfeminine Coloring Book (2020)
Iona Isabella Rivera

Hail weary traveler! Come closer! I don't bite…hard. You lookit poorly, come take a sit by the fire. Rest and grab yourself some stew I got cookin. Tell me, what brings ya my way? Adventure? Hearsay? Curiosity or plain ol' boredom? Well, no matter whence you came, I surely have a story that will peak your delight.

Perhaps a tale of a terrible tragedy? Or a catty, Communist comedy? How about some lore on fallin in love? Or a heroic tale of harrowing a horrible governorship? Or be you one that pines over Power? Maybe a familiar fable of family? Oh! Pardon my rambling. Come tell me your tale, traveler. What colors will you paint with me? Tell, was your way hard, rocky and steep? Show me. Perchance our stories crossed at some point. After all, we have more in common than our differences tell. (https://perceptionspress.ca/cant-her-bury-tales/)

Coming in 2021/2022 from
TransGender Publishing
Publishing Transgender Life Stories and Non-fiction
https://transgenderpublishing.ca/

PUBLICATION EXPECTED IN 2021/22
Life Trips: Navigating LGBTQ+ Aging, Illness and End of Life Decisions
Edited by Jude Patton and Margot Wilson
Volume One: Generations of Hope
Volume Two: Generations of Change
Volume Three: Generations of Pride
Volume Four: Generations of Challenge

Studies indicate that LGBT+ people are still discriminated against in most health care settings and in long term care facilities despite advances made in the past few years in gaining more rights. Evaluating physical and mental health care needs, facilitating access to health care providers and advocating for clients' right as well as end of life decisions and planning for personal legacy options are important aspects of navigating LGBTQ+ aging. Having served as a health navigator for clients with chronic illness and offering end of life doula services to LGBTQ+ community members, Jude Patton collaborates with and advocates for his clients to successfully manage their health care needs. Jude is a proud, open and out, elder trans man, who has worked with under-served populations for most of his career, including LGBTQ+ folks, geriatric clients, developmentally disabled adults, homeless/chronically mentally ill and drug addicted clients. ***Life Trips*** is planned as a series of edited volumes that address the issues of LGBTQ+ aging, illness, and end of life decision-making and will be published by TransGender Publishing. Additional volumes include: Volume II: Generations of Change, Volume III: Generations of Pride and Volume IV: Generations of Challenge. (https://transgenderpublishing.ca/life-trips/)

PUBLICATION EXPECTED IN 2021
Taking Care of Angela
Angela Wensley and Margot Wilson

My name is Angela, and I am a transsexual woman. I have always believed myself to be female, even though I spent the first forty-two years of my life being socialized as a male. To be transsexual is no longer a new phenomenon, although many misconceptions still surround it. One thing has remained unchanged is the great pain and personal upheaval that necessarily accompanies the transition from one gender to another. Looking back now, many years after having had gender reassignment surgery, it seems impossible for me to have accomplished what I have. Changing from man to woman involved no less than a total restructuring of every single relationship in my life, with my spouse, family, friends, workplace, and my everyday interactions in society. For me, being transsexual is a beautiful gift, an honour, an evolutionary jump, as it were, to a higher state of being, one in which I am closer to God and to all humanity.

My personal journey can be likened to casting off in a boat without oars into a swiftly flowing river. Standing on the banks of that river, intrigued but not knowing where it would lead me, I had dipped my toes into the water, even waded out to where it was deeper, where I could feel the tug of the current. How I longed to be swept away by the river: however, my fears kept me from the test, and I always retreated to the security of the shore. Ultimately, spying a rowboat on the riverbank, I climbed in, pushed off into the stream, and waited as the small craft inevitably became caught up in the stronger current of mid-stream. Without oars, I could not return to where I had started and had little ability to control my course, though my direction downstream was certain. I was little prepared for the swiftness of the current, or the treacherous rapids and canyons that lay downstream out of sight. How easy it would have been to flounder in a back-eddy or to wreck on the many rocks that projected from the dark waters. Fortunately, with what little control I had over my course, I avoided destruction and travelled the long and lonely distance. Finally, one day, the current slowed, and I found myself past the mouth of the river, in the ocean that is woman. (https://transgenderpublishing.ca/taking-care-of-angela/)

PUBLICATION EXPECTED IN 2021
Both Sides of the Great Divide
Nikita Carter

Nikita Carter tells her story about awakening. At 60 years of age, a series of shattering experiences led to her being broken open to the awareness that she was a trans woman, and she had to make the changes in her life to reflect that truth. Her life has comprised extraordinary experiences and people throughout, which includes being a musician, composer, educator, Artistic Director, producer, and trans woman.
(https://transgenderpublishing.ca/both-sides-of-the-great-divide/)

PUBLICATION EXPECTED IN 2021
Gender Odyssey: Journey of an Intrepid Androgyne
Ariadne (J. Ari) Kane and Margot Wilson

Ariadne (J. Ari) Kane is a gerontology specialist with Theseus Consulting & Coaching Service. (S)he has developed several workshops focusing on issues of gender, sexuality and health in the latter decades of the lifespan. Many are designed for the LGBT Community. (S)he has been a leading authority on gender diversity in postmodern America and has given presentations at many universities and institutes in the United States and Canada. (S)he is one of the creators of the Gender Attitude Reassessment Program, a workshop on gender for sexologists and healthcare professionals. (S)he co-authored *Crossing Sexual Boundaries* with Professor Vern Bullough. *Gender Odyssey: Journey of an Intrepid Androgyne* is the distillation of 40+ hours of recorded conversation that provide a decadal representation of an intrepid traveler who has forged an idiosyncratic path through gender exploration, variance and expression.
(https://transgenderpublishing.ca/gender-odyssey-journey-of-an-intrepid-androgyne/)

PUBLICATION EXPECTED IN 2021
From Shame to Freedom: A Gender Variant Woman's Journey of Discovery
M. Gayle Roberts

Born in England during WW II, Gayle Roberts immigrated to Canada in 1951 and is an UVic alumnus with an MSc in Physics. She transitioned in 1996 as her high school's Science Department Head and science teacher. Gayle coauthored the guidebook Supporting Transgender and Transsexual Students in K-12 Schools and is author of *From Shame to Freedom: A Gender-Variant Woman's Journey of Discovery*. Gayle feels strongly that trans individuals should document their life experiences. She utilizes specific literary writing techniques (creative

nonfiction) to create factually accurate narratives. *From Shame to Freedom* is one of those narratives.
(https://transgenderpublishing.ca/from-shame-to-freedom/)

PUBLICATION EXPECTED IN 2022
Young Kid, Old Goat: Transgender Journey to Understanding the Man Within
Jude Patton and Margot Wilson

Jude Patton is an elder transman and LGBTQ activist, advocate and educator since before his own transition in 1970. He founded Renaissance Gender Identity Services in the early 1970s and began publishing *Renaissance Newsletter* in the mid-1970s. Jude started one of the first informal support groups for FTM men and incorporated these into The John Augustus Foundation. Joined by Joanna Clark, these became known as J2CP Information Services, taking over Paul Walker's work with Erickson Educational Services. In *Young Kid, Old Goat*, Jude's personal life story and ongoing work is highlighted.
(https://transgenderpublishing.ca/young-kid-old-goat/)

PUBLICATIONS EXPECTED IN 2021
We're Non-Binary:And So are You… No Really!!!
A curated anthology on Non-Binary Identity
RONA MATLOW AND MARGOT WILSON

For almost two thousand years, misconceptions regarding sex and gender identity have abounded. Be it from the limitations of the ancient languages of Scripture, the apparent binary of sex in nature and human biology, societal roles established in Scripture and maintained in Western Culture, or for many other reasons, a binary perspective persists.

During the 20th century, some of these notions have started to break down. With scholarship surrounding the Stonewall era, more barriers have been broken. As transsexual, and later transgender, identity became more widely known, the binary of sex and gender was transgressed and transcended. Still, the binary continued to persist.

And scholars are beginning to take note. What was originally perceived as two opposite forms, one male and one female, shifted to a line segment model, with male at one end, female at the other, and a distribution of androgyny in between. Then, as time progressed and as this model was found to be flawed and limited, a new model emerged, one that recognizes both sex and gender as distributed in multi-dimensional space, with male and female each occupying only single points in that space.

Today, even people in elder LGBTQ circles are beginning to accept the notion of a non-binary identity and are adopting it for themselves.

This perspective is consistent with Scripture, history, nature, culture, human nature, human biology, medicine, and every other area of research that one might consider. Of course, there are many holdouts in the straight world, and in the queer world too, who do not accept this definition of LGBTQ identity. Still, it is here. This new edited volume, to be published by TransGender Publishing, is planned as an anthology that reflects the nature of non-binary identity through original works of scholarship, fiction, poetry, prose, and personal reflections, stories, and anecdotes by and about non-binary people. (https://transgenderpublishing.ca/were-non-binary/)

PUBLICATION EXPECTED IN 2022
Unconditional Love: Stories of LGBTQ+ People and Our Emotional Bonds with Companion Animals
Edited by Jude Patton and Margot Wilson

Our experiences with marginalization often affect our feelings of self-worth. While many people in our lives are unable (or unwilling) to provide the emotional support we need before, during and post-coming out, or transition, our companion animals never fail to see us as we truly are and never fail to express their unconditional love for us. No wonder we love them and derive multiple benefits from our relationships with them. They are woven into the fabric of our lives. *Unconditional Love* is planned as an edited reader that tells the stories of how the unconditional love of (and for) our companion animals has supported, encouraged, confirmed, validated, endorsed and sanctioned our authentic selves. Our reading audience includes those in the LGBTQ+ community who have found sanctuary and validation in the love shared with our animal companions as well as those in the broader community who revel in the company of our non-human loved ones. (https://transgenderpublishing.ca/unconditional-love/)

Coming in 2021/2022 from Stephanie Castle Publications

Publishing Transgender Fiction

https://transgenderpublishing.ca/

PUBLICATION EXPECTED IN 2021
Tips
Newly Chronicles: Volume I
H.W. Coyle

College is a time of discovery, when students find out just what sort of people they are. This is especially true for Andy Newly, a freshman who embarks on a unique journey of self-discovery, one that defies convention and brings into question the most basic aspect of his being. It begins as a bet made between student waiters over who makes more tips, males or females. To determine this, they agree to a rather unorthodox experiment. Though feigning reluctance, Andy accepts the challenge of taking on the role of female waitress as part of the bet.

The original purpose is forgotten as Andy finds that his female persona is more than an act, causing him to question his gender identity. His behavior while Amanda—the name he has given his female persona—does not escape the notice of his friends. Along with Andy, they conclude that their experiment is having unintended consequences. Rather than stopping, Andy uses the opportunity to determine who he really is and where he belongs on the gender continuum. In the process he discovers that there is a vast difference between sex and gender. This already bewildering situation becomes even more complicated when a male college student becomes smitten with Amanda. (https://stephaniecastle.ca/tips/)

PUBLICATION EXPECTED IN 2021
A Different Kind of Courage
Newly Chronicles: Volume II
H. W. Coyle

How does a person go about rebuilding a life that they willingly tried to throw away? For Andrew Newly, this journey begins by realizing it will take a different kind of courage. His efforts begin by returning to where he and a group of friends bought into a crazy bet that changed his life forever. Together with those friends, he struggles to gather up the frayed threads of his life and begin the daunting task of building a new one for himself, this time as a girl named Amanda. Amanda finds that she must not only find a way of dealing with problems that are as confusing to her as they are complex, she must also come to terms with a past that seems to have no place in her new life. This difficult journey is complicated by Amanda's friendship with Tina Anderson, the daughter of an entrepreneur who has accumulated a fair number of enemies who prove to be as much of a threat to Amanda as they are to the Andersons, causing her to draw upon a past that she is trying to put behind her. (https://stephaniecastle.ca/a-different-kind-of-courage/)

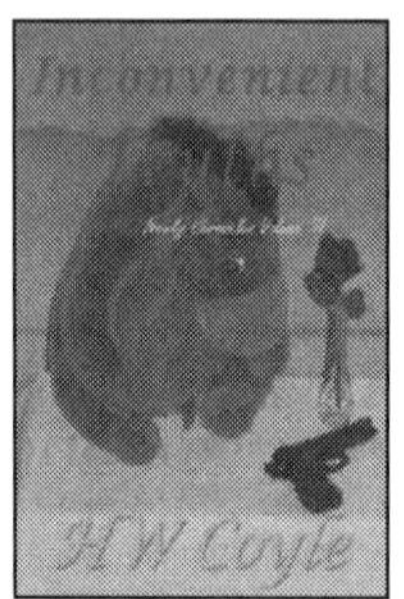

PUBLICATION EXPECTED IN 2021
Inconvenient Truths
Newly Chronicles: Volume III
H.W. Coyle

Living on the edge with nothing but a safety net woven from lies to keep you from tumbling headlong into disaster and disgrace is as dangerous as it is demanding. For Amanda Newly, it is an inconvenient fact of life, one she must deal with every day.

Amanda is a unique college student, bright and intelligent. To the casual observer, Amanda presents the very image of a young woman on the verge of making all her dreams come true. The only thing holding Amanda back from achieving this elusive goal is a past that is totally out of sync with her image as a vibrant young coed, for the girl everyone knows as Amanda started life as Andrew Justin Newly.

In many ways Amanda is still very male, an inconvenient truth she must hide behind a veil of lies as she struggles to reconcile her past with her future. One aspect of Amanda's past that threatens to destroy her chances is not of her own making. Tina Anderson, the daughter of a wealthy entrepreneur and one of Amanda's dearest friends lives under a constant threat of kidnapping, a danger that Amanda once foiled, leaving her vulnerable to retribution from those seeking to bring harm to the Andersons.

Amanda's journey toward a new beginning is one that is as difficult as it is contentious. For she must step outside the accepted norms, which define who and what we are, in order to discover not only what is right for her, but to build a new life for herself. (https://stephaniecastle.ca/inconvenient-truths/)

Coming in 2021/2022 from
Castle Carrington Publishing
You have a story. Let us help you tell it
https://transgenderpublishing.ca/

PUBLICATION EXPECTED IN 2021
Being Happy Matters
Peter Jennings

Being Happy Matters is a re-launch of a previously published book *Why Being Happy Matters.* The updated Introduction references COVID-19 and how happiness can be an antidote to the stress and anxiety people are experiencing right now. The original volume presents interviews with people in Canada, the U.S., Asia, Europe and Australia, each of whom reveal what happiness means to them and why it matters. Readers will meet international PhDs who are actively studying the science of positive psychology (i.e., happiness). This book features Peter Jennings in conversation with 37 intriguing individuals, including John Robbins, heir of the Baskin Robbins empire (who tells Peter about turning down his inheritance and then losing his life's savings in the Bernie Madoff scandal, but still exhibiting a positive outlook of happy perseverance to life's reversals); Roko Belic, California-based Oscar-nominated director of the award-winning film "Happy"; Dr. Christine Carter, sociologist and positive psychology specialist at Berkeley University ; Rolling Stones keyboardist Chuck Leavell (who shared with Peter the joy he gets from working with his buddy former President Jimmy Carter on key environmental issues); Major League Baseball legend Shawn Green; celebrated super-model & businesswoman Monika Schnarre; Time magazine humour columnist Joel Stein; 84 year old Playboy cartoonist Doug Sneyd; Leo Bormans from Belgium, author of the respected "World Book of Happiness"(who explains what lies behind his discussions with global experts); and much more. (https://castlecarringtonpublishing.ca/being-happy-matters/)

Coming in 2021/22 from
Perceptions Press
Publishing innovative, avant-garde (and occasionally provocative) transgender fiction and non-fiction
https://perceptionspress.ca/

PUBLICATION EXPECTED IN 2021
Parably Not
Will2Love Series Book 3
Paul Van Der Spiegel

Parably Not is Book 3 of the *Will2Love Series*.

William Blake wrote in the preface to *Jerusalem The Emanation of the Giant Albion* of his desire to "speak to future generations by a Sublime Allegory." One could also argue that the miracles and the parables of Christ are metaphors, and one of the errors of the religion that bears their name is trampling sublime allegory beneath the heel of process and doctrine.

If *Trans Deus* is Mark, if *7 Minutes* is Matthew, then *Parably Not* is Lucy with the dynamic of "Q Source" thrown in for good measure. "Q" is not a ridiculous conspiracy theory cooked up to delude and obfuscate a population. "Q" is the theory proposed by biblical scholars to account for the shared content in Matthew and Luke, the oral "sayings of Jesus" tradition that is absent in Mark's account. We can only speculate on who Quelle was, but it wouldn't surprise me if they were a woman, or a group of women—a female gospel airbrushed from history by the patriarchy that followed. As someone who passionately believes in inclusion and diversity, it was not too much of a leap to make my Q Source a queer source.

Having written two "text only" books, I wanted to emulate the Prophet of Hercules Road and illuminate these recontextualised parables, continuing the process I had pioneered as a child, cutting up my mum's copies of *Woman's Own* and pasting the chosen pages into my scrapbook.

"We were worried about you for a while," my dad told me as a teenager, as he recollected my enthusiasm for *Woman's Weekly*, sparkly tights, and walking about in my mum's heels, carrying her handbag. I said nothing.

"Poetry fetter'd, fetters the human race," Blake wrote. He's right. But there are plenty of other things that fetter the human race, too.

Our job as sub-creators is to unfetter, to explore, to challenge, to remake. I offer you *Parably Not*, as it is intended: scrapbook literature, unfinished, scruffy, feral, confused, uncertain; ready to be woven into new allegory.
(https://perceptionspress.ca/parably-not/)

PUBLICATION EXPECTED IN 2021
Eman8
Will2Love Series Book 4
Paul Van Der Spiegel

Eman8 is Book 4 of the *Will2Love Series*.
(https://perceptionspress.ca/eman8/)

Coming in 2021/22 from
All Genders Press
Publishing LGBTQ+ fiction and non-fiction
https://perceptionspress.ca/

PUBLICATION EXPECTED IN 2021
Rise of the Magical Three
House of Phoenix Chronicles Book 1
Wilhelm Ostir

Raised by a mysterious grandmother and believing their parents to be dead, Roslynn and her older identical twin brothers, Oliver and Ethan, had only read of magical beings and creatures. But, transitioning into young adulthood, the three embark on an incredible journey as they are introduced to the riddles of their family's past that will forever change who they are and are yet to become. As the three siblings discover the ways of the magical arts, they quickly learn that they are not alone in their quest. Finding help when and where they least expect, the three develop friendships, confront the darkness, work together to save their family from an ancient curse, and learn of a mysterious and ancient bloodline that will forever shape the fabric of time and love. Their fight becomes more significant than even they had anticipated and forces them to make decisions about whether they can effectively save the world, the multiple realms, and magic as they know it. Learning that magic is driven by passion, knowledge, bloodline, and time, will they be the ones to save time, or will they become mere echoes of time?
(https://allgenderspress.ca/echoes-of-time/)

PUBLICATION EXPECTED IN 2021
Secrets Echoed
House of Phoenix Chronicles Book 2
Wilhelm Ostir

Ten years after the events that changed the very fabric of the Arcane and Mundane communities and set a new era of peace in motion, the incredible journey of Rose, Ethan, and Oliver continues. The Noble House of Phoenix, the most ancient of all Arcane bloodlines, must now forge and navigate new allegiances while living among the Mundane.

As the darkness claims control, the three siblings are, once again, thrust into the heat of battle. When multiple disappearances rock the Arcane community, the three siblings put aside their careers, differences, the spaces that separate them, parenthood, and time to join forces, working together again to save their families, friends, and the world as they know it.

In this battle of good and evil, the Magical Three learn of the Curpendulums, a most advanced form of magic. Will the Curpendulums provide the answer to their struggles against the darkness? Or will they prove to be the very weapon that the darkness needs to destroy all Arcane bloodlines and enslave the world? Will magic be lost forever? Lines are drawn, sides are taken, and new secrets are revealed, leaving all to wonder if the echoes of a dark past will remain or be forever changed. (https://allgenderspress.ca/secrets-echoed/)

PUBLICATION EXPECTED IN 2022
The Ignatius 7
House of Phoenix Chronicles Book 3
Wilhelm Ostir

When RJ, a Mundane archeology graduate student, is mysteriously injured during a walk across campus, he makes a discovery that uncovers one of the greatest secrets of the Arcane and Mundane worlds and forever alters how he understands the battle between good and evil.

Learning the truth of Merlin's darks plans and discovering that magic can happen even for those born with no magical power, RJ now holds the key to stopping the destruction of the Mundane across the globe. As time continues to unravel and as missing relics of the past emerge, a bizarre, twisted fate in which the Knights of the Round Table are at the heart of Merlin's plan for total power is revealed.

RJ and his roommate, Dalton, set out to discover their college's history while meeting resistance every step of the way. RJ's journey quickly takes an interesting turn when he receives help from unexpected allies, including the Ignatius 7 and others.

Growing frustrated with the ongoing echoes of time, RJ must formulate a new approach to handling time's bizarre game by channeling the power of technology, mind, magic, and love to bring an end to the battle, save both the Arcane and Mundane, all the while listening to his heart, falling in love, balancing the complex life of a college student, and dealing with his estranged family. (https://allgenderspress.ca/the-ignatius-7/)

PUBLICATION EXPECTED IN 2022
Things are Not What They Seem
House of Phoenix Chronicles Book 4
Wilhelm Ostir

(https://allgenderspress.ca/things-are-not-what-they-seem/)

The **House of Phoenix Chronicles** *is planned as a series of books filled with wizards, witches, fairies, elves, dwarfs, centaurs, mermaids, and dragons in the fight of their lives to protect their ways of life, their families, and the earth. The Phoenix siblings, Rosalynn and her older identical twin brothers, Oliver and Ethan, embark on a remarkable journey of friendship, romance, hatred, and mystery as truths are revealed, challenges faced, and battles with ancient darkness fought. Bending magic* *to their will, Roslynn, Ethan and Oliver, step in and out of time, breaking the rules at every stage of their remarkable journey. Along their way, they meet friends from the past, present, and future, and discover an ancient secret that could forever change the fabric of history, including our understanding of Medieval times and the Knights of the Round Table: a curse sent by darkness to unravel time as it is known. One minute, magic was at its height, the center of life and the community. In the next, cities and villages lay in ruins, a mere echo of a time that was. Can the three siblings channel their family's magic, one of the most powerful magical bloodlines ever to live, for good? Or will their efforts backfire, leading to the destruction of all magical beings? Will they be able to break the curse that affects their family? Can they save their bloodline and the ways of magic? Will they help bring magic back to earth, or will they become the continuation of the curse?*

Made in the USA
Middletown, DE
25 June 2021

42230500R00139